Some Hindustani Musicians

They Lit the Way !

Some Hindustani Musicians
They Lit the Way !

Ashok Da. Ranade

PROMILLA & CO., PUBLISHERS
in association with
BIBLIOPHILE SOUTH ASIA

NEW DELHI & CHICAGO

Published by
PROMILLA & CO., PUBLISHERS
in association with
BIBLIOPHILE SOUTH ASIA
URL: www.biblioasia.com

C-127, Sarvodaya Enclave
New Delhi 110 017, India

First published 2011

ISBN: 978-81-85002-73-6

Typeset in Lapidary 333 BT
Layout by Tarun Beri

Printed and bound in India by
Bibliophile South Asia (Printing Division), New Delhi.

SOME HINDUSTANI MUSICIANS : THEY LIT THE WAY!

Indian music is of course ancient but, in a sense, Hindustani art music is not!

For a generation that began its musical journey in the post-independence era, music does not mean an either/or pursuit! In this era it is not necessary to take to music as a profession to become a competent performer! However, this generation is culture-conscious and seeks history—and therefore demands musical inputs of a wider variety. Unfortunately the generation has also tended to seek more musical guidance from the limited written musicological tradition than from the comprehensive and unique oral/performing tradition—still prevalent in many quarters. Consequently, followers of music in the modern era nearly failed to get to the source of musical knowledge, namely, the performing as distinct from scholastic musical ideas that shaped the tradition.

Under the circumstances (apart from training and performance), perhaps the most concrete way to develop historical awareness, performing wisdom and musical sensibility is to study and analyse music produced by different performers. This kind of study needs to focus on the performing ideas that are best perceived in performances of individual performers.

I have been lucky enough to hear in person some fountainheads of performing ideas. In case of some others, I could receive the ideas indirectly, i.e. through their disciples and recordings. Finally, from some masters I could learn directly!

To place musical contributions of such musicians in the context of the evolution of Hindustani music would be—I felt—an act of expressing personal gratitude. It is also an effort to partially repay the debt we owe to them! Hence these essays. I found the task rewarding—I hope others would find it relevant and useful.

I am deeply grateful to Mr. Ram Kolhatkar, Mr. Sanjay Sant, Mr. Manoj Fulambrikar and Mr. Kundan Ruikar for acquiring and processing appropriate photographs of musicians I have discussed in full articles.

Ashok Da. Ranade

CONTENTS

List of Photographs

Pt. Vishnu Narayan Bhatkhande
(10-8-1860 to 19-3-1937)

1

Pt. Vishnu Narayan Bhatkhande

(10-8-1860 to 19-3-1937)

A Brief Life-sketch

He was born on the auspicious day of *Gokulashtami*, the day when Lord Krishna—perhaps one of the most musical of the Indian pantheon—was born. It is easy to surmise that young Bhatkhande—rightly regarded later as the *Panini* of Hindustani art music during the modern period—was brought up in highly musical surroundings in one of the most contemporary Indian cities, Bombay.

His father managed affairs of the well-known Gora Ram Temple located in Girgaum—one of the older localities in Bombay. Further, this Brahmin family stayed at Walkeshwar, an ancient temple seat in the Malabar Hills, an area heavily populated by the wealthier merchant-class of the growing city. It is noteworthy that music was abundantly and ritualistically used in the temples. In addition, the fairs and festivals inevitably associated with them also provided opportunities for artists and craftsmen of all kinds to come together and to bring to notice their respective skills and expertise. This must have resulted in Bhatkhande's wide exposure to different kinds of music.

Around 1875, as a fifteen year old school boy, Bhatkhande began learning *sitar* from Shri Vallabhdas Gopalagiri, a blind well-to-do Bhatia gentleman and Buwa Damulji—both reportedly disciples of Pt. Pannalal Bajpai of Benaras. The *sitar*-training continued for about three years. In addition, it is also important to note that through Shri Jeevanlal Maharaj, a sectarian *guru* of the Bhatia caste, Bhatkhande began to develop serious acquaintance with the musicological literature. This fact is of central significance as Bhatkhande's life-time work and pioneering achievement was his substantial though selective contributions to the theoretical studies of Hindustani art music. Shri Jeevanji Maharaj was also a disciple of Pt. Pannalal Goswami, a reputed *sitar*-player whose *Nad-Vinod* is one of the authoritative musicological texts of the modern times. By the time Bhatkhande graduated and completed law-studies in 1887, he had become a proficient *sitar*-player. Two emerging facets of the situation then obtained in the region deserve attention: apparently *sitar* was a popular instrument in Maharashtra and secondly, higher castes were clearly and closely involved in music and music-education.

In 1884, i.e., even before he had completed his college courses Bhatkhande had become acquainted with Mr. Shapoor Spencer of the *Parsi Gayanottejak Mandali* (est. 1871), an institution founded by the educated Parsi gentry desirous of arranging music-concerts and conducting music classes on new lines. Bhatkhande became a member of the *Mandali* and was actively involved in its activities. His early and close association with the *Mandali* proved a golden opportunity for the young Bhatkhande to gain immediate exposure to the existing authentic corpus of Hindustani musical compositions and also to learn from the actual performing process.

The *Mandali* employed practising musicians of the caliber of Pt. Ravjibuwa Belbaugkar, Ustad Ali Hussain and Vilayat

Hussain. Bhatkhande went on to learn about 300 *dhrupads* from Pt. Ravjibuwa and 150 *khayal*-s from the *Ustad*-s. It has also been reported that during the period 1900–1915, Bhatkhande could persuade Ashak Ali Khan Jaipurwale to record about 300 traditional compositions. Other musicians who contributed to his repertoire during his entire career were: Pt. Eknath Pandit (Gwalior), Nawab Hamid Ali Khan (Rampur), Ustad Vazir Khan and Muhammadali Khan (Giddhor). It may be said that the basis of his musical knowledge was firmly established because of his varied exposure to and methodical *talim* of Hindustani music that continued till the 1890-s. Of equal importance is his assiduous pursuit of studies in the scholastic tradition of music. Not only did he read the Sanskrit texts but also attended music concerts with a view to document and analyse the wider and prevailing performing tradition. He was able to hear musicians from Delhi, Lucknow, Agra, Jaipur, Gwalior, Patiala, Baroda and Hyderabad (Deccan) at close quarters. As all students of Hindustani music know, these very cities were counted as major seats of patronage to Hindustani music and musicians. Consequently artists hailing from these locations could safely be assumed to represent the very core of Hindustani art music. Bhatkhande also held extensive discussions with them and made it a practice of making detailed notes. Meanwhile, he continued to practise law and became estate manager of the wealthy family of Sukhtankar-s. It is reported that during the years 1890–1905 he lectured on music in the *Mandali*. The exercise obviously gave him an opportunity to organise his musical material, crystallise musicological thoughts and hone a communicative strategy consonant with the modern temper and outlook. It can be deduced that two features of the contemporary musical situation struck him: firstly, the general scholastic tradition and theoretical structures emerging from the Sanskrit musicological texts could not be meaningfully related to the actual practice of music in many fundamental aspects. Secondly, that the prevailing performing tradition, when closely perceived, displayed considerable coherence and uniformity. Hence, it justifiably demanded a theoretical and grammatical statement to be made *ab novo*. Bhatkhande also felt the necessity of getting a first-hand exposure to the prevailing wider and pan-Indian scene. He obviously sensed that, however metropolitan might be the character of Bombay, given the diversity of the country, the city cannot be expected to represent the entire country in all of its musical aspects.

In the succeeding years he appears to have planned pilgrimages of his patrons in such a way as to enable him to collect data on music—the way he liked it to be collected. The religious perambulations of the Sukhtankars thus provided opportunities to undertake musicological fieldwork for the astute mind that Bhatkhande was. In 1896, he toured Surat, Baroda, Bharoch, Navsari, Ahmedabad, Rajkot, Bhavnagar and such other places. In 1904, he set out on a tour of the South which took him to Mysore, Madras, Tanjore, Travancore, Madura, Ittaiyapuram, Trivandrum, Bangalore, Rameshwaram, etc. Of importance is the fact that during his southern travels he became aware of Venkatmakhi's musicological work (especially the systematisation of *raga* in 72 *mela*, etc.) which was to considerably influence his own musical outlook. Similar travels to the eastern (1906-07) and northern (1907-08) parts of the country took him to centres such as Nagpur, Hyderabad, Allahabad, Varanasi, Calcutta, Puri, Vijayanagar and then to Delhi, Mathura, Lucknow, Jaipur, Udaipur, Bikaner and Jodhpur.

During all these travels he established contacts with learned contemporaries such as Pt. Subram Dixit, Pt. Kashinath *alias* Appa Tulsi and Rajah Sourindramohan Tagore. As already stated he recorded and notated 300 compositions of the Manrang *gharana* from Ustad Ashiq Ali and Ahemad Ali of Jaipur in 1906-7. He also obtained about 400 compositions from Pt. Ganapatibuwa Bhilwadikar.

It is evident that Bhatkhande's musical explorations reached far and wide. His probing intellect succeeded in neatly abstracting theoretical structures deeply embedded in the performing tradition. By 1910, his views on grammatical structures, historical evolution, performing norms and aesthetic criteria relevant to Hindustani art music were well crystallised. In this connection, following events from his life are worth considering.

In 1898, he undertook the responsibility to train Vadilalji Shivarm Nayak, who was working as a successful composer for a Gujarati dramatic troupe. Vadilalji had approached Pt. Bhatkhande to acquire 'scientific' training in Hindustani vocal music.

Bhatkhande's responses to Carnatic music in his tour of the South (1904) indicated that he had already evolved a method of comparing musical cultures, notating salient differences while working in the field. In fact he followed a questionnaire consisting of 36 questions to draw a comprehensive profile of a practising musician, including the system of music and musicology he followed and his knowledge (conscious and 'unconscious') in the wider musical perspective (HSP, Vol. II, p. 295-99).

By 1910, *Shrimallakshya Sangitam*, Bhatkhande's treatise in Sanskrit was almost complete. In fact, examples of codification in this treatise were published under the title '*Swaramalika*', thus underlining correspondence between theory and the musical material on which it was based. In the same year he also left practising law, though the career was reportedly proving reasonably lucrative, and devoted himself entirely to the writing, teaching, theorising and organising activities—all related to music. His influence expectably crossed regional boundaries. Due to his industry, analytical approach and ability to convey ideas in English (the language of modernity and wider linkage), Bhatkhande could establish an easy rapport with two major constituents, namely, the enlightened princes and the new educated gentry of the modern British India. These were the classes intensely interested in revitalising Indian culture and establishing its greatness in the occidental eyes. Hence, they willingly came forward to offer affection and patronage to illiterate performers but Bhatkhande won their respect and admiration on account of his deep learning and impressive presentation of the Indian case. He became a spokesperson as well as the leader of a new movement in Music.

One of his pioneering enterprises was annually organising All India Music Conferences which successfully tapped some of the enlightened traditional patronage and created a wide-ranging network of support for music. It is indicative of his modern temper that Bhatkhande advocated discussion, dialogue and conference as the proper mechanism to arrive at a consensus about the nature of *raga* and such other 'technical' issues. In the absence of suitable authoritative texts and because of the extreme divergence between the older textual tradition and the contemporary practice, he obviously considered the modern democratic vogue ideally suited for the purpose (HSP, Vol. III, p. 218). The way he organised these conferences also showed that he was keen on building up a new patronage to music.

Conferences in Baroda (1916, chief patron Maharaja Sayajirao Gaekwad), Delhi (1918, chief patron Nawab of Rampur), Benaras (1919, chief patron Maharaja of Ramnagar), and Lucknow (1924 and 1925, chief patron Sir William Maurice) created a model for such ventures.

While the conferences opened a new channel of dissemination, the establishment of institutions of higher learning proved his pedagogic concerns. Madhav Sangeet Vidyalaya, Gwalior (1918) and Maurice College, Lucknow (1926) were high points in his determined drive to modernise music education. What is significant is that Bhatkhande himself did not run these institutions but had persons he had trained appointed to manage them. For a pioneer, to have a second generation of workers ready to carry on his work is a dream situation come true! Bhatkhande deserves a special praise because he took conscious steps to groom and train his successors. His scholastic work was of course not discontinued in spite of his varied activities. *A Comparative Study of the Music Systems of the 15th, 16th, 17th, and the 18th Centuries* appeared in 1930 and the last two volumes of his *Kramik Pustak Malika* were almost completed by 1932.

At this point it is necessary to move back a little to draw attention to a special feature of the enlightened following music enjoyed in Maharashtra during the period under discussion. When Bhatkhande initiated the movement to organise music conferences around 1916, he left the *Parsi Gayanottejak Mandali*, the organisation which had virtually nurtured him into eminence for more than twenty five years. He joined another cultural body which was also led by Parsi-s! It was called Good Life League. It conducted music classes under the banner of *Sharada Sangeet Vidyalaya* and Bhatkhande continued his teaching activities under its banner. Two features of this situation need to be noted: firstly, the Parsi patronage to Indian culture seems to have followed an interesting pattern. The higher middle class from the community moved to support various facets of culture with a pronounced Indian identity, while the higher aristocracy from the community looked to the West. Secondly, Bhatkhande apparently preferred (or was readily offered) support from people who were not Marathi-speaking! In this connection it is provoking to note that Bhatkhande's chief critics and academic opponents were from Maharashtra. For example, Shri K. B. Deval (1847–1931), Gulabrao Gundoji Mohod (1851–1915) and G.B Acharekar (1885–1939) from Maharashtra were known as his major critics.

A very tangible result of Bhatkhande's zealous scholastic pursuit is of course the great mass of his published work which even today serves as a foundation for any systematic study of Hindustani art music. In volume and variety, relevance and logic his music-literature remains unparalleled to this day. Some salient features of his writings can be noted:

When Bhatkhande graduated in 1885, only five major and important musicological works were available in print. They were *Natyashastra, Sangit Ratnakara, Sangit Darpana, Raga Vibodha* and *Sangit Parijat*. Beginning from 1910, Bhatkhande published 18 more significant musicological works by 1921. The works, he brought into print for the first time, ranged from *Swaramelakalanidhi* (1550) of Ramamatya to *Raga Chandrika* (1912) of Appa Tulsi.

In the six volumes of the series entitled *Kramik Pustak Malika*, Bhatkhande notated compositions circulating in the performing tradition of Hindustani art music as it was practised by major *gharanas* that were accessible to him. He classified a total number of 1800 compositions dividing them in ten *thata*-s as per the codification system he had devised. Clearly the effort was to offer definitive, proto-typical versions of music-compositions traditionally described as '*bandish*' on account of their superior constructional qualities and inherent potentialities to generate music. Because the *bandish* are used by musicians to elaborate, improvise and embellish the selected *raga*, the collection acquired a vital significance when compared with anthologies of mere song-texts. The comprehensive basis of his whole exercise is clearly borne out by an easy break-up. It also points to the representative character of his endeavour.

Thata	Number of *Raga*-s Included
Bilawal	35
Kalyan	14
Khamaj	13
Bhairav	18
Poorvi	15
Marva	14
Kafi	44
Asavari	14
Todi	17
Bhairavi	7
Total	181

Composers included in the collection are:

1. Sadarang (Nyamatkhan)	8. Sanadpiya
2. Adarang (Phirozekhan)	9. Kadarpiya
3. Manrang	10. Akhtarpiya
4. Achapal	11. Amir Khusro
5. Miya Tansen	12. Harrang
6. Ibrahim	13. Chaturpiya
7. Sadakpiya	

Forms or Genres of Music of the Compositions:

1. *Sargam*	8. *Tappa*
2. *Lakshangeet*	9. *Thumri*
3. *Khayal*	10. *Hori*
4. *Tarana*	11. *Ghazal*
5. *Chatrang*	12. *Kajri*
6. *Dhrupad*	13. *Khayalnuma*
7. *Dhamar*	

Languages of Compositions:

1. Hindi	6. Sanskrit
2. Braj	7. Farsi
3. Rajastani	8. Bundeli
4. Punjabi	9. Pushto
5. Urdu	

Tala-**s**

1. *Dadra*	10. *Tilwada*
2. *Jhaptal*	11. *Punjabi*
3. *Ektal*	12. *Ada Chautal*
4. *Trital*	13. *Jhumra*
5. *Tevra*	14. *Roopak*
6. *Sooltal*	15. *Gaj-jhanpa*
7. *Chautal*	16. *Shikhar*
8. *Dhamar*	17. *Matta*
9. *Deepchandi*	18. *Brahma*

It is interesting to note that he appears to have followed a three-language prescription in publishing his own work. He resorted to Sanskrit and the associated tradition of Sanskrit Musicology for structuring and publishing his erudite codification of Hindustani art music (*Sri Mallakshyasangitam*). The explanatory material on his scheme was originally published in Marathi in four volumes. However, he did not hesitate in helping others to expound his ideas in other languages. For example, *Mari Funnagamat* (1913) written by Thakur Nawab Ali Khan of Akbarpur echoed Bhatkhande' influence to a large extent. Published in Urdu this work retained an immense reference value for Hindustani musicians from Northern India who did not know either Marathi or English. Pt. Bhatkhande was also involved in an important publication entitled *Sarode Avesta* by his disciple Shri Pheroze Batliwala, the translator of Bhatkhande's

Swaramalika in Gujrati. Bhatkhande's *Hindustani Sangit Paddhati* (Part 1) was translated into Gujarati by Shri Ratansi Liladhar Thakkar of the *Parsi Gayan Samaj* in 1912.

Bhatkhande's selection of pen-names also suggests a deeper purpose. The Sanskrit writings came under the name of *Chatur Pandit* (a clever, learned man). The explanatory writings were cast in a question-answer format and the provider of answers was named Pt.Vishnu Sharma (a name with unmistakable echoes of the well-known *Panchatantra*, a work designed to turn fools into wise men!) One other pen-name, used very sparingly was Bharadwaj—a major composer of *sama*-s in Vedic music.

It appears that Bhatkhande was not much enamoured with the idea of publishing a magazine on music. He rather chose to concentrate on creating foundational literature on music. Shunning the topical he preferred to regard the strictly contemporary as of secondary importance.

Bhatkhande's concern for music education is forcefully brought home by his attention to developing pedagoic aids. The twenty-four *Geetmalika* booklets, digests of *tala* (*Ashtottarashatatalalakshanam,* 1911) and *raga* (*Abhinavaragamanjiri,* 1921), or his active collaboration with the Bombay Municipal Corporation in preparing text-books on music, are notable instances. Equally significant are examiners' reports that Bhatkhande submitted to the authorities of Madhav Sangeet Vidyalalya during the years 1920-1932. The reports, now available in print, certainly rank high in incisive analysis and attention to details.[1] It is not a coincidence that at the end of *Srimallakshyasangitam*, Bhatkhande avers that "his intention in writing the books is to create good teachers and not to earn money!"

---

[1] *Bhatkhande Smriti Granth*, ed. Chinchore P.N. et al; Indira Kala Sangeet Vishwa Vidyalaya, Khairagadh, 1966, pp. 60-99.

Disciples

As is to be expected, his disciples were from many areas of the country and they were obviously attracted by different aspects of Bhatkhande's work. Shri Shankarrao Karnad, Pt. Vadilal Nayak, Pt. Rajabhaiya Poochwale, Pt. S.N.Ratanjankar and Smt. Khorshid Homji were some of the notable disciples and they made their own respective impacts.

For example, Smt. Homji (with the 'industry-name' Saraswati Devi) had the credit of being the first female, educated music composer for films in Hindi. Shri Karnad was Bhatkhande's confidant and the latter used to send a copy of each of the compositions, newly acquired or processed, to Shri Karnad. Pt. Vadilalji worked in Gujarat and he, along with Pt. Ratanjankar, could be said to have carried on Bhatkhande's torch. Pt. Rajabhaiya was a performer-teacher and successfully created a place for himself as a musician well-versed in nuances of one of the major performing tradition namely, Gwalior, in Hindustani art music.

Bhatkhande's General Theoretical Perspective

Bhakhande's revolutionary and pioneering work understandably aroused keen and considerable controversies in performing as well as academic communities. His work became an inevitable point of reference from which every serious music-person was (and still is) compelled to take one's own bearings. A brief summary of his position may therefore prove helpful in assessing his total contribution.

The basic tenets of the Bhatkhande-ideology or doctrine vis-a-vis Hindustani art music can best be stated on the basis of his four original published volumes of *Hindustani Sangeet Paddhati* published in Marathi during the period 1910–1932. In addition to discussing the strictly grammatical/theoretical issues pertaining to Hindustani art music he also made some pertinent comments/statements that shed light on the intellectual and cultural aspects of the recent and the living Indian past that the 19th century represents.

Grammatical Systematisation : The Main Thrust

What were the major thrusts or orientations of Bhatkhande's investigations into the Hindustani musical behaviour? In spite of his references to history, sociology, psychology, aesthetics, philosophy or mythology as related to music, is it possible to say that his work yielded grammatical results but that he was under the sway of the 19th century zeitgeist of setting up exact sciences on the model of natural and physical sciences? It is notable that in one place he clearly states that questions such as origin of music belong to the domain of history and they are not perhaps highly relevant to understand the contemporary music of the Hindustani *raga* though the *raga*-concept as such has a history! (HSP, Vol. I, p. 27). He repeatedly stated that the system of music which he was propounding afresh was for the contemporary 'classical' music which enjoys no connection with the ancient texts dealing with music. With this view he also emphasised that he was not going into the history of music but dealing with the grammar operating in music (HSP, Vol. I, p. 84). In fact he admits that since his discussion confined to vocal classical music, he has narrowed the traditional definition of music which consists of vocal, instrumental music and dance (HSP, Vol. IV, p. 1). He was also skeptical of the usually given historical accounts of Indian music because they heavily relied on myths, legends etc. (HSP, Vol. III, p. 244). Of course he wrote on the historical aspect of the music he was codifying but that came later.

Interestingly he refers to zoology and botany while discussing the concept of *thata* and *raga* (drawing a parallel with the genus and species exposition (HSP, Vol. I, p.14).

It needs to be added that he was clearly of the opinion that the artistic excellence of Hindustani music and its practitioners notwithstanding, they had lost track of the theoretical foundation that governed this expression as a totality. He also noted that even though the practitioners in the southern system were not actually 'conscious readers' of the old tradition, their music reflected the older tradition. That the rift between the stated *sastric* position and the actual practice was wide open in Hindustani music was his considered conclusion. At times one wonders whether he believed in the general formula of having one nation and one classical music for it! But he certainly wished for a greater musical exchange between the two accepted systems, namely Hindustani and Carnatic. In his view the more scientific vogue of writing on music as in the south, and the more art-oriented music of the north were the aspects to be brought together though in the somewhat distant future! (HSP, Vol. II, p. 216). Expectably he held up Vyankatmakhi's theoretical position as relevant to all Indian *raga*-music, even though Vyankatmakhi wrote only with reference to the Carnatic music in his immediate view (HSP, Vol. II, p. 310 and Vol. I, p.14).

Bhatkhande seems to give a half nod to the position that this happened because music became a preserve of the Muslim musicians who had no access to the ancient tradition. Very logically he goes on to say that there is no reason to believe that even Tansen and other legendary musicians enjoyed musicological knowledge. Finally he nonchalantly stated that Hindustani music is new, hardly 200-250 years old! (HSP, Vol. I, p.15).

Bhatkhande, the astute reader he was of the dynamics of the scholastic tradition, clearly saw and noted that the method of the ancient texts was no more followed and that every systematiser's aim is finally to systematise music of his own times! (HSP, Vol. I, pp. 17, 35). He also firmly stated that medieval writers on music did not understand what the earlier texts said about phenomenon such as colour-music relationship though they went on repeating the traditional position (HSP, Vol. II, p.113). It is symptomatic that he referred to the desirability of knowledgeable people writing on music but also expressed skepticism about a good writer on music being a good performer too! (HSP, Vol. II, p.187). Of interest is his suggestion that modern musicians should explain what they are to present before the actual performance in order to propagate the proper knowledge of music (HSP, Vol. II, p. 273).

Primacy of the Contemporary Music-behaviour

A major governing concern for Bhatkhande's exposition of anything music-related is to continuously refer to the actual musical behaviour around. He is, in other words, practical and preferred to live in the present even at the risk of bringing aspects that may not be complimentary to India, Indians and Indian music!

For example, in spite of the overall priority that vocal music enjoys, he states that instrumentalists' exploration of melodic themes is much more detailed than what the vocalists try to do (HSP, Vol. III, p. 21). He is ready to note how the *dhrupad*-practitioners blame *khayal*-singers and how the latter do the same in the case of instrumentalists, especially the players of string instruments for distorting the purity or authenticity of *raga* (HSP, Vol. III, p. 231). He points out that the prevailing tendency is to put forward the obscurity of musical content or difficulty in rendering as a criteria of musical excellence or high quality (HSP, Vol. III, p. 256). In his practical best we notice how he advocates heightening or lowering the fundamental provided by the *tanpura* etc. depending on the pitch-ranges required to be explored in the music-making concerned (HSP, Vol. III, p. 228). His observation that some musicians prefer to render *raga gaud sarang* in the early hours of the night due to its *vadi* indicates his close attention to the actual practice of music, even when it appears slightly deviationist! (HSP, Vol. V, p. 263). His minute observation also enabled him to note how *raga durga* had become popular in the post-1910 years, or how *raga shuddha sarang* belonged to the category of *aprachalita (*i.e. unknown *raga*) during the 1930's, or how *raga bengal bhairav* was almost not heard from anybody except his *guru* (HSP, Vol. V, pp.297, 309, 332). The same ability to look for performing nuances led him to pithily describe *mand* as a *dhun-raga (*i.e. *raga* that probably originated in a mere *palta*! (HSP, Vol. V. p. 296). The same attitude led to his rather adverse comments on the mode of performers of vocal music from Bengal. (HSP, Vol. IV, pp. 329, 359 and Vol. V, p. 21). It is not surprising that with his frank comments on the prevalent indifferent attitude of properly preserving and disseminating musical knowledge, he comes out as an 'activist archivist' as far as matters musical are concerned! (HSP, Vol. III, pp. 311-12). In fact determined attitude in the work he was carrying out echoes Bhavbhuti—who was pained by the surrounding non-recognition of his work but who was also sure that sometime in future somebody will arrive on the scene to recognise the worth of his undertaking! (HSP, Vol. III, p. 313). Very succinctly he mentions in a positive spirit the major features of the modern music-behaviour and welcomes the inevitable possibility of changes (HSP, Vol. IV, p.133).

Approach to Western Music and Western Writings on Music

As Pt. Bhatkhande was a well-read person, his references to Western writings on music deserve a special attention. On the one hand, there was the prevailing Nationalism which was prone to react against these writings. On the other hand, there was the newly educated energetic Indian mind which positively responded to the breadth and systematic nature of the Western temper as reflected in various aspects of life. Bhatkhande's writings reveal the paradoxical position!

For example, in introducing his own motives in undertaking the task of writing the series entitled *Hindustani Sangeet Paddhati*, he refers to Dr. Burney's *History of Music* with admiration and holds it up as a kind of a model. Another thoughtful reference is to the *Theory of Sound* by Prof. Blasserna. The reference is in the context of the positive use of dissonances in Western music. Bhatkhande however grants that the concept of *Vivadi* notes in Hindustani music may not correspond with it (HSP, Vol. I, p. 22). At one place he specially eulogises the Western writings on music for their clarity (HSP, Vol I, p.129). While discussing the phenomenon of *sruti* he expectably refers to Helmholtz and Ellis, authors in the forefront of thinking on musical intervals and such other issues (HSP, Vol. II). His open stance to ideas from the West and the probable influence of recordings from the same source is clear. Similarly, he is ungrudging in admitting to the import of the Southern *raga* through stage music. He states that though he has not been abroad, he welcomes features of Western music such as descriptions of nature, the spirit of bravery and vigour of musical expression and the notable abundance of instrumental music (HSP, Vol. IV, pp. 337, 343). It is not surprising that in the last volume of his theoretical exposition he reiterates his awareness of the Western progress in music. He specifically lists (1) the development of instruments and their music, (2) advanced choral music, and (3) the Western female dancers' study of Indian dances and their introduction of innovations in them (HSP, Vol. V, p. 287). In this context he also goes on to firmly state that musical nationalism in music is not to be understood as Puritanism!

His views on notation of music indicate that he welcomed the thorough Western approach in this respect. He deplored the half-hearted 'manufacturing of notation' methods in which ancient Indian signage was somehow sought to be accomodated (HSP, Vol. II, p. 167). Adding that no notation can be an exact copy of the actual rendering of music he lauds its role in preserving music as also in its capacity to provide knowledge about how music was practised at a particular point of times (HSP, Vol. IV, p. 399).

It is an interesting nuance that he defines the phenomenon of *Swaradnyana* in such a way that it seems tantalisingly close to the western concept of absolute pitch! (*Hindustani Sangeet Paddhati*, Vol. I, Popular Prakashan, Mumbai, Ed. Prabhakar Chinchore, 1992, IX). A somewhat oblique acceptance of the Western or modern acoustic concept is also detected when he tries to explain the traditional term 'उच्चध्वनिर्मनाक्' employed in explaining the *sruti*-phenomenon. One wonders whether he is referring to the just-noticeable-difference in pitch-perception as it is normally stated in modern acoustics! (HSP, Vol. IV, p.16).

References to Non-Indian Writers on Indian Music

Bhatkhande's references to and quotations from non-Indian writers' writings on Indian music are clear and generous. Thus while discussing *thata*, Capt. Willards' *Treatise on the Music of Hindustan* (HSP, Vol. I, p.10) finds an early mention.

References to Indian Writers on Music

He has made regular and frequent references to Sourendramohan Tagore's writings on issues relevant to the argument in progress (*Hindustani Sangeet Paddhati*, first edition 1914, second 1997, Vol. II, Popular Prakashan, p.1-2, Vol. III, p.32 onwards). He also talks about the increased writing on music in the regional languages and the desirability of having more discussion of these when necessary (HSP, Vol. II, p. 2). While detailing the current *raga*-corpus and its classification, he openly acknowledges the relevance of *Naghmate Asafi*, *Sangeet Sar*, *Sarmaye Ashrat* or *Nada Vinod* (HSP, Vol. III, pp. 80-91, 103, 126). He extensively summarises *Naghmate Asafi* (HSP, Vol. IV, pp. 202-14) obviously because of its contemporary relevance. In fact he tentatively lists useful modern works (HSP, Vol. III, p.106). In the last volume of his theoretical exposition he once more returned to the necessity of tapping Urdu and Persian writings on music as useful sources. He does not fail to mention how his attention was drawn to a Persian work which dealt with the theme of *raga* as a means of curing disorders (HSP, Vol. V, p. 321). His close reading of the Sanskrit musicological texts, his attention to the regional disparities in change and his historical perspective made him notice that Ahobala followed the Hindustani vogue in describing basic notes and their systematisation but still he tried to swear by texts written in the Southern musical contexts (HSP, Vol. II, p.70). Expectably his references to Vyankatmakhi are admiring as well as detailed (HSP, Vol. III, pp. 27-29). So is his admiring reference to Carnatic classification (along with a brief explanation of how the *raga*-name indicates the *thata* to which the *raga* belongs (HSP, Vol. III, pp. 39-41) and to Somnath's detailed enumeration of *vina*-strokes and the signage accompanying it (HSP, Vol. III, pp. 21-22).

How Many Systems of Classical Music?

In spite of his wide travels, correspondence with different authorities and keen observation of the Indian musical scene in general, he firmly held to the view that India consisted of two systems of classical music—Hindustani or *Uttar Hindustani* and Carnatic or *Dakshinatya*. In other words, for him the North-Eastern music or that of the Bishnupur *gharana* in Bengal (to which a brief reference is made in HSP, Vol. III, p. 283) nor the *Sopana-parampara* in the Kerala were to be counted as independent musical systems with sufficiently or adequately codified prevalence (HSP, Vol. I, p.1).

He is however open enough in stating that as in case of languages, it is quite natural to have different systems of music in different parts of the country (HSP, Vol. I, p.13). He repeats the argument with special force in respect of the Southern musical system existing in the same country and yet it's being so different from the Hindustani music (HSP, Vol. I, p.16). Having identified the Northern and the Southern systems as the two main systems of 'classical' music he carefully records clues to interpret the context that determines the northern or the southern allegiance of musicological texts. One such clue is to remember that in the Southern system the lowest state of a note is described as its *shuddha* state and the *vikrit* as the highest, unlike in the North (HSP, Vol. I, p.119). It is with a refreshing openness that he also suggests the desire that Hindustani system should incorporate elements, or features from the Southern system wherever relevant. His special reference is to *raga*-s current in the south but not so in the Hindustani system (HSP, Vol. V, p. 304).

The Method of Discourse

It is interesting as well as intriguing that Bhatkhande described the question-answer method that he followed as something 'new', needing a special mention and an explanation in the very beginning (HSP, Vol. I, p. 1-2). He also reiterates the utility of this method again in a later volume (HSP, Vol. II, p. 2). Was he facing criticism from his contemporaries for following this vogue? The question is: Are not many of the Indian traditional texts in various subjects customarily cast in this mode?

What Music/Sangeet was the Focus of His Theorisation? For Him Music = *Raga*

Time and again he makes it clear that *sangeet* for him was to be equated with *raga-sangeet*. When he briefly refers to folk music, it is only to explain the concept as discussed by a foreign author Perry. (In fact he states that 'this subject is not our concern'.) (HSP, Vol. II, pp. 28-29). Some of his statements are forthright in this respect. In translation they would read:

1. "*Gayan* (i.e., singing) is dependent on the arrangement of the raga." (HSP, Vol. I, p. 2).
2. *Thata* (scale) is the origin of *raga* (ibid).

He proceeds on the basis of three ground-rules: (a) There are in all 12 primary notes—7 of them being the *shuddha* and 5 the *vikrit* i.e. changed. (b) In all *raga*-producing initial manoeuvres—i.e. in the formation of *thata*-frame as also in the following *raga* actualisation process, ascent and descent are the primary essential movements leading to the creation and completion of the fundamental generative framework that *raga* is supposed to be. (c) No *raga* can omit the note *shadja*, this note being the foundation of all melodic and *raga*-creating procedures. With such steadfast fidelity to the role of grammar and procedures based on it, Bhatkhande's view that sub-types or varieties of a *raga* are created by combining different *raga*-s with the main *raga* of a *thata*, seems inevitable (HSP, Vol. IV, p. 4).

Referring to the Southern authority Vyankatmakhi's authoritative position that in all 72 *thata*-s result from the twelve-note-basic-frame, Bhatkhande further points to the logic of selective omission of some notes yielding *raga*-sub-classes namely, *odav*, *shadava* and *sampurna*, etc., and then he could arrive at the staggering figure of the mathematically possible original *raga*-s as 34,848! Of course he grants that all the mathematically derivable *raga*-s cannot prove satisfactory as acceptable and popular music! (HSP, Vol. I, p. 18).

Bhatkhande however argues that the *ragas* in circulation in Hindustani music can suitably be derived from 10 *thata*-s and then he proceeds to do so. He avers that the *thata*-creation has been the ancient procedure and it is also useful for explaining/ teaching the music concerned (HSP, Vol. I, p.15). Obviously he was aware of the possible rejection of the argument assuming the primacy of *thata* over *raga* and hence he sometimes also makes a dogmatic statement about it, asserting that whether it is so in the ancient texts or not he is going to assume it and proceed with the ten-*thata-raga* systematisation! (HSP, Vol. I, p.17).

The point to be noted is that the *thata* system was already a well-crystallised concept though not many Hindustani musicians referred to it. Secondly, in majority of cases the *raga* logically and conceptually pre-existed the *thata*-system as Bhatkhande propounded it. *Thata* do not create a *raga*—contrary to some of his statements! It is however interesting to note that Bhatkhande points to the general prevalence of the term *thata* among the instrumentalists. Obviously with the physical limitations imposed by the breadth of the finger-board or number or fixed frets, instrumentalists had to resort to the procedure of generating a *thata*-framework within the available resources so as to enable rendering of different *raga*-s or providing accompaniment when others explored them (HSP, Vol. I, p. 15).

He explicitly noted 20 musicological aspects of a *raga* which he felt every student of music should be aware of (HSP, Vol. III, p.16). It is notable that a little later (HSP, Vol. IV, pp. 70-74) he becomes more ambitious and literally lists 40 aspects which one must know about every *raga*—this is indeed a *Ragachalisa*! All through his discussions the *raga*-determination is, in his opinion, to be based on the compositions in a *raga*. Hence he is in favour of having a large sampler of compositions at disposal for carrying out this task (HSP, Vol. V, p.1). Logically he seems to allow difference of opinion about the nature of a *raga* if the compositions yield different versions (HSP, Vol. V, p. 294).

Bhatkhande's Statements on the Aesthetics of *Raga, Sruti*, etc.

At the outset, Bhatkhande readily grants that ultimately the criteria or the capacity of a *raga* to offer entertainment ('*ranjakata*') is determined by or is dependent on the society concerned (HSP, Vol. I, p.10). However, he lays down two major rules that are likely to ensure this aesthetic capacity: (1) No *raga* should consist of less than 5 notes. (2) No *raga* should exclude both *madhyama* and *panchama* notes in its scale. Incidentally, it should be remembered that for the first rule or criterion, there is a long musicological tradition from Matanga onwards.

In a non-technical manner Bhatkhande briefly summed up the stages in which performers appear to arrive at valid conclusions with an aesthetic orientation. (HSP, Vol. I, p. 24). He argues that even the illiterate musicians, learning from their experienced *guru/ustad*, initially achieve mastery over 'technical' aspects such as good voice, effective projection and impressive technical virtuosity. In view of this identification of the sequence in learning, it is not surprising that he himself took care to give a brief but detailed description of how to practise, i.e. to do the *riaz* (HSP, Vol. II, p. 320). He pointed out that as the compositions which the disciples learnt from their *guru* are inherently and qualitatively rich, their presentations, based on these are appreciated. Thus the performers arrive at a judgement of taste and through them the society for which they perform also arrives at viable aesthetic criteria. A little later in the same volume (p. 31) he points out that performers follow the well tried out tonal combinations because it is usually risky to introduce new/deviant notes in an already established *raga*. Listeners may not be aware of the grammatical structure of a *raga* but they surely sense what is good to listen to as the taste for it has been already developed over a period. A point is likely to be overlooked here. Even though he states that illiterate Muslim musicians (who formed the main performing music-community) were responsible for the complete break with the earlier tradition that the Sanskrit musicological texts often reflected, Bhatkhande is *not* rejecting the change but merely deploring the fact that the changes were not documented (HSP, Vol. I, p.193).

Even though he specifically refers to questions pertaining to aesthetics of music, on most occasions he chooses to keep away from them in order to focus on his aim of making a clear and extensive statement on the grammar and system of Hindustani art music, (HSP, Vol. III, pp. 5-7). For example, he merely states that the *raga* and *dhyana* relationship as posited in the musical past is no more relevant (HSP, Vol. V, p. 246) but he does not go into the discussion of music-*yoga* inter-relationship. His avoidance of the any detailed discussion of the venerable *rasa*-doctrine is also noticeable (HSP, Vol. III, p.153). He reiterated that it is difficult to establish relationship of the *rasa* theory with the contemporary *raga*. However he appears to give a slight twist to his position when he states that as an unknown learned man has argued that perhaps there are only three *rasa*-s, namely, *Shringara, Veera* and *Karuna* in music and the rest of the *rasa*-s can be included in them (HSP, Vol. IV, pp. 5-6.).

In a similar manner he is not enthusiastic about *raga*-colour relationship or the myth-music connections. He does not reject the phenomenon of sound-colour relationship (and therefore of the *raga*-colour links) but he has no use of it for the task he had in hand, namely to undertake a systematic exposition of Hindustani *raga*-music (HSP, Vol. III, pp. 19-20). The *raga*-myth linkage also meets the same fate. He states that the support for divining the correct nature of the *raga* is to be sought in the texts that codify the concerned aspect or practice and not in the mythology surrounding the phenomenon (HSP, Vol. II, p.170-71).With regard to the effective analysis of *raga* i.e. the psychological effect of raga on listeners—he is non-committal—obviously because of the essentially contested nature of the phenomenon (HSP, Vol. III, pp. 223-24).

Bhatkhande is firm on treating the *sruti*-phenomenon as not being highly relevant to the Hindustani music as practised in the modern times. He states the basic problem about the *sruti*-phenomenon (HSP, Vol. IV, p. 17) and proceeds to extensively summarise Sharangadeva's position (HSP, Vol. IV, pp. 14-32). Further, after quoting relevant passages from the early texts about *sruti-swara* relation, *Grama* and *Murchhna*, he clearly concludes that these and other related concepts, if widely and selectively referred to, enjoy merely historical importance and music, as conceived and presented in the modern period, will not benefit from their discussion. In his opinion, complete disagreement about fundamentals among the authorities themselves and a kind of circularity of argument about critical issues, render the entire debate of little practical significance (HSP, Vol. II, p. 4). He also makes a significant theoretical point that authors or authorities need to be interpreted in the perspective offered by their times and terminology (HSP, Vol. II, p. 52). He held the firm view that the modern way of micro-analysis of the ancient *sruti*-exposition was not of any significance to the early writers because they were more interested in the *raga*-system and that was obviously facilitated by the exploration of the 12-notes-system (HSP, Vol. II, p. 74). He did not feel it necessary to resort to the *sruti*-aspect to explain the performers' use of notes with slightly higher or slightly lower values. He reasoned that these variations appeared because of the concerned note being related to a higher or a lower note in the related progression (HSP, Vol. V, p. 151). In other words, he concluded that the contemporary and acceptable positions about intervals, etc. as sanctified by the Western physics-oriented discussion cannot be foisted with hindsight on the early or ancient Indian authors! For example, he is not ready to accept that the ancient term '*anuranana*' could be interpreted as a reference to the phenomenon known to modern theorists as harmonics (HSP, Vol. II, p. 81). He clearly states that the Sanskrit musicological texts made no reference to the automatic *rishbha* and *gandhar* notes respectively heard from the *panchama* and *kharaj* strings of the *tanpura*. He opined that the term '*anuranana*' most likely and merely meant a sustained note. (HSP, Vol. II, p. 83). He appears to suggest that attempts to justify ancient terminology with modern connotation are probably aimed at winning Western approval for Indian music as such and that is something which may require perhaps many more ages (HSP, Vol. II, p. 53)! (His statement, made in 1931-32, obviously appears to be unduly pessimistic today!)

He is categorical about keeping religion separate from music while thinking on musical matters such as the *nada* (HSP, Vol. II, p. 8).

Historical View on the Origin of Two Indian Systems

The long tradition of music in India was completely disrupted during the medieval times. Since then, music in India changed so considerably that no correspondence between Sanskrit musicological texts and music as actually practised in the post-medieval age could be established. The fact obviously necessitated an *ab novo* restatement of musicological framework underlying the performing tradition. Having made this proposition Bhatkhande added that despite the impressively long list of available musicological texts, none save the following twelve retained relevance in varying degrees for Hindustani art music as actually practised:

S. No.	Title	Author	Period
1.	Sadraga Chandrodaya	Pundarik Vitthal	1556–1605
2.	Raga Manjari	Pundarik Vitthal	1556–1605
3.	Raga Mala	Pundarik Vitthal	1556–1605
4.	Nartan Nirnay	Pundarik Vitthal	1556–1605
5.	Nagmate Asafi	Mohammad Raza	1813
6.	Raga Tarangini	Lochan	1675
7.	Anoop Ratnakar	Bhavbhatta	1780
8.	Anoop Vilas	Bhavbhatta	1780
9.	Anoop Sangitankush	Bhavbhatta	1780
10.	Hriday Prakash	Hriday Narayan Deo	1660
11.	Sangit Sara	Maharaja Pratapsinha	1776–1804
12.	Sangit Kalpadruma	Krishnananda Vyas	1842

All the works listed are post-1600 AD. It should therefore be obvious that the foregoing listing makes contemporary Hindustani musical tradition more modern than ancient! In a country where the temptation is always to trace everything back to Vedic times, Bhatkhande's contention certainly must have rocked cultural self-satisfaction felt by many!

However he does not fail to add *Naradi-shiksha, Manduki-shiksha, Bharata-natyashastra, Sangeet Ratnakara, Sangeet Samayasara, Sangeet Darpana, Swara Mela Kalanidhi, Raga Vibodh, Sangeet Parijata* and *Chaturdandi Prakashika*, as other early important texts though not specifically related to Hindustani music (HSP, Vol. II, p. 3).

In Bhatkhande's opinion, major indications of the clear break that occurred between ancient and medieval musical continuities are easily identifiable as shown below:

(a) The ancient music was based on two parent scales, namely *shadja* and *madhyama grama*, while only the former remained in vogue after about 1600. In the process, the intricate system of microtones, i.e. the *sruti*-s, also went overboard.

(b) In the ancient period, the method/procedure adopted to explore and exploit the available tonal spaces by changing the initial note of the operating scale was known as *murchana paddhati*. This too came to be discarded. In fact, as the two *grama* system gave way to the single *grama*, the principle of tonality replaced the *murchana*-s.

(c) As a combined result of the technical and cultural processes, two musical systems emerged and stabilised in the country. The Hindustani system accepted a twelve-note division of the gamut and the *bilawal thata* as the basic *shuddha* frame in which notes *shadja* and *panchama* remained immovable.

(d) *Jati* and *grama raga*-s went out of circulation with the advent of the *thata*-system. The method of evolving *raga*-s from the *thata*-frameworks assumed full control.

(e) During the course of time, Hindustani art music established many of its distinctive melodic features such as *raga*-s, *vadi-samvadi*-principle and the *raga-samaya* relationship. These features also marked a deviation from the ancient vogue.

(f) Carnatic system differs from the Hindustani system in all major respects such as the basic accepted gamut, elaborational techniques, modes of composing, the manner of evolving *raga-tala* structures and the use of embellishments and formation and presentation of genres.

(g) Despite the technical possibility of evolving 32 *thata*-s and 484 *raga*-s in each *thata*, the contemporary Hindustani music can realistically be accommodated in a framework consisting of ten *thata*-s.

It is touching to read Bhatkhande already referring to his old age and the unfinished music-related tasks in 1932! (HSP, Vol. V, p.347). In fact towards the end in the same volume he lists 15 specific items that demanded further work—and the catalogue needs to be read in the original as it suggests his wide vision and scholastic humility. Pt. Bhatkhande suffered a paralytic attack in 1933, his health continued to fail gradually and he expired on September 19, 1937. Thus ended a glorious career of a modern mind in search of its music! Believing in the value of disseminating knowledge of music, he headed a band of educators whose watch-words were hard work and thoroughness. He laid the foundation of a comprehensive system of music, revitalising in the process a tree which had displayed an erratic and confused growth. To this day the tree continues to flower and fructify. Contemporary minds can make sense of Indian art music *because* Pt. Bhatkhande made available a thought-structure both firm and complex to match the prevalent performing reality. One may disagree with him, or modify what he stated, but one cannot hope to understand Hindustani art music without a reference to his work.

Pandit Ramkrishnabuwa Vaze
(28.11-1872 to 5-5-1943)

2

Pandit Ramkrishnabuwa Vaze
(28-11-1872 to 5-5-1943)

Life Sketch

Born in Ozare, Sawantwadi in Maharashtra, he went through considerable hardships while learning music from many *guru*-s. His early *guru*-s were Balwanntrao Pore and Hadap buwa which is indicative of the fact that probably *khayal*-singing had already penetrated the interior and coastal areas of Maharashtra during the early decades of the nineteenth century. By 1883 he was compelled to marry, but his craving to learn music remained unabated. As a result he left home and went first to Pune in search of a *guru*. His next stop was Bombay where he had the opportunity to listen to Chunnabai and Bande Ali Khan Beenkar who performed in a marriage celebration. Finally he reached Gwalior! There he received training, chiefly from Ustad Nissar Hussain Khan of Gwalior *gharana* reportedly only because one Mr. Bhuskute, Khansaheb's chief patron 'forcibly persuaded' Khansaaheb to teach this persistent aspirant!

As in the case of many of his contemporaries, Vazebuwa had a flair for playing a number of instruments with considerable skill; however he is remembered as a 'classical' vocalist. He was a remarkably eclectic and unhesitatingly learnt *bandish*-s from every possible source. As a result he stands out as a major deviationist from the music-making of the Gwalior *gharana* as usually understood. By 1918 Vazebuwa (age 35), was competent enough to crave for participating in competitive musical events with Rahimat Khan. In 1921 he gave tunes to the play 'Shahshivaji' authored by Tipnis who caused a storm because (while Realism was gaining ground all around) in this play Shivaji was made to sing! Vazebuwa's famous retort to conscientious objectors to the 'singing Shivaji' was "but see in what *raga*-s my Shivaji sings!". He continued to select music for the new vogue Music-drama produced by Lalitkaladarsh company: *Satteche Gulam* (1922), *Turungachya darat* (1923), *Krishnarjun yuddha* (1925), *Sangeet Shree* (1926), [Dinanath—Lata Mangeshkar's father —became his '*gandabandh*' (i.e. ritualistically initiated) disciple in the same year], *Shikka Katyar* and *Randundubhi* (1927) and *Sonyaca Kalas* (1932). At least four of the plays were originally prose, adapted later for conversion into a Music-drama. To that extent, Vazebuwa was blazing a new trail because music-composing in such plays was not a part of the original creative design and process (as it was in films)!

In two volumes, entitled *Sangeet Kala Prakash* (1938), (his age 67), Vazebuwa included many interesting compositions in rare *raga*-s. Prefatory pages of the first volume contain an autobiographical account, which throws fascinating sidelights on the contemporary musical scene. (He had probably been thinking in the autobiographical mode since 1933—when he was 62 ! In that year he wrote autobiographical articles in a magazine called *Vasundhara*.) He was very active till a very late age. His concert in Bombay Music Circle in 1941-42, barely four years before his death, finds a place in descriptions of contemporaries as one of the memorable concerts! One of his forcefully sung compositions—the one in *raga Bhairav Bhatiyar*—specifically mentions on the disc, his age at that time—82! He had many disciples including Pt. Shivrambuwa Vaze (son) and Pt. Haribhau Ghangrekar (son-in-law), Pt. Gajananrao Joshi, and Pt. Bhaskarrao Joshi.

I am not privileged enough to have listened to Pt. Vazebuwa in a *mehfil* as he passed away before I acquired 'musical ears'. The present evaluation therefore falls back on four sources: his gramophone records and two volumes of song-anthology, a few compositions which I have learnt from my *guru*, Pt. Gajananrao Joshi (who had learnt from Pt. Vazebuwa), his stage-tunes and music of some of his direct disciples whom I could hear in several concerts.

Pt. Vazebuwa learnt from many learned musicians but his main *guru* was Ustad Nissar Hussain Khan of Gwalior *gharana*. And yet, it must be admitted that, like many other receptive artists, he assimilated numerous influences from his myriad exposures to music in such a manner that the style he projected can hardly be pigeon-holed as of a particular *gharana*. Therefore it is more appropriate to analyse his music structurally than to examine it as a musical deduction from the Gwalior ideology of music.

His *Khayal* Singing

Pt. Vazebuwa concentrated on singing *khayal*-s. He knew many *thumri*-s, *dhrupad*-s, etc. However, serious and well-trained musicians of those times generally enjoyed an impressive repertoire-width within the general hierarchy of musical genres even though they insisted on exploring in their perfomrances a more restricted genre-pallete. In spite of their wider knowledge they chose to canalise their performing creative expression through one or a few musical forms obviously to ensure an optimum performance-level. The factor of wide-based studies combined with a narrower range of specialisation is worth noting because an artist's study of one or more forms tends to influence his renderings of forms he actually selects for presentation. Thus, though the actually presented form remained in the foreground the rest of the studied forms kept hovering in the background. Chances are that forms thus remaining in the background are nevertheless active in the concerned artists' imagination. Musicians enjoying this kind of abundance are bound to be structurally more complex and musically more exciting.

High Pitch

The first feature one notices in Vazebuwa's singing is the high fundamental pitch he employed. It is easily discerned that he was not at ease while singing at such a high pitch. A listener invariably receives a feeling of hearing a voice under strain. In other words, he could not have attached any musical significance to the high pitch *per se*. In all probability he was resigned to it on account of his asthmatic condition. However, musical consequences flowing from such a basic decision were inevitable and they are worth discussing.

There is no sustained tone-production in Pt.Vazebuwa's music nor are there *taan*-passages of any remarkable length. Phrase-terminations as well as pronunciation of words are characterised by an abruptness. Of course it must be remembered that performing conditions available to musicians active before 1920 in India were, acoustically speaking, far from ideal. It can naturally be assumed that under such conditions musicians' primary concern was to be 'heard' by the listener in the last row, so to speak! In addition, to remain musically intelligible was the critarion to be observed, not just to be heard 'somehow'. Consequently pitch and volume were considered to be the most important dimensions of voice or sound.

Even if the vocal range of the singer did not allow maintaining musical quality in singing the musician was compelled to use high pitches. This means that even if Vazebuwa was not handicapped by his asthama, he would have resorted to the high pitched singing due to the prevailing performing environment. Notwithstanding all such factors, Pt. Vazebuwa had the ability to mould the obtained circumstances in such a way as to ensure high musical returns and that is what should concern us.

Tala and Tempo

On examination it is detected that to offset the disadvantages of singing in a rather unnaturally high pitch, he employed a tempo which was on most of the occasions describable as medium. When set in this tempo, any *tala* becomes more tractable because the temporal spaces that require filling-up also become manageable on account of their shorter span. In this connection, it is to be remembered that the broader and the immediately relevant temporal framework for music is provided by the overall tempo of the *tala* cycle. It is therefore very important to take a proper aesthetic decision in respect of the *tala*-tempo. Further, as far as the perceptual participation of the audience is concerned it is again the *tala*-tempo that supplies the initial clue. In selecting the medium tempo Pt. Vazebuwa made a very vital musico-aesthetic strategic decision.

The matter of the *tala*-tempo cannot of course be considered in isolation. The real question is: medium tempo of which *tala*? Pt. Vazebuwa's inclination was to rely with conspicuous frequency on *teentala* and *jhaptala*. This easily identifiable preference follows almost as a corollary from the choice he exercised in respect of the tempo. As is known, the *tala*-structure essentially depends on the number and distribution of the beats incorporated in the *tala*-cycle. With its four-four beats sections, the *teentala* is found to be suitably structured irrespective of voices, forms, etc., employing it. The other *tala*, *jhaptala* is however of a different type. Pt. Vazebuwa's great predilection for *jhaptala* again proved his unerring aesthetic sensibility. This *tala* has only ten beats and thus has an extremely matching inherent skeleton *vis-a-vis* employment of a medium tempo. In itself the *jhaptala* is neither sprawling (hence difficult to traverse) nor is it too constricting (hence too short for any significant musical patterning). Further, the distribution of beats is 2, 3, 2, 3 — i.e. a pattern which may turn the same *tala* into a rather 'difficult' entity when employed in fast tempo and meaningless in a markedly slow one. It may not be an accident that too slow or too fast compositions in this *tala* are extremely rare in the known general repertoire of Hindustani art-music. Pt. Vazebuwa employed the *tala* very frequently and the frequency is also reflected in the corpus of compositions he has chosen to publish.

Scanning compositions that he chose to publish in the two volumes mentioned earlier one finds that there are 49 *teentala*-s and 40 *jhaptala*-s! Pt. Vinayakrao Ghangrekar, who accompanied Pt. Vazebuwa on *tabla* for a number of years (and whose elder brother, Pt. Haribbau Ghangrekar was Pt. Vazebuwa's senior-most disciple) told me in course of a TV interview that Pt. Vazebuwa sang very often in *jhaptala* and *aadaa* choutala because everybody else was employing *ektala* and *teentala*! In a way, this too is an instance of Pt. Vazebuwa's acute perception. As if to provide us with supporting evidence, his recorded music includes three *jhaptala* compositions and significantly they happen to be the best pieces. The compositions are in *raga khambaavati, khat* and *tilak-kaamod* respectively.

The abruptness evident in his singing was responsible for one more important feature in his presentations: the active role of the element of pause. Due to the high singing-pitch as well as perhaps due to the shortness of breath, Pt. Vazebuwa had apparently developed a vocalising technique in which (contrary to the accepted Gwalior norm), singing did not rely on the vowel-sound 'AA'. Instead, a variant, 'Aw' was employed. This variety of a distorted 'AA' vowel afforded him an opportunity to hold the breath longer. Secondly, it also provided him with more room to manoeuvre the more perceivable emphasis on notes or the desired word-units of the song-text. It is perceivable that immediately after such emphatic points in the rendering; he usually introduced a pause before taking up the melodic thread again. In other words, he did not allow the shadow of the note to linger and consequently the resulting pauses of fractional durations created a chiaroscuro effect of sound and silence. One has only to listen to his *jhaptala* compositions or the famous "*Bol re papiyaraa*" (*teentala*, *miya malhaar*) to appreciate his skilful use of the pause.

The pauses adjacent to *sama*-points in all his renderings, and those located immediately after the introduction of new and intricate musical phrasings are worth a closer scrutiny. All such pauses allowed his music to sink in the listeners' minds. Such pauses make one realise the truth that much more is achieved in music than imagined if sheer uninterrupted vocalising is not equated with musicality! I suggest that his listeners could become permeated with his music on account of the selected *tala*-s and the chosen tempo. Even today these features of Pt. Vazebuwa's music afford us a scope or a breathing space to establish confirmed relationships between the intricate and the non-lingering musical phrases that Pt. Vazebuwa so much excelled in.

Pt. Vazebuwa's choice of the *jhaptala* made it easier for him to apply the suggested chiaroscuro effect. Even a brief consideration of the *jhaptala*-structure reveals that the sonorous and the not-so-sonorous syllables of the *tabla*-language are well distributed, especially those around the *sama*-point. In a *jhaptala* composition, an artist appears to come to the *sama* in a pouncing manner which has an aggressive appeal of its own. In this connection, the author still remembers how an old timer described the *tala*, *jhaptala* and *jhumra* respectively in a picturesque way. He remarked in Hindi, "*jhaptala jhapse aataa hai, aur jhumra jhoomke*". (The *jhaptala* comes in a pouncing manner and the *jhumra* in a swaying manner.) This special quality, traceable to the structural features, was doubly reinforced in Pt. Vazebuwa's singing because the *mukhdaa*-s of his *jhaptala*-compositions never started from the *sama*-points. They invariably began from the eight and a half beat, and the achieved effect was inimitable.

A quality of abruptness in projection and diction was of course not the only characteristic that attracts our attention in Pt. Vazebuwa's music. There was also the important aspect to his handling of the words of the song-text.

Firstly, the words were enunciated with a surprising clarity: surprising because Hindustani vocalists are not generally found to exhibit this quality. It is possible to maintain that Hindustani art musicians tend to take a dim view of the clarity of word-pronunciation because the said clarity may also introduce repeated consonantal terminations in the vocal flow. Yet, Pt.Vazebuwa opted for both clarity and force in the enunciation of words in the song-text. The way he accomplished this (with the accompanying general forcefulness), almost amounted to carving out contours of words in sound. This is observable in all his renderings. Whether it was a *bhajan* like "*Udho karaman ki gati nyaari*" (O Uddhav, the ways of *Karma* are inscrutable) or a *drut ektala* composition like "*Bal bal bal janiye*" (*bhatiyaar*), the words were uttered with strength and deliberateness underlining his conviction that they were the carriers of musical meaning. It may be mentioned here that the style of stage-singing popularised in Maharashtra by the late Keshavarao Bhonsale, Bapurao Pendharkar and Master Dinanath also exemplified a similar tendency. It could not have been a coincidence that all these three regarded Pt. Vazebuwa as their *guru*.

Pt. Vazebuwa treated the words of a song-text as sound-patterns that invited emphasis and employment for their own sake. The role assigned to words in this manner was thus a sound-oriented strategy and not a meaning-oriented one. Perhaps this was also the reason why he frequently ignored uttering words fully. For example, in his otherwise sensitive pieces such as *khambaavati, khat, bhatiyaar* and *tilak-kaamod*, there are numerous instances where words are, semantically speaking, dismembered.

Raga **and Elaboration**

The consideration of the content of Pt. Vazebuwa's music is intrinsically bound with the technical aspects. Hence the nature of his *raga*-elaboration also needs to be looked into. It is in this context that his renderings of *khat* and *tilak-kaamod* are notable.

It is commonly known that during the period Pt. Vazebuwa was active, these *raga*-s were considered *aprachalita* (rare); and further they were also believed to be near-monopolies of the *khayal*-singers of the Jaipur *gharana* as shaped by the late Ustad Alladiya Khan and other disciples. A little exercise of historical imagination would however enable us to realise that Pt. Vazebuwa's interpretations of such *raga*-s at that time in reality indicated that the *raga*-lore in Hindustani art music was very much a matter of general circulation than the impressionistic accounts of the *gharana*-s make out to be. (Perhaps it could even be proved that Pt. Vazebuwa preceded the Jaipur musicians in presenting the extremely complex and challenging repertoire, of rare *khayal-raga*-s.) The author has personally heard rare *raga*-s like *kankan, pradumna-kaanada, mudrika-kaanada, nat-narayani, kaafi-kaanada, khat, saamant-kalyaan* from stalwarts like the late Pt. Shivrambuwa Vaze, Pt. Haribhau Ghangrekar and from the veterans like Pt. Gajananrao Joshi and Pt. Bhaskarbuwa Joshi and all these had learnt from Pt. Vazabuwa. The author remembers how his *guru* Pt. Gajananrao Joshi responded to a query put to him by his father (and *guru*) the late Pt. Anant Manohar Joshi. Pt. Gajananraoji had learnt only a few compositions from Pt. Vazebuwa. Hence Pt. Anant Manohar asked his son, 'What have you learnt from Pt. Vazebuwa?' The latter replied without hesitation, 'I have learnt from him the technique of solving the puzzle that *aprachalita raga*-s are.' (The moral of the story is that to obtain an insight into the nature of *aprachalita raga*-s as a phenomenon is more significant than learning a great number of such *raga*-s or compositions in them from anybody.)

In reality a rare *raga* can be a set of structures actually based on deviations from many other known *raga*-s. It is therefore frequently found that a rare *raga* involves a very subtle balancing of *raga*-forces than a mere rendering of *raga*-phrases of many individual *raga*-s in a certain sequence. It is sufficient to listen to Pt. Vazebuwa's *khat* to discern his bold way of treating this rare *raga*. He conceived it as a melodic interplay of two forces: the forces being the *gandhaar-dhaiwat* pairs and the overall *aasaavari*-mood-orientation in the interpretation. Such a treatment achieved two goals: it enhanced the structural appeal of the *raga* because the paired notes are consonant notes. Secondly, the *aasaavari*-orientation bestowed on the *raga* an emotional appeal otherwise inconceivable. Even today the conventional grammatical interpretation of *khat* maintains that the *raga*-name is a derivation of the Sanskrit term '*shata*' meaning six. The implication is that the *raga* consists of six *raga*-s. If strictly adhered to, this logic would lead to a rendering characterised by a mechanical doling out of phrases of the six individual *raga*-s in succession or brought together in a certain sequence! Thus presented, the *raga* could turn into a colourless patchy entity similar to many of the *patmanjiri*-versions (i.e., *raga*-s reported to have five component *raga*-s) put forward. However, in Pt. Vazebuwa's treatment *khat* escaped this fate. This short analysis of one single *raga* is of course illustrative but it could easily be carried out further in respect of other *raga*-s.

The *Taans*

From his conception of *aprachalita raga*-s to the complex *taan*-patterns is a logical step. As soon as the basic decision about the nature of these *raga*-s is arrived at, the *taans* can hardly remain 'the faster rendering of *alaps*.' The *taans* also have to discharge the function of carrying over the structural and sometimes even the emotional musical content of the *alaps*. The general practice of the Hindustani musicians has been to introduce lengthy *taans* ranging over a span of two or more octaves. In contrast, Pt. Vazebuwa believed a great deal in deploying shorter passages, as also in employing an element of tonal contrast. Therefore, his *taans* do not appear to be an act of reeling off of *palataas* (i.e., traditionally devised scale-patterns used as musical exercises aimed at attainment of technical virtuosity). His *taans* succeed in their truer aesthetic task of becoming significant consolidations of *raga*-images and near instantaneous recapitulations of the more important of the *raga* themes. Pt. Vazebuwa's *taan*-units are generally found to consist of four/five component notes uttered with remarkable energy. In fact, in places he seems to have gone out of tune while executing the *taan*—but this could have been due to his advancing age. (One of the discs has a label mentioning his age to be 82 years when the disc was cut!) The vigour with which the *taans* were presented makes an impact of such a depth that to an extent, the volume seems to compensate for the lack of speed (as otherwise Pt. Vazebuwa's *taans* were not impressive in respect of the agility of movement).

What was Pt. Vazebuwa's contribution? Firstly, he enriched the *raga*-repertoire in effective circulation to a considerable extent. He also presented an alternative approach towards decoding the puzzling phenomenon of the *aprachalita raga*. His singing of the *jhaptala*-compositions showed a perceptive mind which invested these compositions with a new flexibility and also represented a new found artistic alertness that seized upon the structural potentialities of the *tala*. The vigour with which he infused his total singing was a clear dimensional contribution because it carried a hint of substitution of pitch by volume—another dimension of the human voice. In the case of every great artist, his disabilities seem to possess the quality of finally turning into assets. Pt. Vazebuwa is one more example of such alchemy.

Ustad Abdul Karim Khan
(11-11-1872 to 27-10-1937)

3

Ustad Abdul Karim Khan
(11-11-1872 to 27-10-1937)

Brief Life-sketch

Born in Kirana (district Saharanpur, U.P.) he was initially trained by his father Kalekhan and uncle Abdullakhan. It is important to note that the *gharana* was closely involved in playing both *sarangi* and *been*—two major string instruments that can present the melodic aspect of Hindustani art music so well. It is also important to remember that vocalists are always advised to be as tuneful as a string instrument—so true and subtle is their tunefulness. As is usually the case, the traditional wisdom in this respect is pithily recorded in an aphorism and we are repeatedly told "Bring the string in the voice and voice in the string" ("*Gale me tant aur tant me gala lana chahiye*"). The import is that singing should be as tuneful as in a string instrument and music on string-instrument should be as uninterrupted as in singing. It was perhaps inevitable that Ustad Abdul Karim Khan cut a short disc of his *been* playing in the early days of his career.

As per the vogue in those times the Ustad soon took a tour with his brother to announce their readiness for the profession and present his music.They began by visiting known places of patronage. He was barely 18 when in 1890s he was appointed a court-musician in the princely state of Baroda for some time. Due to various reasons he left Baroda and successively moved through Bombay, Miraj and Hubli to spread his musical gospel. One notable event was when Rambhau Kundgolkar—who later earned fame as Pt. Sawai Gandharva—became his disciple in 1903. Next important step was to establish *Aarya Sangeet Samaaj* in Pune (1913) and open a branch of the same in Bombay (1917). He used to organise his own music concerts in which notating feats by his young son Suresh (Mane), (and even a singing item by a dog!) preceded his own performance. Like many other artists he was seeking an alternative to the patronage of kings, the wealthy, etc. He had to attract, create as well as train, his own audience—a task not easy at any point of history.

His work had another important and rather unusual facet. Around 1920 Deval and Clement, the two pioneering investigators in the phenomenon of the *sruti*-s (microtonal intervals) in Indian music began giving lec-dem-s on the theme. The Ustad began collaborating with them in these presentations. Thus by participating in a scholatic event in which music-performance was not at the centre, he gave an inkling of his progressive attitude towards matters musical. To venture into this field with no academic background of university education was certainly an act of faith and courage in those times. Around the same time the Ustad closed the Bombay branch and moved to Miraj in southern Maharashtra. In Miraj too he was at the forefront in giving advice and suggestions to the makers of *tanpura*, the major accompnaying string instrument in Hindustani art music. Obvioulsy he was a musician with a difference. It is also instructive to note that he was popular and respectfully heard in the South by followers and patrons of Carnatic art music, which is indeed a notable musical achievement. He had many disciples, devotees and his way of music-making still enjoyes a large following.

On the 27th of October 1937 he was returining from a tour in the South when feeling uneasy, he got down at a small railway station, offered his last prayers to Allah and bid good bye to the world!

Towards Evaluation

In India, evaluation or revaluation of musicians of the pre-1930 era by the later generation poses special problems—the chief being the impossibility of personal exposure to the musician concerned in a *mehfil*-situation. The acuteness of the disadvantage is however slightly lessened in the case of artists like Ustad Abdul Karim Khan who were recorded not too meagrely. Not only was he recorded fairly well, having about thirty-four discs to his credit, but the recorded corpus is also adequately representative of his art. In other words, it covers all the major (and also some minor) types of his total musical expression. The break-up of his recorded music may prove of some interest. For example one can listen to: *khayals*–14 (including both varieties, i.e., *bada*–6 and *chhota*–7), *thumri*-s–8, *naatyageet*-s–6, *Marathi pad*-s–2, *tarana*-s–2 and Carnatic *raga*-s–2.

It is therefore felt with some justification that the samples of his recorded music may not prove too inadequate for the purpose of analysis. In addition, not to discuss him at all would surely impair the attempted examination of the total musical perspective obtained in Hindustani art music, so important has been his influence through admirers and disciples. His influence has been strengthened by his disciples as well as followers. Roshan Ara Begum, Sawai Gandharva in the first phalanx and Gangubai Hangal, Phiroze Dastoor and Bhimsen Joshi of the later generation contributed to a lasting impress of the Ustad's vocalism and musical thinking.

With this backdrop if one considers the matter of musical genres, the Ustad is heard to revel in *khayal, thumri* and the few stage-songs he sang with relish. The three expressions could of course be separately discussed to an extent. However, in all these renderings he exhibits certain common features. It is therefore advisable to discuss the common features prior to devoting attention to the other traits of his art, specific to particular musical forms.

His Vocal Tone

Irrespective of the form of music involved, the overall vocal tone that the Ustad employed attracts immediate attention. His vocal tone could be described as thin, pointed, resonant in segments, slightly nasal and occasionally a little hollow. It also gave an abiding impression of a high fundamental pitch. His voice could be technically classified as an 'upper register voice' that excelled in accentuating those brilliant overtones usually available in abundance in the higher portion of the scale. Unless one is also in possession of a matching lower register, such a voice is naturally weak in the lower ranges. The Ustad clearly lacked the lower register and the musical consequences flowing from this partial vocal development proved inevitable. It is therefore not surprising that most of his pieces were better elaborated in the upper reaches of the scale. The pieces in *bhairavi* ("*Jamunaa ke teer*"), *jogiya* ("*Piyaake milanki aas*") and *tilang* ("*Kaaheko naina lagaaye*") are worth noting in this respect. In fact the *sama*-s of the compositions in *jogiya* and *bhairavi* are on the *taar saa* (the octave note). To carry the point a step further, one notes that generally the spots of unmistakable musical impact in his renderings are also located in the upper reaches of the scale. This is of course not to suggest that he was out of tune in the other parts of the scale. It only means that due to an adherence to the vocal tone as described above, the Ustad was not able to extract the same results in the lower ranges which he could obtain in the upper reaches. A similar lack of appeal was also evident in his execution of the progressions in faster *tempi*. Apparently, an exception is detected in the tonal space, around *madhya gandhaar*. Even though this note is located in the lower stretches of the scale, the Ustad was surely able to invest the singing with appeal while he was engaged in elaborations around this note. In this connection the author has a hypothesis which can accommodate the present exception. Due to the fascinating acoustical qualities (inadequately analysed so far) the last string of the *tanpura* (an instrument which provides the drone to all Hindustani musicians) produces a *gandhaar* which is known to Indian musicology as *swayambhu gandhaar*, i.e., the self-existent *gandhaar*. It is suggested here that by virtue of the Ustad's nasal and upper registered voice-production, the overtones of this note received reinforcement, thus enabling him to retain the musical appeal in an area which would have otherwise remained out of his effective orbit.

The vocal tone so uniformly applied by him was further characterised by superimposition of the compound vowel-sound 'o' or a variety of it on the entire vocalising process. Pressed into service in this manner, the vowel-sound proved a very reliable aid in maintaining '*aas*' in his renderings. The importance of this quality in a solo, melodic tradition can hardly be overestimated. It was due to the '*aas*' that the Ustad was able to maintain vocal connections between the successive musical phrases. The slow fade-out quality realised because of the '*aas*' prevented occurrence of breaks in the intended vocal flow. Of all the vowel-sounds, 'o' has the maximum resonance except in the tonal area above the octave (where in fact all the vowel-sounds tend to lose their respective individual identities). It is instructive to note that the term '*aas*' is derived from the term '*ansha*' meaning a part. Thus to have '*aas*' in music means that instead of a sudden and certain secession music fades off wihtout our becoming aware of its stoppinng or ending. The total situation obtained in the Ustad's music could therefore be interpreted as an application of a two-fold strategy: use of a uniform vocal tone and reliance on a compound, resonant vowel-sound which was a deviation from the normal practice of Hindustani practioners of vocal music to insist on the use of the vowel sound 'AA'. From the dual strategy two musical consequences followed directly: the experience of continuity and generation of an evocative quality.

Both the formulae served him well when singing in slow tempo and at least in respect of the higher notes. In addition, the strategy also blurred the consonantal edges of the words of the song-texts and during the process made the words sound rounder—a musical gain to some extent. But unfortunately the operation also made all the words non-starters as far as etching their individual sound-contours was concerned. Therefore, whether it was a Marathi stage-song ("*Ugich kaa kaanta*"), an art-music composition in *bilawal* ("*Pyaraa najar nahi awandaa*") or a *thumri* ("*Kaaheko naina lagaaye*" or "*Paani bhareli*"), the projected words were unfailingly appealing though utterly indistinguishable from one another.

The foregoing argument has an interesting counter-proof available in the performing techniques of some of the other major followers of the Kiraana *gharana*. As is known, from Ustad's male followers the late Pt. Sawai Gandharva and Pt. Behrebuwa 'sounded' appealing *a la* their *guru*: one could easily detect in them the same vocal techniques as the Ustad had applied. It consisted of: the superimposed compound vowel-sound, abundant use of the upper register and the uniformity of vocal tone irrespective of the genre. On the other hand, Roshanara Begum (who later shifted to Pakistan) and Pt. Bhimsen Joshi (a well-known disciple of Pt. Sawai Gandharva) do not create the same kind of appeal because both these artists do not 'sound' like the Ustad. The reason is that these singers use a projection strategy consisting of a two-registered voice and employment of multiple vowel-sounds. Such changes were imperative for these artists because without introducing them they would not have succeeded in executing the fast *taans*, an act they perform so effectively. It is in fact a vindication of a performer's logic to see the same two artists also abandoning the use of a uniform tone.

Accent on the *Bol-alap*

Another commonly traceable feature of the Ustad's singing was his total reliance on the *bol-alaps* and the proportionate paucity of the use of *aa-kaar* (utilisation of the vowel-sound 'AA') in his musical elaborations. This was casually connected with the continuity of tone that he so firmly believed in. Musical continuity of the type described earlier would not have been possible if the vocalisation was to depend on vowel-sounds (and especially on that of 'AA'). The simple and unexceptional reason is that vowel-production by itself means spending more breath than what is necessary for producing consonants. Even a non-technical, commonsense definition tells us that vowel-sound is heard when an uninterrupted, outgoing, air-flow is used for producing voice, while a consonant-sound is created when the flow is stopped at various points in the oral cavity in different ways to produce linguistic sounds. The Ustad's accent on the *bol-alaps* is to be viewed in this context. Words were used copiously because using them meant exploiting the consonants as devices for shaping and maintaining the voice-flow for longer durations. However, this manner of giving importance to words is not the same as the other two modes of according recognition to words as musical forces. (The two other modes of giving musical importance to words are to pay heed to them as meaningful units and to use them as sound-patterns.) As the Ustad used them, they were more of voice-savers and colouring agents than being vehicles of meaning or patterns in sound. Almost as a rule, words were formed tentatively rather than definitively in his music and their aura was regarded more important than their clarity. There was a pervasive blurring of sound-contours of the individual words and in place of their purposeful differentiation (either meaning-based or sound-based) listeners became conscious of a continuous musical flow.

His Position on *Tala*

The third recurrent characteristic of his music was the Ustad's notion about the role of *tala*. To judge from his music, the Ustad definitely assigned a subservient role to *tala*. He took the first step towards making the *tala* less important and less obtrusive, barely perceptible and considerably lenient or less rigorous when he slowed down the tempo of the accompanying rhythm in his music-making. Nothing could have been more effective in attenuating the impact of the individual pattern of any *tala*. It is certainly significant that even today those responsible for a further slowing down of the tempo of *khayal* music are also followers of the Kirana ideology. In such instances today the tempo has been slowed down to such a (crawling) pace that it has caused a near-total obliteration of the design of individual *tala*-s. In the Ustad's music this slackening of the general tempo of the *tala* was further followed by a consistent reduction in the variety of the *tala*-s kept in circulation. The Ustad confined himself to a very few *tala*-s and in the process totally ignored the effect of the diversity of patterns made available to us by the structural peculiarities of individual *tala*-s. In sticking to *ektala* and *teentala* he in a sense proved logical, and his usage exemplified his position. If the pattern of a *tala* was not worth noticing, there was no need to use a variety of *tala*-s as basic frames. This same scant respect for the *tala*-entity was also evident in his noticeably sparing use of *taans* and *bol-taans* that enjoyed a pronounced rhythmic orientation. His avoidance of the conventional tempo-doubling at the closing stages of *thumri*-singing could also be traced to his basic reluctance to allow any scope to the *tala*-element in music. It is known that the doubling of the tempo in *thumri*-singing ensures a temporary shift of emphasis to the *tala*-frame which is otherwise kept dormant. The Ustad did not concede to *tala* even this momentary glory! He was reported to have favoured the traditional aphorism "*Tala gaya to baal gaya, sur gaya to sir gaya*"! Roughly this means in translation, "if a musician loses in respect of *tala*, it is comparable to a mere loss of hair but if he goes out of tune, it is like losing one's head!"

It was on this background that irrespective of the form of music presented, the Ustad's music recognised only those beats which were adjacent to the *sama*-point. As far as other sub-sections of the *tala* or other contributory time-points like *khaali*, etc., were concerned, no special care was taken to build any relationship with them. It was obvious that *tala* was regarded as a constraining force rather than as a co-operating component of the patterning activity that music ceaselessly tries to be. *Tala* was treated as less than equal, though peaceful co-existence with it was not totally ruled out. For the Ustad, it was the tempo and not the *tala* which was material. He was traditional enough to employ a *tala*, yet he was a rebellious soul in the sense that he voluntarily denied himself the exciting possibilities and appeals of rhythmic variations as well as their interplay with the changing tempi. Listening to him one always gets a feeling that had he been living today, he would have hardly hesitated to banish the *tala* completely, even at the risk of making music unvaryingly smooth and therefore undesirably satiating. It is no secret that between the tonal and the rhythmic variations, the latter are conveyed and perceived universally and with more facility. In fact, it is maintained that even in the case of transcending the intercultural or cross-cultural barriers, the element of rhythm crosses them with more sureness. The stakes involved in playing down the role of *tala* were therefore very high. It may of course be possible that on the Ustad's part this was more of an intuitive choice than a conscious aesthetic decision. Yet the consequences were aesthetic and are to be considered as such.

A Kind of Non-Academism

Finally, his entire music was also imbued with a spirit of non-academism. The observation perhaps needs some explaining.

In this context two terms and the related concepts must be clearly distinguished. They are: academism and pedantry. Pedantry is a dry (or puritanical) adherence to the scholastic tradition of music. In contrast, academism is a positive recognition of the scholastic tradition. Academism views scholastic tradition as a musical force that stabilises the performing tradition and provides a continuous base for deviations. Having a wider perspective, an academic musician becomes the chief protagonist in an effort to realise the aesthetic paradoxes. A true academic successfully strikes a balance between conformity and innovation, stability and dynamism and lastly between craftsmanship and creativity. For example, in the matter of *raga*-renderings an academic musician tries to project a grammatically correct image of a *raga* and yet takes care to suggest the possible and perhaps musically attractive deviations. It is in this sense that the Ustad lacked the academic outlook. The grammatical outlines of his renderings were often confused or they lacked definition. For instance, his *sarparadaa* could hardly be endorsed by the established interpretation of the *raga*. It also happened that his *taans* would disagree with the *raga*-interpretation as put forward in *alaps* (e.g. his rendering of *raga basant*). All these musical *faux pas* could take place not because he was not aware of the core-deviation phenomenon but because he had accorded an aesthetic priority to the particular general tone of his music and also because he regarded individual notes as more important than the collective *raga*-image that the notes stood for. In other words, effectiveness of the musical tone reigned supreme in his musical logic and correctness-core and the deviational periphery remained on the sidelines. It is therefore not surprising that his published correspondence with disciples reveals his preference for intensive practice as opposed to the theoretical concern for the correctness of *raga khambavati*. Of course, to have such preferences was not unique in his times. A majority of musicians always regarded effective performance as more relevant to genuine musicianship than accquisition of theoretical insights. Though exonerable, the sort of either/or attitude exhibited towards musical matters in such preferences was in the ultimate analysis, a lop-sided response to the total musical reality. It is naive to equate grammatical correctness with pedantry and to dissociate knowledge of music from its practice. However, as such opinions were almost universally detected in his times the Ustad need not be singled out for censure.

His Singing of *Khayal* and *Thumri*

Discussion of these general characteristics of the Ustad's music prepares us for a more technical analysis of two particular musical forms the Ustad selected as vehicles for his musical expression namely, *khayal* and *thumri*.

Even a cursory hearing makes it clear that in his renderings *khayal* and *thumri* came so near to one another that they became practically indistinguishable.

To start with, the singing of a composition in both the categories was replete with the same uniform, appealing tone, described earlier. The consequence was predictable. In this connection it must be remembered that one way of keeping musical forms separate is to vary the emotional appeal with which they can be infused. It can be safely generalised that, those art-musical forms categorised as 'classical' in India are cooler, less sensuous or less emotional in appeal and presentation than those categorised otherwise. The classical forms tend to attract the listeners by the arabesque quality of music. The Ustad's strategy of investing both *thumri*, and *khayal*-singing with the uniform tone resulted in uniform appeals and similar musical appearances. The act was a musicological taboo as it was an aesthetic risk. But the choice, in the final analysis, was his to make and he made it unequivocally.

There was also a possibility of keeping the genres separate by keeping a watchful eye on the 'definition' of structures of the individual *raga*-s. This would have made the contours of *raga* a little more resistant to effacement. In each *raga*, the primary building-blocks of set melodic phrases are clearly identifiable. Such phrases are often exclusively attached to a particular *raga*. Thus to emphasise these phrases is a very efficient course open to a musician interested in *raga*-individuation. It may be said that of all other distinguishing factors, it is the *raga*-individuation that effectively separates 'classical' from the 'non-classical' music in India. However, it is clear that on account of his overall musical strategy both tone-differentiation and the *raga*-individuation were denied to the Ustad. His *khayal* and *thumri* therefore produce a near-identical musical impact.

In addition, the Ustad also refrained from employing the words of the *thumri*-text in a meaningful manner. A *thumri*-singer (as contrasted with a singer of *khayal*) could be said to orient all his musical elaborations on the lines suggested by the emotive drift of the *thumri*-text. There are many *thumri*-types in vogue but all of them agree on the point of putting performing and musical emphases on the words of the text. For example, in one type of *thumri*, the words are arranged, rearranged and distributed in the main stream of music. This type is aptly known as *bol-baant*. In another type the singer of *thumri*-s laces the emotive appeal of the words with matching tonal and gestural variations. This type is appropriately known as *bol-banav*. *Thumri*-singers are also prone to recite matching lyrical couplets in between their main musical elaborations. All such devices undoubtedly bring the word-meaning to the fore. In fact, *thumri*-singers are so conscious of their use of words that they are also aware of the sameness of musical effect that the word-orientation might produce. This unrelieved dependence on one single element of music they seek to diminish by bringing in the elements of tempo (through the *dugun*-phenomenon), rhythm (through the centreing of the *laggi*-pieces reeled off by the *tabla*-player during the *dugun*) and *taan* (through the flourishes coming at the phase-terminations during the presentation).

One finds that all such features were absent in the Ustad's renderings. In their place was installed a uniform, enveloping tone which blurred the word-contours as well as the structural lines of the presentation taken as a whole. *Thumri* as a musical form had already crystallised when the Ustad was active. (Even the *thumri-gharanas* had come into their own.) Under the circumstances the Ustad's neglect of the accepted conventions of *thumri*-singing needs to be explained. Was it the Ustad's lack of academic outlook that led to the 'blurring'-effect referred to?

To be fair to the Ustad, another possibility also needs to be considered. That possibility was of deliberately introducing the 'blurring' as a measured step towards modernity. It is known to all students of arts that merging the prevailing art-forms or initiating processes that accentuate or accelerate their overlap is very often regarded as a major characteristic of modernity. The Ustad's music could be construed as a prominent example of such a phenomenon in Hindustani art music of the present times made of the immediate past, continuing present and the closely following future. His tendency to blur the dividing lines existing between two forms could be interpreted as an operation that denied the validity of the traditional hierarchy of musical forms. For him musical forms were only carriers of musical messages. His music as such had one message and hence followed the equality of treatment and temperament in respect of *khayal*-s and *thumri*-s.

The Ustad's preference for the 'blur' effect was also discernible at one more level. It has already been seen how he had burnt his boats as far as *raga*-differentiation according to structural and codified features was concerned. He adopted a similar attitude in respect of the emotional appeals or the evocative identities of individual *raga*. In this context it is instructive to examine the way he handled the matter of *raga*-dynamics which is a very effective device of *raga* individuation. *Raga*-dynamics can be described as the cumulative result of volume-variations and the condensation-rarefaction of the note-clusters involved in a particular *raga*. The

Ustad was deprived of these devices because his motto was fidelity to every note in near-equal measure and also because he was insistent on maintaining a high degree of melodiousness throughout a rendering. Sincerely pursued, the resultant policy placed him in the predicament of a lyricist who insists that every word in his composition should be lyrical! Such a literal 'single'-mindedness achieves artistic success of a 'monochrome' variety. Inevitably, *bilawal*, *shankara*, *basant* or *jogiya* all sounded alike in the Ustad's music. Irrespective of one's position on the interrelationship of *rasa*-theory and Hindustaani music, it is clear that *raga shankara* has a mood that is markedly different from that of *raga jogiya* or that *raga basant* possesses an atmospheric effect of its own which is qualitatively and radically different from that of *bhairavi*! In the Ustad's music, however, there is only one deep hue of anguish all over and in all *raga*-s. In view of the unvarying vocalising techniques he adopted, the general attitude he held about the nature of musical appeal and the treatment he reserved for words in all categories of music—this was inevitable.

Response to Carnatic Music

Of his musical personality one facet needs to be considered before a settled opinion about his contribution can be recorded. The matter of his responses to Carnatic music deserves a special mention. His responses were more positive and deep-seated than responses of many other musicians of his times. To 'import' Carnaatic *raga*-s into the Hindustani fold, to author new compositions in them and in this manner to totally acclimatise Carnaatic *raga*-s in the Hindustani vogue is perhaps too obvious and easy a response to merit analysis. What the Ustad tried was however more fundamental and subtle. What he did was to incorporate certain

Carnaatic patterns of phrasing the *sargam* (i.e. the *sol-fa* singing) in his Hindustani elaborations and to employ them without the colour of the Carnaatic *gamak* style. To all purposes, a major way of enriching the available, total and performing musical repertoire of any culture is to induct new performing patterns into it, and this was what the Ustad tried and achieved. The patterns he brought in could be well assimilated because they were not accompanied by the Carnatic way of intoning them. At the same time, the quality of novelty was unmistakable because the patterns did not belong originally to the Hindustani progressions and were an outcome of their deft removal from the original matrix. He had, in other words, transplanted them and placed them in a different but conducive context. His action was therefore not an attempt of wholesale borrowing of Carnaatic structures, nor was it a fashionable or a 'gimmicky' move. It was a deliberate and a skillful measure of introducing new resources by way of re-creation. As a result, the new patterns could serve him as generative moulds which were neither restricted to the particular instances of their original appearance, nor were they confined to Hindustani musical examples similar to them in structure, *raga*-phrasings, etc. In other words, the Ustad's *sargam* with the Carnatic contours was a veritable feat of musical bisociation. It was logical that these moulds were used in all forms of music he selected to perform.

Conclusion

Ustad Abdul Karim Khan surely belonged to the category of the non-conformists. His musical accomplishment was twofold. Firstly, he was responsible for throwing a strong challenge to the dry (though grammatically correct) *khayal*-singing that was in vogue. When most of his contemporaries were interested in systematising the available corpus of Hindustani *khayal*, he stressed the role of 'appeal' in music. It is true that many other musicians too would have sworn by the same credo. But in reality very few took the risk of changing the traditional orientation of the actual performance in pursuance of the musical ideals they preached. The other genre he chose to perform was *thumri*, and in his singing of it he registered an interesting deviation. He chose not to cling to words in an obvious, literal fashion in the name of emotional appeal. Under the circumstances he could be credited with liberating the *thumri* from its word-dependence. Without having recourse to the word-meaning, he succeeded in retaining the emotional quality of music by virtue of his 'tone' and his attitude towards musical material in general. His achievements as a *thumri*-singer stand out as a valuable addition to the established dimensions of the form. He could be emotional without being sentimental and sweet without, being cloying in his *thumri*-s. This was not a minor feat to perform.

Some of Ustad's presentations are briefly analysed here to provide additional material to evaluate his achievements. Intentionally the material is chosen from recorded music available to all.

Darbari Kaanada

As the name suggests the *raga* is connected with kingly courts. The *raga* is associated with Miya Tansen, the legendary vocalist who was Emperor Akbar's court-musician. The *raga* can be accepted to be fairly old as it has compositions in most of the durable genres of the Hisdustani art music such as *dhrupad, dhamar, khayal, chaturang, tarana,* etc. This aspect also points to its musically accomodative nature as well as structure.

It certainly lives up to its name as its internal tempo impresses by its majestic slowness. The elaboration takes place mainly in the lower and middle octave ranges. If rendered with adequate attention to all its important notes, it can certainly be expansively presented over an hour's duration. The mood is grave and contemplative. Due to its inherent potential it can easily project the compassionate mood of a tragic hero.

The note *komal gandhar* in the *raga* tests the ability of a musician to note nuances of intonation. This note in this *raga* demands vibration without trembling. The concerned artist's perception, skill as well as the depth and rigour of his training, are all put to test simultaneously! In other words, even the concerned performer's *guru*'s effectiveness of teaching is put to test! Normally the *raga* is presented during midnight hours and no particular season is associated with it. Even though the name is also suggestive of the South, no *raga* of southeren origin tallies with *darbari kaanada* in toto.

The following varieties of the *raga* are well-established in the tradition: *Adambari, kolahal, kaushi, khamaji, chandra-mukhi, jayjaywanti, devsakh, daulati, nagdhvani, nayaki, naubatkhani, panchmukhi, palasi, bageshri, bilaskhani, bhhop, mudriki, vasanti, shuddha, sindhura, 'sughrai, suha, suha-sughrai* and *sorathi*.

The *chhota khayal* composition—"*Zanak zhanakwa tore bichwa*"—that the Ustad has presented could be said to reflect well the personality of the *raga* as well as the genius of the artist. With a few haunting initial notes we are acquainted with the grave and sad mood of the *raga*. A definite and yet oscillating intonation of the note *komal gandhar* he reaches us with a light and moving manner. He achieves the miracle of keeping in tact the evocative power of the note in the middle as well as in the high octave. In the lower ranges the intonation is rounder while in the higher ranges it is thinner, piercing and yet sweet. Both heaven and the earth are easy to access in his music! His *alap*-s, i.e. the melodic musical elaborations are generally lingering if not too slow. Yet, often his way is to include fast paced clusters of four-five notes while moving towords a note he wants to emphasise on which he wants to stop. In the present case we hear this happening in relation to the note *Komal Gandhar*. Without the requisite unimpaired tunefulness this would have remained an empty gesture. The Ustad has avoided this harm. In fact, in his rendering he also has executed some fast and forceful *taans*. And this raises an issue.

On account of this *gharana's* oath-taking loyalty to the evocation in music and the emphasis on the slow tempo elaboration, it limits the *raga*-s the artists from this *gharana* would take as relevant. The corroboration of this statement is found in the *raga*-s the *Kirana* artists favour. *Raga*-s such as *kalyan, puriya, lalat, darbari kaanada, miyaki todi, abhogi kaanada* would find favour. These are appropriate for *alap*, i.e. not specially suited to *taan* and other similar elaborational procedures. In addition, the position of the *gharana* regarding intonation, importance of *alap*, place of emotion in music etc., also makes the role of *tala* rather subsidiary. Thus a routine use of *tala*-s such as *ektala*, *jhumra*, etc., is expectable.

Sarparda

This morning-*raga* is derived from the *Shankarabharan thata* known to most Hindustani musicians as *bilawal thata*. *Sarparda,* regarded a sub-variety of *bilawal* is also credited to Amir Khusro as one of his creations. Some treat it as a bringing together of *yaman, alhaiya* and *gaud* but there are others who do not adhere to this opinion. The internal tempo of the *raga* could be said to range between medium to fast. A controlled feeling for the pain of seperation and the readiness to acccept whatever takes place characterises the mood of the *raga*. It needs to be kept distinct from many varieties of *bilawal*, and *bihag*, a night-time *raga*.

As far as the Ustad is concerned one ever-present mood of his music could be described as a combined mood inclusive of pathos, pain and peacefulness. Additionally the mood is not explored on a personal basis. When the Ustad's rendering of "*Gopala karuna kyon nahi aave*" (O Krishna, how is it that you do not feel any compassion!) in his rounded, somewhat nasal and fading-out intonation one is convinced that this is the only way for everybody to invoke Lord Krishna!

The Ustad moves in all spaces of the octave with extreme confidence. Through subtle variations he creates shades of the main emotional thrust. The intensity of emotional anguish is often localised in high notes. Yet even when one is listening to the moving music one notes that his rendition is thin on the established/codified nature of the *raga*. He appears to change/mix *raga*-shades as if he is presenting a *thumri*! His aim is not elaboration of a *raga* but to permeate the atmosphere with emotion and evocation. The echoes of *bhajan* or *thumri* are heard in profusion. The Ustad makes an excuse of a *raga*-scale to generate a state of mind. May be the Ustad is taking advantage of the fact that *raga*-s such as *sarparda* are less than definitely entrenched in the codified hierarchy.

The kind of music he creates tempts me to look for more of such deviationist attempts!

Abhogi Kaanada

This is one of those *raga*-s that has been imported from the Caranatic art music. Even if the name suggests it is a sub-type of the *darbari Kaanada*, in reality it is derived from the *mallar raga* in the *kafi thata*. Perfomred during earlier part of night its predominant mood is of quiet, sweet feeling of expectancy. Elaboration takes place mainly in the lower and middle octve-ranges. It has no special connections with any particular season and the internal tempo ranges from slow to medium. The *raga* offers scope for *alap*. The phrases linking notes '*Dha*' and '*Ma*' are characteristic. Its vogue in the Hindustani art music is comparatively recent.

The Ustad presents the *raga* in his own way. It is perhaps an instance of his ideas about how to stabilise Carnatic *raga* in Hindustani music-making. Even though *darbari kaanada* and *abhogi kaanada* share ideas about internal tempo, mood, etc., the responsibility to maintain their identities distinct is thereby increased. The Ustad has achieved this goal to some extent. Though the tempo of the *tala* is not very slow the Ustad has opted for a slower tempo in his own singing. The vocal tone is kept rounder everywhere and words are not too emphatically pronounced, thereby maintaining an accommodative evocative projection throughout the rendering. The *taan* becomes a jarring feature in the total context. It is surprising that even the Ustad should consider *tana* an integral part of the *khayal* singing.

Gara

Gara is a representative example of what happens in case of many other Hindustani *raga*-s. The name does not suggest region, season or any such feature as the generating agency. *Gara* includes all the seven notes and also allows roles to the *komal* (flat) varieties of notes *gandhar* and *nishad*. In addition, the genres with which the *raga* is mainly associated are not inherently keen on adhering to the *raga*-rules. In fact they are keen on making deliberate and frequent deviations from any melodic frame which constitutes their compositional skeleton. The *raga gara* is often employed by shifting the fundamental note '*Sa*' to '*Ma*'—a procedure facilitating the creation of shadows of many other different *raga*-s. The procedure is known as modulation (of keys). The fact that *thumri*, *dadra* and 'lighter' genres of music-making in Hindustani music are closely associatd with the *raga* seems natural, inevitable and also desirable due to the intrinsic capacity of *Gara* to allow musical freedom to the artist. The internal tempo ranging from medium to fast seems conducive to the liberated elaborations of the *raga*. The mood is peaceful and happy. Special-effect musical embellishments known as *khatka*, *murki* that are not easy, but provide accessible sense of pleasure to listeners, are profusely employed. Thus in a rather paradoxical manner, though the *raga* is associated with many seemingly non-restrictive features it is not an easy job to put forward its rich quality.

The Ustad's performance makes a gift of two moons! Firstly, the pleasure of listening to a 'classical' maestro singing a 'lighter' piece which goes to prove his versatility. And secondly in the rendition *dadra* as a genre and *gara* as a *raga* are experienced in their glory.

It is to be noted that *dadra* is the name of the genre as well as the *tala* in which it is presented. Thus the specific *tala* is an essence of the genre. The *tala* is of a very limited expanse as it consists of only six beats. Naturally, individual cycles of the *tala* get over very quickly, thus not offering much time to elaborate musical ideas. The *tala*-structure is also very simple and easy to follow and the intrinsic tempo is medium to fast. It is instructive to note that often in the related grammatical expositions the *tala* is described as *ardha-tala*. All these features of the *tala* reach the listeners easily through the Ustad's music-making.

A damsel going to the river in a graceful manner to fetch water, is a favoured theme of Indian music-makers. Through the singing the lilt of the *tala* and the seductive gait of the damsel both are conveyed well. Intonation, pronunciation of words, melodic patterns with a capacity to reflect the attractiveness of the whole scene—all move together to make the piece a memorable musical presentation. The Ustad succeeds in creating evocative music that is not tied down to a classifiable emotion!

Malkauns

In the tradition *raga*-names such as *malkosh*, *malavkaushik*, *mallkaushik* are mentioned. Interesting information that Kaushik refers to the Satpuda mountain ranges known as *mala* is also provided. On the other hand, it is also argued that the *raga*-name directly points to Malav region. What is however most instructive is that the present-day *raga malkauns* derived from the *bhairavi thata* has no musicological support in the ancient works. Some have suggested that the *raga* can be derived from the *asavari thata*. With the note '*ma*' as its *vadi* and '*sa*' as the *samvadi* the *raga* flowers in all tonal ranges and genres such as *dhrupad*, *dhamar*, *khayal*, *tarana* etc, all circulate in it .It has varied internal tempo and both vocalists and instrumentalists are keen on it due to its wide expressive spectrum.

It is grave, mature and has a tinge of majestic sadness but does not emote pathos. It is philosophical or contemplative and non-dramatic acceptance of the fate seems to be its bearing.

In the season-*raga* context the *raga* is associated with *Shishir Ritu,* i.e., autumn and the late night hours are allotted for its performance in the tradition.

Ustad has presented the popular *khayal* "*Peer na jani*" and it certainly is a memorable rendering—intense as well as evocative. The song-text has the usual thrust—"He does not understand how much pain he causes by not coming to see me. His behaviour is strange and since when he has become so ascetic as not to turn my way—I fail to understand !" Now the text is so phrased that with a little stretching of imagination the 'He' of the composition can also be considered a reference to God!

The emotional ambiguity of the text is consonant with the Ustad's own position on the *raga*-emotion relationship. He is known to sound intense, pleading, full of anguish even when rendering near-amorous texts and while engaging in aggressive melodic designs such as fast *taan*. One can lose something precious whithout knowing what has been actually lost! This is what this *malkauns* appears to project.

Jogiya

The meaning of the word *Jogiya* in Hindi is "of the *yogi* who has renounced the world". Jogi is a word derived from the Sanskrit *Yogi*. The *yogi*-s in many sects employ music but the *raga* under discussion is not a favourite item in their repertoire.

The *raga* is also not from the ancient corpus of *raga*. The compositions in circulation in the *raga* are not varied. Though the *raga* frame is not very restrictive the *raga* mainly explores the middle and high octave with notes '*Sa-ma*', or '*Ma*-high *Sa*' as its *vadi-samvadi*. Obviously and characteristically, the Ustad prefers the second opinion. Internal *raga*-tempo is medium. In the final analysis, it is appropriate to classify the *raga* as a *dhun-raga*. Its strength is not in expansive possibility or codificatory definiteness but a clarity of thrust, attactive melodic framework are its strong-points.Some linking movements (*Ma-re*)contribute to its musical stature.This *raga* sounds similar to the Carnatic *raga* called *Saveri* to some extent. It is therefore interesting to consider the suggestion that *jogiya* be seen as a combination of *raga bhairavi* and *saveri*. It has a non-commital, philosphical mood in which turning away from the mundane world is a primary factor. To project the sentiment is not easy.

The *jogiya* derived from the *bhairav thata* is alotted morning-hours as performing-span of time though no specific season or region are connected with it. Due to its musical profile very often it takes the place of *Bhairavi* which is the last *raga* to be performed in a concert in the Hindustani tradition.

All the perfomring merits of the Ustad's musical personality have found a place in his rendering of the *raga* with the composition "*Piyake milanki aas*" (I have still some hope of meeting my beloved). Right from the beginning the Ustad emotes intensity, anguish and a sense of pathos. A call to the beloved subtlely becomes a prayer to the God! How the artist achieves this marvel, one wonders!

Pt. Vishnu Digambar Paluskar
(18-8-1872 to 20-8-1931)

4

Pt. Vishnu Digambar Paluskar
(18-8-1872 to 20-8-1931)

A Brief Life-sketch

In the 19th century an enveloping musical renaissance was trying to take charge in India and Maharashtra was no exception. Sometimes the 'realness' of the renaissance has been questioned. For example, doubts have been raised about whether reinterpretation of older texts to provide guidelines for contemporary action can be described as a true reform as the basic strategy of preferring texts to life-pattern as decision-makers remained untouched. However, the work done in the field of music by Pt. V. N. Bhatkhande and Pt. Vishu Digambar Paluskar has been accepted as fitting examples of renaissance and reform related to music. If motivation, the scope of the intended and achieved work, and the intensity of efforts to accomplish the ideals set forth as life-work and all such factors are considered, it can be rightly claimed that these two Vishnu-s from Maharashtra were glorious reformers of Indian music in many respects. In this attempt, the work of Pt. Vishnu Digambar Paluskar is sought to be evaluated.

Under the Maratha rule many small princely states were active centres of culture and Kurundwad, with Patwardhan-s as its ruler was one of them. Vishnu's father Digambarpant was a practitioner of *Naradiya keertan* in this Brahmin State. As this kind of *keertan* invariably included philosophical-religious discourses permeated with music Vishnu could be said to have enjoyed religion and music as his staple food from the childhood. Indeed both music and religion are understood in the Indian tradition as forces to bring the society together. Vishnu's vision became too weak very early and the normal school-education had to be ruled out. Perhaps this was the reason why Vishnu decided to pursue music as a career. At the age of 15, Vishnu shifted to a nearby larger State called Miraj to receive better music education. After a brief stint with one Pt. Maheshwarbuwa—known as a good singer of *tappa*—Vishnu received good *talim* from Pt. Balkrishnabuwa Ichalkaranjikar, who was the person responsible for firmly establishing the Gwalior *gharana* of Hindustani art music in Maharashtra. About the time Vishnu also had to get married according to the conventions of the time.

> A symbolic coincidence was that Wajid Ali Shah of Lucknow staying at Matiya Burj in Calcutta during his exile died the same year. Wajid Ali had come to Calcutta with a retinue of musicians under his patronage in the older style, lived and encouraged music for nearly 30 years before his death. In his later life Pt. Vishnu Digambar was to prove a pioneer in the movement aimed at creating a new kind of music with a new kind of patrons!

In 1896 at the age of 25, Vishnu had decided to move out to test professional waters as a musician and a vocalist. According to the established customs he had to begin by performing for the wealthy, feudal lords and rulers of the princely States to get patronage and recognition for launching his career. For example, in this first tour he visited Satara, Baroda, Kathewad, Rajkot, Gwalior, Aligarh, Mathura, Delhi, Jalandhar, Amritsar, Lahore, Jodhpur,

Montgomery, Jaisalmer, Udaipur and Bombay. But it is noteworthy that in 1897 he organised a ticketed public performance of music because, as hinted earlier, he was keen on finding a new kind of patronage for music and musicians. In the same year in a memorable revelatory incident a *sadhu* he met in mount Girnar advised him to go and explore the North, and go to Punjab to attain his aims. Vishnu Digambar performed impressively in the famous *Harballabh Mela* in 1898 and he started receiving invitations to perform. It is obvious that while handling a busy performing schedule he was also closely observing the social and cultural scene, analysing the musico-social behaviour and deciding on one of his more specific goals in music and related fields. He decided to work simultaneously in music-performance, music-eduacation and music-propagation and made this a mission of his life. This is the background on which he opened a music-teaching institution in Lahore in 1901 when he was about 29. In a prophetic incident in 1902 one of his admirers presented him with a copy of Tulsi *Ramayana*! If music shaped Vishnu's life, the *Ramayana* and Vishnu's devotion to Rama determined the nature and shape of Vishnu's music! Both were much more than influences.

It is instructive to note some other events that took place in his life during this early period. Appreciated together they give a better idea of the scope of his total achievement. For example, in 1904 he joined a procession taken out in Lahore demanding freedom from the foreign British rule. He was engaged in singing patriotic songs in the procession and one famous song had a line criticising the ignorance of the people (How long will you remian in ignorance, O inhabitants of my Bharat! कितने दिन ज्ञानहीन रहोगे). Much later in 1921 he acceded to Gandhiji's request and sang *Ramdhun* to quieten a restless crowd attending a meeting. As an activity linked to his multi-aspected task of music-propagation and music-eduacation, he also founded an instrument-making factory and a printing press along with the music-school. Mr. Daulatrao Shinde was put in charge of the factory and Mr. Narayan Khandekar looked after the press. A separate section was opened in the School to look after music-teacher's training. In 1905, he launched a magazine devoted to music—appropriately and ambitiously naming it *Sangitamrutpravaaha*. During 1908-1913, branches of the School were opened in Bombay, Pune, Nagpur and in 1915 the music-classes run in Bombay were relocated and turned into an impressive looking Music Institution. (A notable coincidence was that Lokmanya Tilak's *Geetarahasya* was published in the same year.) The Institute awarded dimplomas and degrees in music with great fanfare and ceremonies for the same dazzled the music-community in the years 1911, 1915, 1919 and in 1921. The regularity of the occasions bring home the success of the venture. In between Panditji also established *Ramnaam Aadhaar Sangeet Mandal* in 1918. A son, Dattatreya was born in 1921. He was Panditji's only son who survived and earned a name as a musician though he too died early, leaving behind a tragic feeling of so much unrealised potential amongst those who followed his short career and Panditji's ordeals.

It is indeed true to say that events in Panditji's life give an impression of an embattled tragic hero in a Greek tragedy. Even after achieving so much in so many music-related fields he was forced to close his Institute in Bombay and auction off all his property in the multi-coloured city of Bombay in which he had created deep imprints. (Was it a presentiment that prompted him to begin donning a *Kafani*—a known traditional sign of renouncement since 1922?) Attempts were reportedly made to reopen the Institute in 1929 by securing a place in Khetwadi and then in Banam Hall Lane but all that was in vain as far as Panditji's institutional life was concerned. He was merely 52 at that time!

His heroic struggle seemingly continued on a personal basis. For example, a Women's Music Conference was organised under the leadership of Shrimati Petit in Bombay and Panditji perhaps formulatd the basic idea and also participated in her conference. The first Music Teachers' Conference organised in Nasik (1928) also had his inspiration and participation. During the same year he visited Sri Lanka and delivered lectures in English. In Pune the issue of employing Marathi for making Hindustani art music was being hotly discussed and Panditji was in the forefront of the discussion. In 1929, he was planning to visit England and also to act in a film of Sant Tulsidas. However, while engaged in all these and varied activities he was becoming more and more detached. He had accepted the fate of facing countless defeats and yet to continue working in music-education, propagation and institutionalisation of music. He died in Miraj when he was only 59.

Evaluation as a Vocalist, Music-Educationist, Music-Propagator and Music-Organiser

It can be stated that Panditji's work in the field of music could be classified as that of a vocalist, music-educationist, music-propagator and a music-organiser.

Panditji as a Vocalist

Unfortunately there is no direct evidence today such as audio-recording etc. to enable us to arrive at an independent evaluation of Panditji's music-performances. This is rather surprising as even a traditional perfomer such as Ustad Rahimat Khan was recorded in 1920. Prof. Deodher has noted that Panditji was rarely heard in a *mehfil* because Panditji demanded Rs. 500 as a honorarium at that time and secondly because he did not accept invitations to sing at celebration of marriages, etc. As a cumulative effect his music is not available to us. Secondary evidence of descriptions of his singing by his disciples, admirers, etc., is not of much use as such descriptions tend to be similar even when compared with writings on other musicians. As a result Panditji's specific qualitative contribution as a performer cannot be imagined from a perusal of such sources. Panditji had also published some booklets that consisted of notation of musical elaboration of certain *raga*-s —almost trying to produce scores of music as in Western musical tradition. However, the notation system was too skeletal for the purpose and such publications were not numerous. So this unique attempt is useful not for getting an idea of his performing prowess but his thoroughness as a music-educator and propagator.

Panditji as a Pioneering Music-Educator

Fortunately there is ample evidence of his achievement as a music-educator. Perusal of what his disciples have written about him, books that Panditji authored and contemporary accounts —all bear testimony to his immense and multi-directional work in the field of music-education. It is interesting to note that even before he established his music teaching institution at Lahore in 1901 he was already thinking about evolving a mechanical aid for keeping *tala*. Western musicians have been using metronome as a rhythm/tempo keeping mechanism from the 18th century and Panditji must have been inspired by this vogue. He also evolved and finalised a notation system which carries a clear impress of the Western staff notation. What emerges is that he was thinking and working on evolving modern means of teaching and learning music even before he began the actual campaign.

Of course what is more fundamental than the matter of educational means is the phenomenon of shaping an appropriate musical pedagogy. Essentially what strikes in his attitude is his conviction that music education needed to be rescued from *guru*'s/*Ustad*'s whims, disciples' fate/destiny and divine coincidences. Having done so, it can be transformed into a disciplined approach which is irrespective of the persons concerned. This seems to be his basic faith and he worked accordingly. Panditji believed that the revered *guru-shishya parampara* was appropriate to music but a change in the framework in which the *parampara* functioned was needed. Hence he tried to reorganise different aspects of music education. Thus, even though there was a *Gurukul* and the staying of the disciple with the *guru* in his model, it was minus the usual excess of domesticity etc. and the attempt was to enable the disciple to be near the *guru* while he was engaged in his music-related activities. He insisted that his music-teaching institution must have a character of a platform that allowed an intense exposure of trainees to a wide-ranging musical behaviour accompanied by a rather impersonal process of learning and teaching.

He also devoted considerable attention to the matter of what is to be taught through the institutional infrastructures which he so hopefully erected. He had divined two fundamental principles in this respect: firstly, all students of music need not be and cannot be performers, and secondly, all those who desire learning music must have an opportunity to do so. For this purpose, a certain body of music from the rich musical culture must be made accessible to them. He was aware of one of the proud features of Indian culture that there cannot be an Indian who is entirely non-musical owing to the very richness of Indian music understood in its larger sense. Once having grasped this truth, the question "what is to be taught?" was solved immediately. Yet another facet of Panditji's response to this question is to be noted. It is easy to conclude that all musical genres and the Carnatic system of art music are to be included in the scope of music-education taken in a wider context.

However, to pay attention to Western music and Western musical instruments showed a rare and a desirably modern as well as a somewhat exceptional perception. This is why in the 1921 Music Conference he organised in Bombay, he invited the well-known, Bombay based pianist Prof. Scrinzy to present an item. Prof. Scrinzy was a celebrated music-teacher and he also reviewed 'programs' of Western music for *The Times of India*. Further as was natural to the musical activist in him, Pt. Vishnu Digambar gave a schlorship to one of his young disciples, B.R. Deodher, to learn Western music from Prof. Scrinzy and with a similar scholarship, sent Mr. Dhundiraj Paluskar to an Italian violinist to learn *violin*.

Once the content of what is to be taught was decided upon Panditji turned his attention to details such as drawing up of the required curricula, creating means and literature appropriate to the curricula, and imparting the necessary training to selected teachers for implementing the designed courses. From his campaign to propagate music on the widest possible scale, he did not exclude even the task of introducing music to amateur music-lovers. His astonishingly comprehensive attitude is apparent in the fact that he clearly recognised the fact that motives of those who take to music are bound to differ and therefore courses etc. have also to be extrememly varied. Traditional or authentic *khayal*-music, elementary as well as artistically rich *bhajan*-compositions, music fit to accompany physical exercise and music to divert attention of the crowd or mobs—all found a place on his musical spectrum. He was aware of the cultural fact that music which is not musically rich can however be socio-culturally legitimate as well as valuable. He was able to step beyond the narrow confines of personal likes and dislikes or individual capacities and capabilities and hence he was able to think of, and see beyond, the immediately visible horizon. This is the reason why he can rightfully be regarded as a revolutionary, reformist and a socio-culturally relevant musician of a whole nation.

Publications

Perhaps it is helpful to consider in some detail the musical literature he created in this context. It must be noted that the immense, fundamental and grammatically oriented literature authored so ably by Pt. Bhatkhande has been rather incorrectly considered as the only relevant music-related literature. This has been the view because out of ignorance, generation of means of music-education and production of pedagogical literature is not considered 'scientific'. A reference to Mr. Govindrao Paluskar's article in the *Sangeet Kala Vihar*, May-June 2001 provides valuable information in this context.

Panditji's 60 publications can be broadly classsified under 9 headings:

1. On culturing voice and undertaking melodic elaboration with the help of embellishments
2. Introductory study of music
3. On *gayaki ang*
4. On *hori* and such other musical genre
5. *Khayal*-presentation and elaboration according to the Gwalior *gharana*
6. Patriotic songs
7. Bengali and Carnatic music
8. Music to accompany physical exercise
9. Singing of Tulsidas's *doha* and *choupai*.

Four books deal with selected muscial embellishments, their use and role in elaborating musical ideas. His suggestion is to study embellishments along with linguistic vowels 'aa', 'u' and 'ee' and further to use them in connection with different *raga*-s as also to the accompaniment of rhythmic patterns. Panditji also referred to the permutation-combination of 7 notes yielding 5040 elaborations as noted in the *Ratnakara*. All these were published around 1900 and this certainly proves him to be a discerning pioneer.

Baalodaya Sangeet (3 parts), *Sangeet Baalaprakash* (3 parts) and *Swalpalaapgayan* are introductory volumes to music-making. The target audience is clearly mentioned as children below 10. Interesting features of the *Baalodaya* are: songs composed with a sequential inclusion of 5, 6 and 7 notes, and information imparted through a question-answer method. *Sangeet Baalaprakash* consists of 44 *bhajan* compositions of 11 saint-poets, three *sargamgeet*, 8 *tala*-s, and 28 *raga*-s that are more commonly used. The publication *Swalpalaap* consists of *alap-taans* of compositions included in *Sangeet Baalaprakash*. It is obvious that the books are useful even to those whose mental age in music matches the group described as "below ten". The methodical appraoch to music-making and opening up of the concerned students' vision is obvious.

Similar compositions by saint-poets are also included in publications on music for women.

Raga Pravesh Maalika (19 parts) and *Sangeet* (5 parts) provide basic compositional material to more advanced practitioners of music. In the *Raga Pravesh*, each part deals with one *raga* and one *Bandish. Bada* and *chhota khayal, thumri* and *bhajan* are the genres included. The compositions explore in all 7 *tala*-s and notation of the *bandish* is given. Phases of elaboration identified as *alap*, *bol-tana*, *tana* and *sargam* are included. The assumed performance is structured as a more or less sequential rendering of

1. Ascending-descending patterns in nom-tom
2. *Sthayi*

3. *Antara*
4. Variation of *mukhda*
5. Short and longer *alap*
6. *Bol-taan* of the *sthayi*
7. Ascending and descending *taan*-s
8. *Mukhda* variation of *antara*
9. *Bol-taan* inclusive of employment of 'aa' and 'ee' vowels
10. *Taan* in double, treble tempo, etc.
11. *Bol-taan* on selected syllables or words with emphasis on vowels
12. Virtuoso *taan* (i.e. ranging over multiple octaves)
13. *Taan* in increased *tempi* and conclusion.

It is obvious that changes could be and would be made according to the composition, *raga* in question. These manuals consist of notations of music actually performed for the purpose because performing competence is the aim. The notated performances are on average of duration of 15 minutes each. It is to be mentioned that many of the compositions explored in this effort are traditional. For the second series entitled *Sangeet* (with one *raga* each for the five-part series) it has been specially mentioned that singing of *khayal* is kept in mind. Each item consists of a *sloka* of *Ragadhyana*, a *bada khayal*, a number of *chhota khayal*-s, *tarana*, *dhrupad*-s and *dhamar*. Compositions in medium tempo, *alap*, *bol-taan* and *taan* appropriate to them are notated. It is stated that the material provided would be of the duration of about 30 minutes.

In the volume respectively entitled *Hori* (1923) and *Tappa* (1927), information of the genres and notation of 22 and 23 compositions is given. The former includes two compositions by Panditji and the genre-specific *taal deepchandi* is introducecd. The second, reflecting the compiler's honesty notes that the *antara* of one traditional compositon is not given as Panditji himself did not know it! *Sangeet Baalbodh* consists of *jod-raga*, introduces *tala Rupak*, compositions employing *tala* such as *savari*, rare form such as *ashtapadi* in a addition to *khayal*, *tarana*, *sargam* and other genres in circulation.

Volumes on Carnatic and Bengali music brought out in 1923 included 7 and 15 compositions respectivley. Books titled *Rashtriya Sangeet* and *Vyayam ke Saath Sangeet* include 4 compositions and marching music respectively.

One of his disciples, Mr. Dhundiraj Paluskar had compiled an anthology of *doha* and *choupai* compositions that Panditji used to render.

Some generalisations about the publications seem necessary.

1. These are designed to provide detailed performing maps to music-makers of all sorts. (They can loosely be described as music scores.)
2. *Sangeet* (music) is nearly equated with singing.
3. However music is not equated with or confined to classical or art music. This is a revolutionary step in the Indian contexts and needs to be acknowledged as that.
4. Writing on music in India, due to overemphasising the grammatical aspect of music overlooked that theoretical writing can be much more wide-ranging. It is also not recognised that music can also be 'applied', that writings on these aspects is also important and authors of this kind of literature are not given their due recognition. Not only that, Panditji produced written material that was performance-centred but he also put forward a very wide spectrum of music as an expression.

The New Patron

Whether performance or education Panditji understood the term 'patron' in a different light and accordingly took positive and imaginative steps to attract a new patron. It is obvious that he took deliberate steps to reduce the dependence of all music-related activities on the support received from princes, wealthy families and the like. He consciously developed the notion that the receivers of the new British-inspired education—the 'middle class' can and does function as patron. In this light, it is interesting to note that in 1912, along with some 30-40 students he undertook a nation-wide tour to raise building-fund for his Mumbai-based music institute. The stops were Nasik, Amaravati, Nagpur, Kharagpur, Calcutta, Patna, Benaras, Ahemedabad, Kanpur, Delhi, Lahore, Ludhiana, Jalandhar, Amritsar, Ajmer and Jaipur, etc. On account of his consciousness of the new patron he did not hesitate to introduce changes in the performing menu. Prior to the classical items he presented physical exercises by children, orchestral music or *Ramayana* recitation, etc. It is revealing that he had commissioned a *sarangi* 8 feet high to parallel the bass section of the Western string instruments. In addition, when he found that the *sarangi* though impressive looking produced no sound he calmly said, "But have it on the stage in the orchestra, it looks so impressive!". In one of his early self-advertised and self-organised music programmes he also had an item of *tabla-tarang* with the same concern for attracting a new audience-patron.

The way he valued the role of school/institute-based teaching of music, it is clear that he was aware of the practical aspects of all educational activities. The traditional patronage often created an overawed sense of abashment/embarassment for the receiver and those who tried to receive *talim* without patronage had to pass through a long waiting period full of anxiety till a warm fruitful relationship developed between the *guru* and the disciple. Panditji hoped to cut across such difficulties through his own institutions.

It can easily be deduced that the general lack of education of musicians was what Panditji viewed as the main reason and cause of the defects in the prevailing music education. If a musician is educated, it enables him to see how music is related to other departments of life and how the relationship can be maintained to make both more meaningful. Obviously the contemporary custom of entirely segregating musicological and performing aspects and be rather contemptuous about the roles of theoreticians, musicologists, educators, etc., was unacceptable to him. He must have been plagued by the question: if in ancient India, Bharata could be both a practitioner as well as a theoretician, why should this not be possible today? From 1918, he was particular that those who became his disciples should also get school-education. For him performance and theory was to be taken as a unit and this faith made him bring out an annotated edition of an ancient musicological work such as *Naradiya Shiksha* with a Hindi translation. It can be imagined that he did not have the expertise, experience, training and the time needed for such a task and hence the publication is not a satisfactory product. Yet, the motivation and the amazing foresight he displayed is unmistakable and he deserves a respectful praise for it.

For him to create and train teachers capable of passing on music as a *sanskara* to women from respectable families, children and school-going young population as well as to those who merely wanted to know more of cultural aspects of Indian heritage was the need of the hour. The teachers, apart from being able teachers also had to be well-behaved and honourable human beings to ensure that music, musicians and the profession regains its largely lost social prestige. This is how he viewed the multi-faceted challenges faced in the field of music and all his varied and simultaneous activities are to be interpreted as cumulative effects of his wide reformist, renaissance vision.

Panditji as a Propagator of Music

As an educator of music, he worked in pedagogy and published a varied literture on music. The other aspect of his unceasing efforts was directed towards propagation of music. In brief, the dual aim he set for himself in this regard was to educate the musician and make the educated sing. This is the reason why he undertook the complex task of evolving a notation system, notate simple/complex as well as representative compositions in genres such as *bhajan*, *hori*, *tappa*, and put down in notation complete performing profiles of important *raga*-s. One concern he had was to insist that those manifestations identified as scientific/classical should be classical enough. To put forward this view could not have been exactly a popular move. For example, he heavily criticised the diluted / distorted classicism in singing in the extremely popular Marathi music-drama titled *Manapman* (1911). His concern was to maintain the 'origianl' codified integrity of the classical idiom. He did not hesitate to advertise himself for his own ticketed performances. In other words, he did not think this was commercialisation of music.The same 'practical' propagator's temper allowed him to precede his musical-performance with items such as '*tabla-tarang*' for recreation or children's drill accompanied by music. It is a hard truth of life that a propagator cannot be too finicky about 'purity of means'—and he appreciated it.

In his vigorous music-propagation he did a kind of tight-rope balance. On the one hand, he was hand in glove with parties engaged in various movements launched for liberation of the country from the yoke of the British political rule. On the other hand, he was also in close touch with the ruling British power and its administrative machinery. In other words, he was not touchy about the finer sense of propriety. Almost echoing the devotional slogan of the ancient Indian God "I am whereever my devotees are", he followed the motto 'wherever people come together music has to be there'. In the final analysis, propagation of music was an article of faith with him. In this context, it is interesting to note that even before a sense of renunciation sounded in his personal life, Rama, importance of his name, *Ramayana* and its recitation, registered a deep impression in his musical behaviour. It must be admitted that exploiting the name of Rama to acquire all sorts of material benefit has a long and pervasive tradition in India. Panditji unhesitatingly used the easy acceptance of Rama-phenomenon in India to propagate music. In India, for ages the sentiment of *shringara* has been purposefully used to arouse Divine Love, and fables and stories harnessed to inculcate wisdom and knowledge. In a similar manner, Panditji harnesses *bhajan*-s *et al* for generating wide-based interest in music. From 1910, he began giving discourses on *Ramayana*. From 1913 he presented *Ramayana* before presenting classical music. From 1921 he began using *Ramnaam* for the free *alap* portion before the rhythm-accompanied singing of *khayal* commenced. He opened some doors for music through music-conferences and through setting-up of committees consisting of officials, inviting Governors for convocation and making important social personalities or political leaders, his patrons. As early as in 1906, he had not hesitated to organise a special music-programme in honour of the visiting British monarch—George the Fifth. Similarly, he employed *Ramnaam*, one's own sage-like appearance and ascetic costume for popularising music.

Panditji as an Organiser

Most of the times musicians are loners. It is also to be admitted that usually their agenda has themselves as the main if not the only item. However, the propagator in Panditji was interested in setting up a network of institutions and this inevitably meant drawing together as many like-minded persons as possible. Establishing an instrument-making factory, running a printing press, feeding, teaching and training disciples and also appointing them later to head various institutions in different places (and relinquishing all personal control over these)—all these were pointers to his ultimate goal. His goal was to be a multi-faceted organiser fired by an impersonal ambition to create a live or a charged field of musico-cultural ideas. He never avoided meeting people who were working on music. When he met Pt. Bhatkhande in 1912, Panditji was 40 years old while Pt. Bhatkhande was 52. It is interesting to know that in the same year Pt. Bhatkhande had delivered a lecture on notation in the well-known and prestigious *Vasant Vyakhyan Mala,* i.e. The Spring Lecture Series in Pune. Panditji was present in the famous 1916 Music Conference that Pt. Bhatkhande had organised in Baroda. It is significant that during the Conference he registered a protest against the proceedings being conducted in English because that excluded most of the practising musicians from understanding what was happening. All these details merely confirm that to understand Panditji's life is to understand his readiness to accept all that happens when a person takes a life-mission and sticks to it through thick and thin.

Conclusion

To make a conclusive sense of Panditji's life-work in the field of Indian music, it appears that perhaps the roles of educator, propagagator and organiser in Panditji's life overshadowed the musician and the artist in him. What he achieved opened up new vistas, laid down a comprehensive plan of action and it meant looking ahead of his times. It is noteworthy that his main disciples such as Omkarnath Thakur, Vinayakrao Patwardhan and Naryanrao Vyas earned name as vocalists. His writing work and analogous activities undertaken with a broader understanding of the theoretical aspects of Indian music did not get the recognition that they deserve. He simultaneously worked on different fronts and tried to take into account the rich past, exciting present and the challenging future. To understand such an achievement needs different sets of evaluative criteria. Overlooking this fact has led to a lop-sided appreciation of Panditji's pioneering accomplishments. Addressing India in Hindi, planning activities out of Maharashtra and trying to yoke together religion and politics in service of music was certainly a cultural undertaking with music as an important component.

Pt. Anant Manohar Joshi
(8-3-1881 to 2-9-1967)

5

Pt. Anant Manohar Joshi

(8-3-1881 to 2-9-1967)

Pt. Anant Manohar Joshi was my first *guru's*—Pt. Gajananrao Joshi's—father. It means he was my *guru*'s *guru*—thus occupying a very prestigious place in my personal and musical hierarchy. We all called him "Baba". I began my *talim* from Pt. Gajananbuwa in 1947 when I was about 10 years of age. This was the time when Baba had staged a kind of come-back in the world of music. Therefore, there were occasions to meet him under diferent circumstances—sometimes when he came to our home in Girgaum, or later in Dombivali, near Bombay at Pt. Gajananrao's house. Sometimes I saw him at close quarters in his *Daataamandir* in Oundh or sometimes whenever he was giving performaces at places near Bombay.

He was always dressed in *dhoti*, long coat, *uparane*, traditional *pheta* over the head and held a long walking stick in his hands. He always stood or sat errect and looked impressive, dignified and almost from another older period. At Girgaum I was often dispatched to bring a taxi for our honoured guests and personalities. They stood in front of the building where we stayed while I was engaged in the task of hailing the cab, etc. While standing thus in front of our building two personalities—Ustad Ahemadjan Thirakwa and Pt. Anant Manohar Joshi—always attracted attention of the entire middle class lane—so striking were their appearances and bearings. Both obviously exuded majesty and glory of the adjacent past. In addition, due to my rather adventurous temperament I used to 'talk' to Baba with a sense of freedom not always considered proper. As an upshot of all this background the present essay may echo some non-related or extra-musical features of Baba's life and work.

A Brief Life-history

Baba was born on 8th March 1881 in Kinhai, a village in the erstwhile princely State of Oundh, Satara district of Maharashtra. The Goddess-temple in Kinhai was also a well-known place for the devotees. Baba's father, Manoharbuwa was, from his 11th year, a keen devotee of Sant Narayanbuwa in Kinhai. Manoharbuwa was a favourite in the Oundh court because of his sweet renderings of devotional music. His kind of musicianshsip attaracted the attention of another court, Sangli in the region and he was invited to join the latter court, which he soon did. Here he had greater opportunities of meeting and interacting with musicians of known calibre such as Pt. Ravjibuwa Gogte (Ichalkaranji), Pt. Mahadevbuwa Gokhale (Miraj) and Pt. Bhaurao Kagwadkar. Reportedly he also received some training from Pt. Ravjibuwa. His musical renderings used to prove so attractive or effective that he was always asked to sing last in a concert where other musicians were also participating. This honour is normally accorded to a musician who is regarded the best in such get together-s. In fact, impressed by his growing reputation the Oundh court invited him back and he finally stabilised there.

However, he died in 1888 and his wife (i.e. Baba's mother) and son (Baba) had to move back to Kinhai again in rather strained circumstances. Baba was then merely 7 years of age. Some schooling and learning music from a local musician called Mr. Bapurao

Ayachit decided young Baba's routine. His progress in music was remarkable and everybody felt that he should concentrate on music. His mother therefore took a bold decision of shifting to Miraj where Pt. Mahadevbuwa Gokhale had settled and his wife was distantly related to Baba's mother. Obviously Baba's mother hoped that Pt. Mahadevbuwa would take Baba under his wings. However, Pt. Mahadevbuwa categorically announced that he would teach only his sons—and no one else. This was certainly a bolt from the blue to Anant and his widowed mother. Yet as luck would have it, Pt. Balkrishnabuwa Icalkaranjikar, a prominent vocalist of the Gwalior *gharana* in Hindustani music had just arrived in Miraj after completing his *talim* in Gwalior. Anant and his mother lost no time in approaching Pt. Balkrishnabuwa who agreed to teach Anant and his mother could heave a sigh of relief.

At that time, two future musical celebrities—Pt. Vishnu Digambar Paluskar and Pt. Gundubuwa Ingle were also receiving *talim* from Pt. Balkrishnabuwa. Vishnubuwa Paluskar had the Chief of Miraj as his patron and his *talim* nearly took place directly under royal supervision. Anant also received a small stipend from the Oundh court and he was permitted to have his food in the Palace. (Only Gundubuwa had to depend on free food offered to him by some private houses as an aid.) In other words, Vishnu Digambar was the leader of the pack. This went on till 1896. In that year Vishnu Digambar decided to test the waters of the outside world to estimate his own musical prowess. Baba also accompanied him. They roamed for about 2 years performing and putting their musical abilities to test. After two years Baba however felt that he needed some more training. (Perhaps he also felt that Vishnubuwa's influence did not allow him to come into his own.) Whatever the reason might have been Baba came back to Miraj only to find that Pt. Balkrishnabuwa had by that time shifted to Ichalkaranji—a nearby princely State. Baba with some support from the Oundh court shifted to Ichalkaranji and trained for two-three years before finally deciding to launch his own career with the *guru*'s blessings. However, the Oundh court had helped Baba on the condition that he came back to Oundh and worked for the Court till the Raja who had helped him was on the throne. Baba did so. At that time Pt. Gundubuwa and Pt. Nathbuwa Pakhwaji were also employed by the Oundh court. The three enjoyed music and each other's company, and made music happily.

Then came an important turning point in Baba's musical journey. A news reached that Mr. Vishnupant Chatre, the famous and pioneering circus-owner and a great lover of music has succeeded in tracking down Ustad Rahimat Khan, the elusive son of Ustad Miya Haddu Khan, the latter being one of the originators of the Gwalior school of Hindustani music. Not only that, the news was that Prof. Chatre has 'brought' Ustad Rahimat Khan to Satara where Ustad Rahimat Khan was soon to perform. To cap this all, the musician-trinity from Oundh was invited to the concert. The three were of course elated and walked 25 miles to Satara. Needless to say, they were transported to another world while listening to the self-absorbed Ustad. Suddenly Vishnupant asked Baba to take up the *tanpura* and accompany the Ustad. Vishnupant's words were orders and Baba, though with some hesitation took up the *tanpura* and sat behind the Ustad who probably was not even aware of the changes taking place in the performing set. Not only Vishnupant but the Ustad also liked Baba's accompaniment. During the concert the Ustad had looked back once or twice with approval in the direction of Baba and that was enough. Everybody was surprised as the Ustad was mostly in an other-worldly state. He never spoke on his own and rarely answered others unless he himself wanted to do so. He was extremely whimsical and everybody agreed that only Vishnpant could have humanised the Ustad to this extent. Vishnupant told Baba, "Listen, he has liked your accompaniment. If you stay with him for some time you will be able to learn so much." Fortunately the Oundh King with whom Baba had the contractual obligation had expired by 1901. Baba also did not find the atmosphere in the 'new' court very conducive. So Baba was a free agent now and he agreed to enter the Ustad's roving discipleship. This stint continued approximately till 1905-7. However, he could not continue further as he did not have any financial support. So Baba decided to camp at Bombay and established a music school in 1907 naming it *Shri Guru Samartha Gayan Vadan Vidyalaya*. As coincidence would have it Baba's senior *Gurubandhu*, Pt.Vishnu Digambar had also established a music teaching institute in the town. Baba's school soon attracted attention and the early disciples included Acharya S.N. Ratanjankar, Mr. Chaugule, Mr. Godbole, Mr. Gokhale. (The latter three were to contribute to the music education in the municipal schools in the early days.) Pt. Antubuwa brought out three parts of *Sangeet Pravesha* and two of *Harmonium Delighter*. Unfortunately the First World War and the influenza epidemic took a toll. Pt. Antubuwa left Bombay and shifted to Wai, a place in the interior of Maharashtra but lost his wife and three sons. The lone surviving son was Gajanan who went on to become an ace pioneering *violinist* in Hindustani music and a highly respected *guru* as well as a knowledgeable *vocalist*. Pt. Antubuwa then tried to settle in Sangli, a princely state with a cultural background. However, he was for all practical purposes a shattered person. As luck would have it, the then ruling prince of Oundh, Shrimant Balasaheb Pantpratinidhi who was a cultured patron of arts again extended support to Antubuwa. So Antubuwa came back to Oundh and settled down with Gajanan who was already showing promise. The Maharaj used to perform musico-religious discourses and he told the young Gajanan to provide accompaniment on *violin*. Gajanan took up the challenge to study the new instrument on his own and learnt from Pt. Antubuwa. However, the latter was advancing in age and moving towards an ascetic way of life. He had met Shivanand Swami, a saint and becoming his disciple, Antubuwa built a Datta Temple away from the main part of the Oundh and shifted there, this time for good. He was nearly lost to the musical world outside and the world was for him too far away to be bothered about. Antubuwa built Shivanand-Swami's *samadhi* when the latter passed away. In his memory Pt. Antubuwa began to hold the annual music celebrations from 1940 and that has continued since.

In 1947 Pt. Gajananbuwa and others who knew his music coaxed Pt. Antubuwa out of his musical retirement and he broadcast his 'remembered' music at the age of 66 ! Numerous cognoscenti in the city were overwhelmed with the authentic music and the unknown artist. Consequently, there was a considerable renewed interest in his music. He was honoured by the Central Sangeet Natak Akademi and performed in many places. Years rolled on with a newly acquired fame and prestige. He was in the Dombivli, at the residence of Pt. Gajananrao and suffered the old-age gracefully. When he expired at the age of 86, he was fully conscious till the end and his last words were, "*Swamimaharaj ki jay*!".

This is the background against which one notes some significant features of his musicianship.

The Undiluted Gwalior-way of His Music-making

As many perceptive listeners have noted, the first characteristic of Pt. Antubuwa's music-making was the Gwalior idiom in its purity and its confident approach to the undisputed glory of *khayal* music. This was evident in every component of music namely, in matters of *raga*, *tala*, composition, musical elaboration, tempo, the climatic *taan*-phase and also in respect of the musical genre chosen as a vehicle. One cannot say that Antubuwa had heard no other music but it appears that he deliberately kept other fragrances out of his own musical boquet. An interesting detail needs to be mentioned in this contrext. It is that the Gwalior music in Maharashtra is not exactly similar to the Gwalior-music in vogue at Gwalior itself. For example, the embellished *tappa*-way of music-making that adorns the singing of Pt. Krishnaro Pandit and Pt.Rajabhaiya Poochwale is not present in the Maharashtra based Gwalior-music. Pt. Paluskar and his disciples, Pt. Antubuwa, Pt. Mirashibuwa and all other Maharashtra based Gwalior musicians provide instances of this non-*tappa* music. It is generally true to say that the Gwalior based idiom makes music more unpredictable while the Maharashtra based idiom is replete with a musical poise. On the other hand, both the expressions emphasise fluidity and dynamism in music than a step-by-step elaboration of musical ideas.

However, due to his close association with Ustad Rahimat Khan, Pt. Antubuwa distinguished himself from the other Maharashtra based Gwalior musicians. To maintain a musical flow in a medium tempo along with an enveloping resonant tone was the strategy. The main feature of the idiom was to focus on elaboration of notes or their clusters but without a step-by-step approach. In his music, the *bol-taan* entered the scene and freely moved in it as if it was not aware of the existing and constricting *tala*-frame. Unlike in case of many other musicians, the *bol-taan* did not appear in Pt. Antubuwa's 'Rahimat Khan-inspired' music with a conscious emphasis and stress on the *tala*-slots or by referring to their divisive functions. It is symptomatic that in his music, very often the *sama* does not stage or announce its dictatorial arrival! It is no doubt registered but music passes on with a pleasant nod to it. The same logic applied to the *taan*-phase. It recognises the boundaries of *tala* and *raga* but without restricting its motion and design. A straight *taan* was a favoured entity as also a movement in more than one octave. In this respect, Pt. Antubuwa's favourite *sutra* was, "All *raga*-s become straight in the *taan*-s". The Gwalior idiom certainly loved this variety of *taan* just as numerous people love straight drives in cricket. In addition, Ustad Rahimat Khan's music hovered around higher notes and especially around the *tara shadja* (i.e. the high octave note). The music in this case moves around the note in an absorbed, introvert manner.

In sum, Pt. Antibuwa could draw his own musical map and differ from the other Maharashtra based Gwalior musicians because of the deep imprint he carried from Ustad Rahimat Khan's music making. Once Shri Narayanrao Rajhans, the epoch-making actor singer known as Balgandharva had told Pt. Gajananbuwa, "Your father sang just like Ustad Rahimat Khan." Pt. Antubuwa's was a rare example in which a genius cast a creative shadow over another genius to create different music.

Yet another important feature of Pt. Antubuwa's music can be better described in his own words. He used to say, "Our music begins from the *antara*." He obviously referred to his avoidance of the slow, systematic, step-by-step melodic elaboration of *raga* from the lower to the higher notes. His music did not place any premium on slow-paced, gradual upward movements from the *madhya* '*sa*' in every *raga*. He felt that this way of singing is nothing but warming up exercise preferably to be done at home. In a *mehfil* the direct approach should be to locate *raga* with immediacy and not to search for it through the individual notes—this seemed to be the unstated philosophy. Like a Shakespearian play, his music making took a direct plunge in music. His was a case of musical '*in medias rex*'.

His musical repertoire was limited to *khayal, tarana* and rarely a *sargamgeet*. When I heard him in person or when he was recorded, he was well-advanced in age and this also meant that he could not use and stick to the clearly produced vowel 'aa' though he always spoke in favour of this practice otherwise.

Yet another important feature in his presentations was the effortless music-making which did not bring about facial and body distortions, so depressing to the listener. One of his favourite recollections in this respect was about Ustad Rahimat Khan's way of singing. Pt. Antubuwa who accompanied the Ustad used to tell us, "I did not see any extra movement of his back even when he executed a fast *taan* spanning many octaves!" He believed that music is to be primarily heard and not seen.

I wonder whether there wss an inter-relationship between Pt. Antubuwa's strong and durable physique and the easy flow of his Rahimat Khan-type music. For years he looked after himself and the temple-affairs and these tasks must have been demanding in their own way. And yet his music-making never appeared to be weak. Once, after he had begun broadcasting again—in his old

As stated, his repertoire consisted of *khayal* and *tarana*. However, under unusual circumstances we, to our astonishment, learnt something that opened our ears. He was ill and during his recuperation we were dusting and cleaning his room and cupboard at Oundh. In a corner of the cupboard we found his notebooks full of *bandish*-s. Examining them we found that he had meticulously written down many *dhrupad* compositions. Espying a favourable moment we asked him about them. And he said, "In our first tour why did we camp so long in Mathura? The aim was to improve our knowledge of Hindi and learn *dhrupad*. You should always learn more than what you yourself prefer to perform. That is called education!" Indeed an important insight into completing one's vision of music.

age, he started from Oundh and missed his train at Rahimatpur. Without batting an eyelid he hired a porter to carry his luggage and walked to the other station, Koregaon to catch another train and see the broadcast through as scheduled. To use the Akashvani terminology, due to his efforts 'deviation' from the planned programme was avoided.

As a Teacher of Music

As a teacher he was exceptionally patient and tenacious. His famous 'short-temper' which was so prominent in his non-musical life, was entirely absent when he taught. One of his much-trusted instructions to the disciples was, "Do not imitate me but sing like me!" In other words it was not reproduction of his music but a response to his way of musical thinking that was expected from his disciples. This method meant a unique combination of a discipline to be followed and a freedom to be enjoyed. The disciple was simultaneously initiated into both strategies of the music-making venture. Antubuwa sought to arouse the disciple's consciousness of what was appropriate or artistic. A *talim* was intended to enable a disciple to find his own voice. This interpretation is corroborated by the fact that Antubuwa always allowed and often encourged accompanists by giving them ample opportunities to sing.

Much later I could comprehend a significant feature of his teaching strategy. As is known, who should be taught, which *raga* and when, is usually decided by the *guru*. But Pt. Antubuwa apparently also thought about the sequence of compositions (*bandish*) in the same *raga* to be followed in case of particular students. For example, in the *talim, raga yaman* is to be taken up early for teaching but the *khayal* would be, "*Kah sakhi kaise ke kariye*" set in *tala ektala*. Once the disciple had attained the desirable standard

Pt. Antubuwa would go back to *raga Yaman* and then take up another *khayal 'Banre Balaiya'* set in *tala jhumra*—for the *talim*. A particular disciple's standard would be judged by looking to the *raga* and the kind of *bandish* he sang in it. Obviously the main thrust was not the correctness or otherwise in the disciple's singing (the correctness would be similar to knowing the dictionary meaning of a word). But the concern was whether the disciple was mature enough to take up an equally mature composition in a *raga* known to him. This would refer to his relationship with the musical content of the *bandish* as contrasted with the meaning. This way of thinking certainly showed an aesthetic insight.

Popularly, the tendency is to rate/rank or place a musician by applying the criterion of his knowledge of rare or unknown *raga* described with words such as *anvath*, *achop* or *aprachalit*. Pt. Antubuwa surely had an enlightened view on the matter and this was reflected in his teaching. Most of such *raga*-s are attractive deviations from other known or generally circulating *raga*-s. If such deviant melodies are codified in great detail then in order to understand them as performing realities, it does not really amount to musical analysis but a pedantic exercise reducing notes to nothingness. In other words, Pt. Antubuwa felt that to classify or codify such *raga*-s is to destroy their creative capacity, their power to colour music with emotion etc. As a result, Pt. Antubuwa rested content by describing or naming such *raga* merely as a variety of some prominent *raga*. For example, he used to describe the *raga* of the multicoloured *khayal*-composition "*Kaise daras paras yeh tum*" as "*Yaman ka prakar*". This same way of thinking propelled him to lay down another golden rule for melodic-rhythmic elaboration in singing of *khayal*. He used to advise the singer "Sing in accordance with the *bandish*". His perception was that even in the same *raga* different compositions usually stress or re-emphasise different

Outside music and in day-to-day life, his temper was proverbially extreme and unbearable. For some time, a student (who had an excellent hand on *tabla*) from a nearby rural area was engaged to stay at the temple to help Pt. Antubuwa. Once he was doing some work in a room and from the nearby room Pt.Antubuwa called him. He did not hear the call and continued his work. Suddenly he heard some crashing sounds made by things dashing, bumping against the ground. When he looked out of the window he saw that his bed, clothes, etc. were flying out of the window of the first floor. He immediately knew what was happening and immediately ran away to his home only to return at the time of the annual music festivities when Pt. Gajananbuwa (Pt. Antubuwa's son, and many others were also present!

elements of music to register a musial nuance. Hence individual compositions may bring in subtle variations about the descent-ascent, tonal movement, employment of grace notes or of musical embellishments, etc. On this background, to impose on each of the compositions the same generalised musico-grammatically codified musical contours is to effectively negate the special contribution of the specific composition. This is to be avoided if musical creativity and not the ability to be a consistent codifier is to be encouraged. His strategy to sing as per the *bandish* selected enabled rendering different *raga*-images through different compositions. He used to explain this very eloquently to the urban disciples—"Raga is not a flat in Bombay with only two doors—*raga* is a palace with hundred doors!". It is not a coincidence that the music-tradition has always insisted that every musician should know as many *bandish* as possible to enable him to be a complete musician. In fact the greater the number of compositions a musician knows the higher is his place in the hierarchy of the musicians.It is to be expected that these views influenced his work as a composer.

As a Composer

Pt. Antubuwa has successfully placed before us one more facet of his musical personality through the *bandish*, he composed. As noted earlier, in his very first tour of the North India he sensed his own lack of knowledge of Hindi (as also of *dhrupad* as a genre). He assiduously studied the Saint's devotional literature in Hindi, Braj as a dialect of Hindi, and Surdas and Tulsidas appear to be formative influences in this regard. His compositions are not much different as far as their literary content is concerned. But they are not poor patchworks of stock-words or rhyming compulsions. Song-texts full of words such as *sainya, guinya, painya* or *avo, gavo, javo* to "hang the melodies on", are not encountered in his compositions.

Secondly, the compositions are not forced somehow in *tala*-frames. "*Jhan na na na na na na na payal baaje*" (*raga marwa*, *tala jhumra*), or "*Albelo mero"* (*raga bibhas, tala jhumra*) skillfully use the gaits of the specific *tala* and touch the prestigious *sama*-point with great lilt and delicacy. Some other compositions take off from difficult and unexpected *tala*-points and yet attain the *sama* with remarkable ease and naturalness. For example, "*Meelanko jiya mera chahat hai*" (*raga komal rishabh asavari, tala trital*, the *mukhda* takes off from the 11th beat), "*Painjaniya mori bajan laagi"* (*raga hindol, tala trital*, the *mukhda* takes off immediately after the 13th beat), "*Nanadike bachanuva*" (*raga yaman*, *tala trital*, the *mukhada* takes off from the 4th beat.) "*Madan Mohan kabahun gokul aave*" (*raga malkauns*, *tala trital*, *mukhada* takes off from the 5th beat)—are some of such compositions. The last *bandish* in *malkauns* has one more attractive feature. In it the *tala* divisions are of four beats each while the text proceeds in words that consist of three letters each. In sum, Pt. Antubuwa believed in maintaining a close but unstressed relationship with the rhythm. This also enabled him to be playful with the rhythmic cycle in the composition itself. "*Nahi bin dekhe chain nahi aave*" (*raga alaiya bilawal, tala trital*), or "*Eri malaniya gunde lavori*" (*raga chayanat, tala trital*) are distinctive in this respect. Additionally, there are cases of his composition in *raga*-s in which there are no worthy compositions in circulation. For example, "*Rain kari darawan laagi*" (*raga chhota khayal* in *malgunji, tala trital*) or "*Bhaj man Ram sumir*" (*chhota khayal, jaytashri, tala trital*) are thus contributions of fundamental importance. In some other compositions he succeeds in making the mood of the concerned *raga* very deep through recourse to meaningful text. Examples are: '*Soch nahi mohe Maatpitako*' (*chota khayal, bageshri, tala trital*) or "*Chalori maai Ramsiya darsanko*" (*raga chhota khayal, shri, tala tritala*). It is thought-provoking that he never used a *nom de plume* in all of his compositions!

Some Sidelights on Pt. Antubuwa

It is indeed difficult to trace with certainty some facets of an artist's life or personality directly to his art. However, his experiences manifest themselves in his art in subtle ways. Some such events I noticed in Pt. Antubuwa's life and living.

- When I was a student, I won a competition in Classical vocal music of the All India Radio and I had felt great while receiving the award from the hands of President Rajendra Prasad. To celebrate the achievement we organised a ceremony to honour my *guru* Pt. Gajananbuwa—and my small concert was to precede the ceremony. The audience consisted numerous persons who were like *guru*-s to me, including Pt. Antubuwa. I was extremely nervous and this must have shown on my face. When I walked up to Pt. Antubuwa to offer obeisance to him, he spoke to me in a reassuring tone and said, "When you are on the stage consider yourself the wisest person and all others to be big, uncomprehending fools and then sing freely and without tension!" I sang *puriya* and the audience reactions boosted my confidence. Now Pt. Antubuwa called me and said, "Remember, once you have come down from the stage consider yourselves the fool and all others to be wise!" This was a gentle slap in my face and I knew it to be so.

- On another occasion, in my first participation in the famed and annually organised Swami Shivanand Utsav in Oundh I had presented *raga bhairav bahar* and was feeling happy about it. I offered my respects to Pt. Antubuwa who was sitting in an easy chair near the fountain outside and waited for some complimentary comments. Now the brief and a rather chastening dialogue went off like this:

  "What did you render?" he asked.
  "*raga bhairav bahar*", I said.
  "You rendered a *raga*, now; when are you going to sing music?" said he.

  Fortunately, I have heard such aphoristic aesthetic *sutra*-s often and from many!

- For a long time, Pt. Antubuwa used to cook for his own lonely self in the Oundh temple. Hence expectably he was frugal and kept measured quantities of everything he needed—milk, ghee included. If there was a drop of ghee left in the pot he will not prepare the next lot. Once, even though I could see some ghee in the pot he said, "I must prepare some fresh Ghee". I looked at him askance in surprise. Smilingly he said, "The ghee in the pot is slightly smelly and Bandya does not tolerate even this much of the smell ! The catch was that this Bandya was a male cat ! He was non-violent. He looked beyond killing mice, etc. If he was served anything smelly he walked away indignantly, climbed up the fountain and sat there with a philosophical indifference to the world.

- Once Pt. Antubuwa had come to Bombay and was staying with his son Pt. Gajananbuwa in Dombivali. He lived on the first floor. He once told me, "Go down and bring some tobacco from Gajabuwa—I know he eats it when I am not around!" I went down and brought the '*dibbi*' (the tobacco container) with me and offered to pour tobacco in Pt. Antubuwa's hand. He glared at me and said, "Are you my equal to pour tobacco thus in my hand? Hold the container open in your right hand, touch the right hand with your left thus and wait for me to take what I desire!" Thus was given to me a lesson in courtesy and protocol that enrich Indian musico-cultural spectrum.

Ustad Faiyaz Hussain Khan
(1886 to 5-11-1950)

6

Ustad Faiyaz Hussain Khan

(1886 to 5-11-1950)

Background

He was born in Agra and spent his growing years and impressionable age surrounded by families of musicians. From his father's side, he was the great-grandson of the famous composer Rangeele and from his mother's side, he was the great-grandson of the originator of the Agra *gharana,* Ustad Gagge Khuda Bux. Thus music ran in his blood. He received training mainly from Ghulam Abbas (grandfather) and Kallan Khan (granduncle), both of Agra *gharana*.

He was appointed State-musician in Baroda in 1912, awarded the title of *Aaftaab-e-mousiki* by the Maharaja of Mysore in 1925. Since then Ustad Faiyaz Hussain Khan was popularly known as *Aaftaab-e-mousiki*, 'the sun in the world of music'. For once, the praise was not hyperbolic though it did describe a musician! He was well-known for his ability to sing a variety of musical forms. Moreover, he was known for his prowess for being always immensely successful in *mehfils*. He invariably created a state of *rang* (colour) in his music-making and presentation. As is known, *Rang* is the term used to describe the high success of a performance in performing arts such as dance, drama, music, etc., in India. The Ustad belonged to that rare category of musicians who not only won admiration but also earned affection from the audience because he brought so much cheer to them through his music.

The Extrovert Attitude

Does 'cheer' as a quality belong to the extroverts among musicians? It might be so, because in a very marked way, the Ustad's music displayed an unmistakable outgoing quality. His music was very openly directed at the audience with an express purpose of involving it in the musico-cultural processes that every musical concert in India promises to be. For the Ustad, the number of listeners present hardly mattered. A presence of a few attentive ears was enough to spur him on. At the same time the Ustad (like Prime Minister Pt. Nehru, who was an improviser in speech,) loved crowds. In the company of a participating audience the Ustad's music acquired an easy flow and a conquering edge. Very aptly he was often referred to as *mehfil ka baadshah* (king of concerts).

The Bass Voice

How did the Ustad elicit this intense and qualitative involvement of his audience? His first asset was an unabashed projection of a bass, booming voice. To describe his use of the bass, as 'unabashed' has a special propriety because in his times and among his contemporaries, employment of a high fundamental pitch by vocalists was in itself regarded a virtue and a custom religiously followed. To a certain extent the absence of sound-amplifying gadgets certainly made the practice necessary. But it is also true that to sing in a low key was not highly regarded. To do so was almost taken to be an admission of some weakness in the musical make-up of the artist. It is on this background that the Ustad's decision to sing in a low-keyed fundamental could be regarded as courageous.

It means that as a performer he was not interested in the empty heroic gesture of singing in high pitch, whatever may be his own preference. He used the bass and in doing so exploited the volume-dimension of the voice as opposed to the pitch-dimension that was routinely utilised by a majority of his contemporaries. It followed logically that in his music the aesthetic principle of musical contrast came into operation. Whether it was the *nom-tom* (e.g., *lalat* and *darbari*), his famous rendering of the *antara* in *raga barawa* or his pieces in *bhairavi,* it was the *fortissimo-pianissimo* effect that was repeatedly employed. As an expressive dimension the volume of human voice has fewer potentialities than the dimension of pitch. In the light of this acoustic fact the Ustad's choice spelt an aesthetic risk. In all probability he accepted it because he was aware of the limited pitch-range of his voice, had weighed the total consequences and had ultimately decided in favour of a low-keyed but strongly projected voice as against a voice that was high-keyed but strenuously produced. The Ustad's use of the voice was validated by his music. He could reach the audience to the last man and could also simultaneously envelope the listeners in music that was always surging-forward. It was a sense of power that one primarily experienced in his music. As his expression was directed at the audience, the power-element was entirely in place. His aim was to gain ascendancy over the audience—either by conquest or through persuasion. To achieve an 'effect' was of primary importance to him and he was hardly satisfied by an aesthetic 'realisation' of musical ideas in isolation.

The low-key base and the accompanying projection in vocalisation were also associated with a marked superimposition of the vowel-sound approximate to 'a' (as in 'man') instead of the usually advocatd 'a' (as in father). This must have proved a valuable aid in projecting voice effectively because the vowel-sound 'a' (as in 'man') is certainly less open than 'a' (as in 'father')— the vowel-sound, customarily insisted upon in Hindustani vocalisation. Consequently, his vowel-sound 'a' was easier to control. It is clear that what was involved here was a performer's musical logic, not an accidental choice.

Preference for the *Nom-Tom*

An important clue to his musical logic is to be found in the overall *dhrupad*-orientation of the Agra *gharana*. Ustad sang *dhrupad dhamar* in accordance with all the established norms. However, listening to him in between the notes we find that in his *dhrupad-dhamar* renderings, the weakest was the *dhamar*, in the sense that it was uninspired. On the other hand, he seemed to relish the singing of *nom-tom* to such an extent that he went on to record *nom-toms* alone in *raga*-s *darbari*, *ramkali* and *lalat*. The deduction is that he valued *nom-tom* singing as an unfettered way of elaborating the *raga*-s or of creating the *raga*-mood in a more immediate and comparatively unrestricted manner. In this context, it is interesting to note that he did not restrict the *nom-tom* to the *dhrupad-dhamar* genre. He employed it even before rendering a *bhairavi dadra* ("*Banaavo batiyaan*") or prior to presentation a *drut khayal* composition (*Jaunpuri,* "*Phulwanki gajare*"). This only strengthens the view that he had divined the wider potentialities of the *nom-tom*: it could evoke a *raga*-mood and it also allowed the musician a free hand in doing justice to the thematic complexities of a *raga.* It is no exaggeration to say that he sang *dhamar*-s out of a sense of musicological loyalty to the accepted repertoire of the *gharana* and in conformity with the performance-norms of the genre. Yet the artist in him keenly felt the aesthetic possibilities of *nom-tom* which could be brought to the forefront only when this phase was employed in isolation or independently. This was the reason why he employed it irrespective of the form presented.

The Ustad's penchant for the *nom-tom* and the superimposition of the vowel-sound 'a' (as in 'man') were intrinsically and mutually related features. As a detailed elaboration of *raga*, *nom-tom* aims at constructing a complete structure with the help of a perceptive use of meaningless syllables. In other words, this phase is also marked by a vocal flow which is intermittent in contrast to the *raga*-elaboration presented with the help of the vowel-sound 'aa' (as in 'father'). In *nom-tom* the interest is therefore not centred on an experience of continuity but on making listeners feel the tonal movement realised through succession of units. It was this punctuated phrasing which was facilitated by his favoured vowel-sound 'a'.

His Versatility

The discussion of the Ustad's ability to involve the audience is directly related to the projection techniques he pursued. However, the projection techniques were not the only tools he had. His success in establishing a rapport with his listeners was also greatly aided by his mastery in presenting a variety of musical forms. He was at home in *dhrupad-dhamar, khayal, tarana*, *thumri* and *dadra*. In fact it was due to his versatility that he was called a '*choumukka*' artist, i.e., an artist who could see in four directions like the lord Brahmadeva of the Hindu pantheon. His *repertoire of ragas* too was very wide. He relied heavily on the *prachalita raga*-s like *darbari*, *yaman, kedar, basant, todi, lalat, jaunputri,* but equally expert was his exposition of *raga*-s like *paraj*, *nat-bihag*, *gara-kaanada*, *suhag, barwa, bhankar,* etc. To have *aprachalita raga*-s in one's repertoire and yet to insist on presenting the *prachalita raga*-s was undoubtedly an indication of his desire to bring music nearer to the general audience. Presenting *prachalita raag*-s was to all purposes a musical strategy he used for taking the audience into confidence. But whenever the occasion demanded he sang the rare *raga*-s with a stamp of authority that only deep knowledge could bring out. In this context it becomes more important to study how he managed to create and sustain the listener's interest in the *prachalita raga*-s he sang so frequently.

In order to achieve this he used a number of devices. A very distinctive device was the pronunciation of the words in the song-text in *khayal*-singing. The author is inclined to characterise his manner of pronunciation as 'speech-oriented' or 'conversational', that is, the pronunciation was so shaped and projected as to convey the meaning through patterns of intonation, inflexion, etc.—usually associated with speech or conversation as distinct from music-making. As already said, he used the volume-dimension of the voice by making it sound soft, loud, tender or vigorous, etc. He brought this same skill to the utterance of words according to the requirements suggested by the linguistic meaning of the word units. The actual process was in fact comparable to clothing the dramatic categories of speech with musicality and using the resulting total phrasing as a part of the musical idiom. For example, in his *drut khayal* in *lalat* ("*Tarpat hun jaise jal bin meen*") the vocal tone-modulations introduced after the word "*sainyaa*" (meaning 'beloved') are expressive in a manner reminiscent of a dramatic presentation. Remaining true to his perception of the musical appropriateness of a dramatic tone, he is heard to repeat the device with a telling effect in *thumri-dadra* renderings too. For instance, the words "*vahin jaavo*" (meaning "go only there") were almost spoken and not sung ("*Banaavo batiyan*" in *bhairavi*). In addition one also encountered the use of words—like '*are*', '*haan*', etc.—i.e. words which are the distinguishing marks of day-to-day conversation. Employment of such exclamatory class of words moves music closer to the first, intuitional impact which is so vital for a deeper and better understanding of music. His way of rendering made music more concrete because his presentations contained inbuilt clues useful for initiating a listener into music.

These and similar devices are in fact used abundantly by *thumri*-singers. Their incorporation in *khayal*-singing was a daring if not an altogether original act of intra-genre transfer of musical devices. Perhaps a rarer feat of a similar quality was the Ustad's resorting to speech-tone for the *nom-tom*. The meaningless syllables of the latter were articulated as if they had definable and communicable meaning (viz., *nom-tom*, in *lalat*). Treating them as 'words' enabled him to combine freedom from the worldly meanings of the words and yet simultaneously suggest shadow-meanings through 'tones'. When meanings were hinted at in this manner, they did not become shackles on musical manifestations for musicians as well as the listeners. This could be taken as an emotive use, as against the more obvious emotional use of words and the material they are made of. Poets are known to have taken pride in their stylistic achievements because of their success in realising linguistic and stylistic approximation to the colloquial. The Ustad could have made similar claims. He brought the musical experience nearer to speech-tones without sacrificing the distinctive elements of the musical act.

Bol-alap, Bol-taan and *Taan*

Under these circumstances it was very logical on his part to stress the *bol-alap* portion in his elaborations. In fact a musical chain-reaction was observed here. He could afford to give short shift to *alaps* in *aakaar* because of the extremely detailed presentation of *nom-tom* which preceded his singing of *khayal*. Further, as he had modified the usual vowel 'a', to suit his purpose, he could switch over to *bol-laya* (i.e., rhythmic variations on the words of the song-text in slower *tempi*) and then to *bol-taan* and the *taan* during the singing of *khayal*. For the climactic *taan*-portions he usually employed a not-so-fast-rendered *drut khayal.* The total situation was therefore an example of judiciously done transplantations and inter-mixtures of musical genres or specific vocal techniques associated with them. His *khayal* used *dhrupad* techniques for laying bare the total and tonal structure *of raga,* exploiting in the process, the special attributes of his natural voice: low-keyed fundamental and sonority. His *khayal*-singing also employed speech-tones to make the words dramatically appealing. Finally, he rounded off by improvising extraordinarily varied rhythmic patterns in *bol-taans* and *taans*.

This brings us to the discussion of his *bol-taans* and *taans* regarded as specialities of the Agra *gharana* even today. The *talim* of the *dhrupad-dhamar* genre imparted with a syllabic regularity in this *gharana*, obviously helps the followers of the Agra *gharana* to conceive and execute *bol-taans* and *taans* which possess astounding variety and power. Some of the easily identifiable *dhrupad-dhamar* orientations in the *bol-taans* and *taans* can be enumerated as follows:

i. Majority of *bol-taans* employ the method of '*pat*' while formulating a *bol-taan*. *Pat* is doubling, trebling, etc., of tempo associated with the original setting of the units (i.e., in the present context, *bols)*.
ii. There is an abundance of *tihai*-s designed in the manner of *dhrupad*-singing.
iii. The *gamak* is used in profusion as in the general *dhrupad-dhamar* idiom. *Gamak* is an act of intoning every specific

note along with the context of the adjoining notes. Thus intoned, the individual notes are less sharply defined.

iv. Very often the *taan* patterns begin from the successively changed starting points of the *tala*. Consequently, the whole *tala*-cycle undergoes a process of re-segmentation. This too is a *dhrupad*-feature employed in that genre in respect of *bol-taans*. (The genre does not allow the use of *taans*.) By merely changing the point of beginning the concerned rhythmic pattern gets a new look and the sin dreaded by all musicians, that of repetition, can be easily avoided on account of the new patterns put into circulation.

v. The overall bearing of Ustad's singing was comparable to the singing of *dhrupad-dhamar.* This was so because he relied more on robustness of expression and a ponderous musical movement. Listening to Ustad's *taans* it becomes evident that they were not dazzling in their speed. Their main impact was one born out of a controlled dynamics. Gradations in volume were so discriminatingly used that the lack of speed was not felt.

Foregoing analysis helps in understanding the logic that motivated his use of *prachalita tala*-s and moderately slow/fast tempi. Music of his extroversion did not allow pauses. His *bol-taans* and word-play also could not afford inordinately distanced *tala*-points. Even during *alaps* his non-use of a clear *aakaar* denied him continuity. Altogether there were many effective arrows in his performing armoury to be used as and when required.

All these virtuoso characteristics were matched by a unique sense of freedom in his demeanour on the stage. He was not inhibited and enjoyed having a central presence. Neither was he shy of using facial expressions, hand or head gestures to underline a musical effect. Perhaps this was what helped him in establishing an immediate contact with his heterogeneous audience. He loved every moment in the process of music-making and was eager to openly invite others to sense it as also to participate in it. Like a *thumri*-singer, the Ustad sometimes sang with his body. All said and done, not everything that a vocalist wants to convey is understood by the audience through the actual rendition. A lot more could be communicated through the accompanying factors. Ustad Faiyaz Hussain Khan wanted to communicate his musical involvement, his happiness in music-making as well as his considerable ascendency over the abstract material of his art to his heterogenous audience. If there was any secret of his artistry, this was perhaps the clue.

In 1921 the great singer of *thumri* music Siddheshwari Devi gave her debut concert at the age of 18. She ended the presentation with the evocative composition in *Bhairavi* ("*Kaahe ko daare gulal*"). Her music was overwhelming. Ustad Faiyaz Khan was scheduled to follow her performance. Unlike many others the Ustad was frank in his appreciation. He said, "After this singing nothing can be done" and then told Siddheshwari Devi, "After Gauhar Jan, the crown of *thumri* singing rests on your head."

So generous was he even to the junior artists! The way he complimented Pt. Gajananbuwa Joshi at Mysore is noted in Chapter 16 on Pt. Gajananbuwa, who was my first *Guru*.

BALGANDHARVA
(26-6-1888 TO 15-7-1967)

7

Balgandharva—A Great Actor-singer

(26-6-1888 to 15-7-1967)

A Brief Life-sketch

His full name was Narayan Shripad Rajhans and he was born on the 26th June 1888. When he was about 10 years old in 1898, Lokmanya Tilak, the great freedom fighter and leader in Pune, blessed Narayan with the honourable name Balgandharva (the young celestial singer) and the name became Narayan's identity for the rest of his life. He is known as that even today because of his epoch-making achievements. Narayan suffered from a slight deafness in his left year and hence was sent to Miraj in south Maharashtra for treatment. Things took a different turn and he joined the prestigious and pioneering music-drama company, the *Kirloskar Natak Mandali* on 25th Octobar 1905 on a monthly salary of Rs. 75/-. He also got married in 1907. Ironically, the same *Mandali* had earlier shown him the door because he had just broken his voice and they compared him with a cracked pot! But now the things had changed completely. His sweet music, looks and the artistic temper was of such calibre that the *Mandali* thanked its stars to have him. Balgandharva went on to create a challengingly creative prototype of a *Stree*-party singing actor (i.e. a male playing 'singing' female roles) and enrich the Marathi music-drama for over 50 years. To this day any aspiring singing actor/actress has to establish his or her bearings by referring to him. To be like him or different from him is the first decision such a person has to take. Evaluation of an actor-singer's abilities is invariably done with a reference to Balgandharva's music.Though he played his last role as Rukmini in 1955, his performing *avatar* had ended around 1937. By a rough count he created 35 roles in 27 plays by 10 different authors. (The exact number of performances he gave would prove to be a theme for some arduous research—so scattered is the data.) His singing was so effective that it is tempting to say that his music created the characters he portrayed. After being continuously on the boards for over 29 years, V. Shantaram of the pioneering Prabhat Films, brought Balgandharva on the silver screen in the film *Dharmatma* (1935). But the venture barely lasted till Balgandharva realised that he was not made for the cinema. As coincidence would have it, years ago, with Balgandharva's active help V. Shantaram had attempted a foray in drama. But he had realised that he was not made for the stage and had left.

Balgandharva went on drawing his furrow in Marathi music-drama despite the notorious internal sqabbles in the profession, indebtedness, insolvency, illness, dometic difficulties, etc. His financial conditions had worsened so much that in 1940 he declared insolvency. He was respectfully invited to join the theatre centenary-celebrations in 1943-44. Balgandharva was busy performing for fund-raising for the Red Cross till about 1947. His wife died in 1951 when he was in strained circumstances. After his wife's demise he married Goharbai. From 1952 onwards he experienced extreme difficulties in body-movements. The Central Sangeet Natak Akademi honoured him in 1955. His 75th year (1964) was celebrated all over. His illness was however consuming him and he died on 15th July 1967. His life cycle was directly related to the biographical graph and the historical march of Marathi music-drama. Against this background, while evaluating his musical contribution one has also to remember that the stage-music that he practised and raised to a high status aimed, realised and propagated different goals than art music of the times.

At the outset it must be admitted that my generation was not fortunate to see him in full glory on the stage and we could hear his music when his powers were waning. But whatever I heard from him in a concert and then in recordings left me speechless with wonder and wistfulness. In addition, my *guru* Gajananrao Joshi used to play Balgandharva's songs with unimaginable involvement, impact and truthfulness in his violin-programmes. Balgandharva's moving musicianship was also discussed otherwise. Marathi stage-music has acquired its multiple attractions due to its assimilation of music as expressed in *khayal, thumri, Qawwali* and Marathi devotional music. Balgandharva's proficiency and creativity in performing this multi-coloured repertoire can be experienced even today in the available recordings.

Reportedly Balgandharva played the *sitar*. His uncle has learnt to play the *mridang* from Pt. Balkrishnabuwa. Balgandharva's mother and aunt used to sing women's songs with great appeal. His maternal uncle was one of the early founders of the famous theatre group known as *Natyakalapravartak Mandali*. Balgandharva had some rudimentary training under a musician called Mehboob-khan at Jalgaon. But after joining the profession, Balgandharva's real training was under Pt. Bhaskarbuwa Bakhale and later he received guidance from Pt. Govindrao Tembe. However in the final analysis one can say that his extraordinary musical aptitude and talent led him to newer musical achievements. While assimilating the Goharjan touch or while selecting and modifying tunes or music with the help of Janakibai and Sundarbai for his own purpose, Balgan-dharva's unerring musical sense and skill to learn as one works with the material proved the most useful educative tool he could have hoped for.

The Drives Behind the Stage-music

Several different results are possible when the twin arts of theatre and music combine. The precise nature of the results depends on the nature of the concerned culture. For example, when such a combination takes place the following questions become relevant: To what extent the audiences have a taste for music? What kind of music is already prevalent in the concerned society? Who is the patron of music and to what extent the patronage offered is by the middle or the white-collared class? While theatre and music are seeking a combination do they in their manifestations, indicate awareness of other forms of entertainment in society? In the literature current in the times, is there an evidence of a developed prose? Is there a noticeable increase in the population and what is the distribution of the increase at a point of history when music-drama is emerging? Are there efficient, general and rapid modes and means of transport available for all? These and such other issues actually shape the combined *avatar* of music and theatre. Opera in the West, Music in America, Kunfu in China and *Sangeet natak* in Maharashtra could beocme strong realities with definite and considerable aesthetic consequences because answers to these and such other issues differ from culture to culture. Such manifestations inspire repeated inquiries because today the mutual dependence of music and culture is being increasingly realised and understood. Of course all such inquiries reach an intriguing phase because of the mercurial phenomenon of the individual artist. When a miracle takes place, it is a cumulative result of active combination of mind, moment and the surroundings. Study of the Moment and the Surroundings can perhaps be helped by scientific, methodological strategies but what about the mind? And Balgandharva was nothing but a mercurially musical mind in the world of Marathi music-drama.

The Firm Grip on the Musical Content

Yet to describe Balgandharva's music as mercurial may be paradoxical or it may only be a half truth. This is so because his artistic mind was very stable in the sense that he was very sure about what is music and certain about what and how to present it to covey the content he had in mind. He was never tentative in the act of final music-making. *Ragas* such as *bhop, bhimpalas, yaman, bihag, pilu, jangla, bageshri, malkauns, des, deskar, mand, pahadi, kalingda, lalat, tilakkamod, bhairavi, sindh bhairavi, deshi* or *shankara* were goddesses pleased with him. The role he played lacked victory or valour-oriented compositions. Perhaps he could not have done justice to them even if he was allocated such songs. Whether in a *bhajan*-concert, or one devoted to stage-songs, recording or just humming songs without accompaniment for others, musically he was never unsure, tentative or hesitant. He was able to introduce last minute changes in the matter of vocal intonation, selected tempo, chosen composition, *bandish* or devotional songs such as *abhang*. Whether it was Pt. Mallikarjun Mansoor's iteration of the *sthayi-antara* in his performances or Balgandharva's seemingly repetitious singing of song-lines, the basic aesthetic *sutra* (or *mantra*) was the same—to concentrate one's own and listener's attention on the proposed musical content of the endeavour. While singing, many things are simultaneously taking place. Elaboration of musical ideas, *bol-taan*, *taan* or *tihai*, contestful dialogue with the *tabla* player, exchanges with *sarangi* or *harmonium* accompanist. Sometimes the performer may also have exchanges with the audience. Thus music may go on but rather hastily. A good musician is able to slow down the flow of music and make it fuller and linger back a little. The abiity to take repeated musical bearings or restoring the subtly lost balance actually declares a performer's proficiency as well as the strength of the original structure of ideas. Music was always a well-established entity in Balgandharva's presentations.Often I am tempted to describe his musico-aesthetic sense as the unblinking eye of the tornado or as Eliot phrased it, "Still point of the turning world."

Not Singing but Song-making

From about 1910, Balgandharva was very popular among the student-population (which included Gujarati and Kannada speaking students too). He used to give numerous performances of 'non-stage' music-making. Such music I would like to describe as song-making and not as singing, as the latter is framed in the provided theatrical contexts and had thus to be purposeful for non-musical or extra-musical considerations. The 'songness' of these presentations brought out how his music-making can be without deliberation or without a conscious effort to 'create' music. It also means that there is a qualitative continuity or uninterrupted exploration in song-making as contrasted with "singing". His non-stage music-making was a subtly projected experience of eternity. Nobody failed to notice the sustained quality of his music-making. Prof. Gangadhar Gadgil, a sensitive major writer of fiction in Marathi has depicted a character which perceptively describes Balgandharva's music-making. It says, "This man is always singing in his stomach, we hear the music when he opens his mouth, that is all!"

What were the main components that made for this quality of musical continuity? Firstly, it was the selected tempo, which was not slow and generated an impression of being fast-paced. In the 78 r.p.m. recordings it certainly appears to be fast but even in live presentations Balgandharva believed in the musical efficacy of medium tempo. At least till the 1930-s musicians from Gwalior and Agra *gharana*-s maintained a steady preference for the medium tempo while making their music. Once the basic temporal map of music-making is established as the medium tempo, distances, spaces or durations become shorter and intrinsically more manageable. Mainly depending on successive arrangements of melodic production, Indian music places great value on the continuity of music leading to a continuity of musical experience. *Naradiya Shiksha*, the ancient musicological text has beautifully described how notes should follow one another: "like a shadow that follows the sunlight!" Balgandharva's selection of tempo was thus a decision of great aesthetic consequence.

To use the terminology of Yoga, Balgandharva was blessed with the *siddhi* of *laya,* i.e. rhythm. Once a *tala* was brought into play he was permeated with the pulses of the selected *tala* and its aesthetic aspect—the rhythm. No *tabla*-player could mislead him. Further he could 'catch' any *tala*-division with precision. But all this would only mean that he could maintain the *tala* i.e. he was a *layadar* artist. However, to be a *layakar* (creator of a *laya*) is something different, subtle and more aesthetically inclined. This required a keen perception of the nuances in the temporal design and an ability to 'play' with the micro-divisions to create sophisticatd designs that enrich the music-making activity. One major strategy he generously used towards this end was of introducing minute changes in the placements of individual words in a song within the *tala*-frame. Consequently, the entire *tala*-cycle was in a manner of speaking 're-lit' in a different fashion. He certainly opted for recurrence and not for repetition. As somebody has observed even a small hand-gesture by a good actor may charge the entire stage-space! It was not different in Balgandharva's music. For example, one may listen to the famous song "*Nath ha maza*" (from the play *Swayamvara*) as rendered by Smt. Manik Verma and earlier by Balgandharva. The former's approach to '*sama*'-point is tentative because she could not emulate Balgandharva's creative use of a playful deviation from the stated framework of the *tala*.

Voice and Intonation

However, this could not hacve been adequate to maintain the musical continuity or flow presently under our discussion. For example, musical continuity will not be created if individual notes are held over a longer duration. Balgandharva had the skill to collect four to five notes in one swift, uninterrupted vocal movement to create a dynamic cluster. In fact one does not find him camping on any single note. (He preferred *Bhamini*—one of his heroine-roles who liked a garland—to Noorjahan who was intent and content on inhaling fragrance of one single rose!) In sum, his music was experienced as dynamic or moving because of the selected tempo and also because his melodic phrases were dense.

Briefly and rather simply, it can be said that to follow the principle of melody in music making means one note at a time, and one note after another. Most of the Asian musical cultures follow this system of tonal organisation. There are also many which follow the performing strategy of 'one throw, five notes'. However, the strategy may not produce undeniably acceptable results. It does require a certain kind of voice along with the skill of 'throwing the voice'. Balgandharva's was not a thin voice but the intonation was delicate. His pitch was neither too high nor too low. His voice was naturally quick in movement but was never unstable nor too hurried. Sometimes voices are such that if you hold them for a while they dig themselves in (so to say) and then to move them becomes a laborious task. To avoid this difficulty some performers never plant notes firmly. They use a voice which is on a note but hoveringly so, to enable a quick movement. To me this appears to be a second choice! Whatever that may be, those who have a clear notion of correctly pitching a voice and applying the right proportion of force would do so in such a way that it allows them to plant themselves firmly and yet whithout any perceptible heaviness. Balgandharva was a master of this technique. This is almost a 'singing' parallel to what Hamlet advised the players about the delivery of dialogues—"Say it trippingly on the tongue." Medieval Indian musicology devoted a good deal of thought to the specific merits of a singing voice. One of the merits listed is called *sharir* (*sharir* = body). The term invites a simplified explanation—that which comes with the body (*sharir*) is *shareer*. However, the texts go further and explain that the vocal merit '*sharir*' means that a voice endowd with that quality is able to realise and concretise the *raga* without difficulty. In performing arts there is so much that can only be experienced through 'action or doing'. Such actions are psycho-physical and a performer is hardly able to control them from outside. In an actor, facial expressions or the eye-movements, for a dancer the hand movements and gestures, in an instrumentalist, his touch and strokes and in a vocalist, the intonation etc. consist of an element which almost appears to suggest that the body itself thinks of the performing ideas (or the body dreams of them). It is possible that the term *shareer* is suggesting the quality of a genius as discussed in literary epression. Without such a concept it should never be possible to describe the expressive miracles brought about by voices of artists such as Balgandharva, Bade Ghulam Ali, Pt. D.V. Paluskar or Lata Mangeshkar!

This discussion needs a reference to Balgandharva's tunefulness. It is not that he could be so tuneful due to his 'natural' musical aptitude. He was consciously tuneful. He was partially deaf in his right ear and probably because of this defect he had shifted all his accompanists to the 'front of the stage' locations. It must be remembered that in 1919-20, when he was to stage the play *Draupadi*, he replaced *harmonium* with the *pedal organ* and added two *sarangi*-s. It was obvious that overcoming all physical impediments he wanted to be extremely tuneful and hence this kind of all-sided efforts. As a consequence, people noticed his ability to unerringly intone and hold on to even the nuances of notes involved. That his admirers' spectrum included persons from Bhatia, Multani, Gujarati traders to Ustad Alladiya Khan (who was a fan of Gandharva's music-making nearly from 1916) was not in a small measure due to his tunefulness. In a way, natural aptitude and conscious artistic intent together lead to the tunefulness that we are talking about. And yet the question remains, how to distinguish between tunefulness as attained by different artists? It is tempting to come out with a flat answer that either an artist is or is not tuneful—no in between stage is possible. One may therefore state that the ability to perceive, attain and hold on to a note that is relevant in a particular manifestation is the first step towards tunefulness. Further, to be able to achieve this whenever required, with ease and maintain the pleasantness for the receivers constitutes the second step. To this extent, all artists who are tuneful are on a common ground. But beyond this is the province of the enveloping mood of the artist in whatever he does. This is where each artist can be different (at least he should be able to do so). Fresh learners often err at this point. They try to produce, intone and use their voices as per the model voice in their mind. In matters of the fundamental pitch, volume, attack and fade-out procedures they may be able to create an impression of exactly being 'another so and so'. But the question remains, what about the enveloping mood? For example, even if one gets the high pitch and ease of voice-production *a la* Lata, this will not bring along the mood of intense longing which Lata's singing invariably projects. Ustad Abdul Karim Khan's tunefulness has anguish and compassion while Ustad Bade Gulam Ali's tunefulness has a deep impress of an intoxicating richness. Smt. Heerabai Badodekar's or Smt. Manik Verma's tunefulness brings forth an attractive innocence, Master Krishnarao projects delight, Master Dinanath focuses with an aggressive brightness and Balgandharva persuades with a pleading, and intense devotion.

Perhaps due to the mistaken belief that Indian vocal music lives on its content, music-thinkers have avoided analysing voice as a quality-imparting agent or component. (Inevitably this view has also led to sidelining a serious study of voice-culture). In an age of abundant and sophisticated sound-projecting and amplifying technology as well as mechanism it is obvious that timbre is likely to be the most expressive and therefore most important dimension of sound. It is hence high time that analysis and evaluation move beyond the use of usual adjectives and refer to more sensitive criteria.

Balgandharva was also prone to a manner or mode of intonation in which there was an initial recourse to an 'H' sound. This consonant is known for the extra breath it requires and the greater reach it ensures. Expectably in Balgandharva's singing it appeared before a fast *taan* or a cluster of high notes was to be executed. Obviously his need to effectively project his essentially soft music, made him use this technique. However, later with the ageing process and health-conditions taking their toll, this was overdone .He was not able to control the unmusical aspects of the vocal technique he was using. His imitators made matters worse by treating this emergency-use as a feature of his patent "style"! (In Marathi, such gross imitators were described as "*Ha Ha Gandharva*" or even as "*Kha Kha Gandharva*"!). The feature became intolerably apparent as the advanced public address systems inclusive of good microphones became available. Barring this one feature, Balgandharva's music was always made with remarkable ease and impressive effortlessness. To hold a note, to move from one to the other, to arrive at the *sama* or just to fly past it gracefully, everything was accomplished with great ease. Till very late in his age, there was no gap between the emergence and execution of musical ideas in his performance.

The Musical Content

One feature of his singing that determined the musical content was intensity in his music-making. It may be that his being an actor contributed to this characteristic. (In a way, this kind of creative intensity characterises all creative activity.) In every kind of performance, acting, acting-singing or singing Balgandharva was intense and communicated this ethereal state to his listeners very effectively.

A very major feature of his musical content was that it was not 'classical' or art music as these terms are generally understood. It is true that most of the standard repertoire of stage music in Maharashtra is closely mapped on classical compositions. As Balgandharva himself explained often, the method of musical training of the majority of actor-singers (including himself) in stage-music involved teaching of the 'classical' composition prior to the training in the stage-music version based on it. Interestingly, even in concerts Balgandharva would often sing the classical composition first and then follow it up with the stage-song based on it. On examination of his repertoire, it becomes clear that it consisted of an admir-able variety of *raga, tala,* form and style. (To that extent he could be described as a Nayak i.e. a musician who is a rich store-house of *raga* and compositions and knows them well.) Not only did he know them—he was also able to effectively present them and elaborate the musical ideas contained in them, as a *khayal* singer would do with facility.

Balgandharva was able to correctly project the *raga*, and then he could also skillfully, momentarily and purposefully deviate from the *raga*-map to add colour to the proceedings. This phenomenon known as *tirobhav* of a *raga* suggests knowledge of codification in *raga*-music as well as the artistic ability and courage to move away from it to create meaningful music. For example, in "*Jo lokklayn sadhavaya jan*" (*bageshri, Sharada*) he used to introduce the note *shuddha gandhar*, or in "*Swakul tarak suta*" (*Bhimpalas*) he used to bring in notes *komal dha* and *shuddha gandhar*. On some other occasions he employed the note *shuddha nishad* in *raga Bhimpalas*. In "*Vairi marayala*" (in *raga Malkauns*) his employment of note *shuddha* '*re*' was also of a similar vintage. All these are instances of deviations from the *raga* concerned. The deviations were registered as musical features beautifying the presentations because they were born of a rare sense of balance, musical design and emotional enrichment, combined to delight all listeners and aesthetically provoke the knowledgeables in the audience.

Yet Balgandharva was a great actor-singer and not a classical singer (it must be admitted that he never claimed otherwise). The point to be stressed is that the term actor-singer does not indicate a lesser kind of artistic stature. Music conceived and performed in both genres generates different kinds of music, leading to distinctly identifiable qualitative musical features and criteria to evaluate the resultant expressions. Unless this is remembered both classical and actor-singers and their respective art is not likely to get analytical justice. The point is that Balgandharva's music was shaped according to an actor's sensibility. The theatrical mode determined and controlled the content of Balgandharva's music-making and music. It is instructive to understand how the feature of musical intensity mentioned earlier appeared in this context.

In brief, I would suggest that the theatrical strategy of achieving contour-touching identification with the character or role brought the intensity into activity. Simply stated, he imagined himself to be *Chokha Mela* while singing the evocative "*Johar maybaap johar*". Similarly, in case of singing the compositions of his female roles (e.g. of a heroine in love or the one suffering from separation), he superimposed moods and motives associated with the concerned characters on himself and thus enabled the intensity to shape the musical content. I would suggest that this vogue can safely be described as *natanmarg*.

In contrast to actor-singers, generally a classical singer does not have access to the *natanmarg* and they rarely insist in having recourse to it. The matter can be easily understood in the way they use the musical component of a linguistic word. It is true that while singing *thumri* or similar other forms of music, classical singers use the linguistic word evocatively. However, this evocation is of a different kind. Firstly, even if the singer invokes the said '*natanmarg*', yet in view of the ultimate goal the singer is bound by the codified norms and rule of the genre involved. In other words, the exploration of the *natanmarg* by a classical singer is limited, occasional and under constraints. If it is more than that, the most likely comment would be "He/she is more dramatic/theatrical in singing!" On the other hand, the actor-singer's composition appears within the emotional framework related to the dramatic requirement. He is thus expected to sing in a manner parallel to the dramatic structuring. This being so, Balgandharva was on his musico-dramatic alert while rendering songs such as "*Prem nach jaai*", "*Avaghachi sansar*", "*Baghu nako majkade*". In all the phases of rendition, e.g. in melodic elaboration, rhythmic variations, faster *taan*-s, etc., he was aware of the musico-dramatic genesis of what he was presenting. Even in concerts this approach was not abandoned, the musico-theatric moorings were never lost.

To explain the differences in the discussed approaches, it can be said that a classical singer, even when he renders his music with awareness of the evocative power of the word, his aim is not to set up a framework of feelings that runs parallel to the specific thrust of the composition-text. His appeal is to the broad or a general mood of the composition. He is trying to direct the flow of musical ideas to arouse the related stock-responses for some time. His music tries to establish a perceivable relationship with situations such as seperation of the lover and his beloved, or their union, stylised love-exchanges between Radha and Krishna, the heroine's loneliness or the hero's love at first sight, etc.

In contrast, in the play, *Saubhadra*, Krishna-Rukmini's love for each other, or Sindhu's anxiety about Sudhakar in a play called "*Ekach Pyala*", Balgandharva's music is moving parallel to what the concerned incident/event is emoting. It is symptomatic that in classical music concerts, even top-ranking vocalists are heard to non-chalantly 'break' words or phrases to suit themselves! (For example, for the classical singers words/phrasings become sound-patterns and hence they are heard to sing "*Sajanaa ye ghar*", or "*Neekeghun gariya*", or "*Chameli phulicham pa*" instead of "*Sajan aaye ghar*" and "*Neeke ghungariya*" or "*Chameli phuli champa*" respectively.) In a dramatic presentation, dismembering of "*Prem nach jaai*" into "*Premna chha jaai*" would be regarded a culpable act.

It is easy to understand the reasoning behind these basic differences in the approaches. A concert of Hindustani classical music i.e. *Baithak* or *Mehfil* is a format that associates with it extensive elaboration of *raga*, *tala,* etc. through the performer's tools, such as voice and imagination. In other words, the format makes specific demands on the artistic techniques employed, genres selected and all such matters are determined accordingly. In these and all such other matters, Balgandharva as an actor-singer and drama-music as the musical content differed from the classical contexts. In *raga* for example, Balgandharva's interest lay in 'colouring' the important aspects of *raga* as an actor-singer would do, to ensure effective rendering of the selected 'song'. Roughly it would be true to say that a classical singer draws a parallel with a novelist in expanding the tale, while the actor-singer, like a dramatist, is interested in making the impact more intense and quickly. In the final analysis, music and theatre are performing arts and hence enjoy certain similarities in functioning and goals set. But they follow considerably different paths. (Therefore, it is not surprising that there are instances of classical musicians who managed to create a final impact mainly through virtuosity or technically impressive renderings.)

Balgandharva's music also marked a change from the classical music in respect of the emotional content. This emotional content is not to be confused with the Balgandharva's musical intensity referred to earlier. In order to ensure generating an impact of the scene directly involved and to help the final effectiveness of the performance as a whole, the dramatic-song and the actor-singer concerned try to establish a relationship between music and the emotional content of the scene. This use of music can be described as evocative. Initially the dramatic incident along with music that is intended to be parallel to the import of the scene; this is to be followed by the dramatic progressions. This is the total setting in which dramatic music operates. It is obvious that classical musician does not proceed with music in this mode.

Yet another feature of actor-singers' craft is that the total effect intended also partakes of some results obtainable from other extra-musical factors such as the reality-effect created by the mounting of the play, fall out of dialogues, the pulls exerted by the plot. In addition is the specific character of the Marathi music-drama. Music and drama have come together in Maharashtra in such a way as to register deviations from many other combined *avatar*-s. Hence it is different from opera, musicals or from folk presentations with their combination of dance-music and drama. Putting aside the wider concept of theatre, Marathi dramatic sensibility opted for the rather limited proscenium versions of dramatic performances, mainly of two kinds: prose-drama and music-drama. This is why Balgandharva's music-making assumed its specific character. Some obvious norms he observed were to sing less but intensely, not to forget that the voice belongs to a character, to be aware of the story-line as well as particular incidents, etc.

Obviously these or similar restrictions and criteria born thereof will not suit classical singers' music-making. A classical musician is an explanatory commentary on the *bandish* he is rendering. He is supposed to expand the musical ideas present as a seed form in the *bandish*. On the contrary, an actor-singer states the musical idea and tries to elaborate the dramatic seed-form. It is interesting that Balgandharva followed the drama-music conventions even when he rendered an original *bandish* on which the particular drama-song was mapped. In sum, the Marathi music-drama carried on a battle with doctrines such as naturalism or realism, on the one hand, and the codificatory aspects of classical musical traditions on the other. What emerged was not an opera, or a musical, it was music-drama. It represented a cultural consensus of a people.

In the end, Balgandharva's music presented a dramatic-music with a Marathi character. Pt. Bhaskarbuwa's classicism, Pt.Govindrao Tembe's northern touch of *thumri, qawwali, ghazal* and similar semi-classical genres, Master Krishnarao's *bhajan*-idiom—all were turned into Marathi-coloured *pada, varkari abahang* or *baithakichi lavani* etc. No culture is easily inclined to change its own music and music is the last to change in the totality of cultural components that inevitably undergo changes. In modern Maharashtra too, all social strata changed their music in various ways and at varied intervals. In case of music and drama, the former is more abstract and the latter more representational and hence these changed in different ways. If one concentrates on music-drama,

> Around 1954-55, my father was an employee of the Maharashtra State Cooperative Bank. The bank-staff had organised a *Satyanarayana Pooja* (worship of God Satyanarayana) to celebrate something. They had also organised a *bhajan* concert by Balgandharva. I had begun my music-studies under Pt. Gajananrao Joshi who always praised Balgandharva's music very highly. So I had accompanied my father to the concert. When I saw Balgandharva, I was a bit shocked! He was clad in a white dhoti, simple white shirt and wore a Gandhi cap. He had difficulties in movements and looked nearly helpless. He had to be lifted to sit on the platform and within minutes he was rendering the famous *chhota khayal* in *raga bageshri* ("*Kaun gat bhaili*"). He was effortlessly tuneful. There was an overwhelming intensity in his singing and he appeared to do everything classical musicians do without much ado. Then followed a stage song based on the *bandish* he had rendered. The music continued flowing. He then sang some *abhang.* Again the absorbing quality of his music was not lost on me. I wondered how he achieved all this and much more with so much of ease and pleasantness. His music still remains with me and strikes me as mystifyingly simple and beautiful.

one may say that there were at least three basic idioms/styles that came into prominence. These were exemplified by Babajirao Rane, Patankar-Mandali and Balgandharva. The three were respectively liked by the general people, the mill-industry-related crowd and the middle class. It stands to Balgandharva's credit that those who admired his music considerably outnumbered those who patronised and liked his music-drama. That spoke of his ability to transcend the limitations of time, space and language, every great artist testifies.

SURASHRI KESARBAI KERKAR
(13-8-1892 TO 16-10-1977)

8

Surashri Kesarbai Kerkar
(13-8-1892 to 16-10-1977)

A Brief Life-sketch

Born in Keri (Goa), Surashri Kesarbai Kerkar shifted to Kolhapur for some time at the age of ten, where she received some training from Ustad Abdul Karim Khan. Later on serious (though often interrupted) training that she received was from Pt. Vazebuwa, when she returned to Goa from Kolhapur in 1901. In 1911-12, she left for Bombay and after one year's guidance from Ustad Barkatulla Khan (*beenkaar*), her real *talim* from Ustad Alladiya Khan of the Jaipur *gharana* began and continued for about fifteen years (from 1920 onwards). By the time this phase reached completion, she was in her mature forties. She was recorded for the first time in 1933 but that recording never reached the public.

Rabindranath Thakur awarded her with the title *Surashree* in 1938 and this title has since become etched in peoples' memory though she was also a recipient of many other honours. From about 1965 she stopped giving public concerts.

Smt. Kesarbai Kerkar was one of those artists who exercised an undisputed sway over at least two generations of musicians in the 20th century. The lay listeners equated her with majesty and strength; for the discerning she was a measure of greatness and excellence. To practising vocalists, she was puzzling and challenging and to students of music she was a role-model. How could she register simultaneous victories on so many diverse fronts?

Voice and Melodic Elaboration

Perhaps the foremost striking feature of her singing was an almost masculine breadth of her voice. The impression one received was of a very low natural key being used as the fundamental. However, even a casual check revealed an interesting fact: her fundamental key-note was always between *G* and *G*-sharp. This means that in reality her singing-pitch was not very low. Female singers in India usually employ the same key. Hence, the impression of the low singing-pitch was to be explained by some non-pitch factor. A little attentive listening revealed the reasons for both of these easily and primarily perceived qualities: breadth and the low-pitch. The reason was her undistorted vowel-sound 'aa'.

Irrespective of the tempo of music, the part of the octave-range under exploration, or the *raga* presented, she employed a flawless, unattenuated 'aa'. The special acoustic qualities of this vowel-sound are well-known. It has a better reach and it allows greater continuity of musical effect. It is instructive to note that the Indian musicological term for melodic elaboration, namely *alap* is often explained as directly derived from the vowel 'aa' ! Whatever that may be, the vowel-sound is also more manoeuvrable and it facilitates changes in tempi and especially *taan* and other 'fast' progressions. The primary importance of the vocal reach for a singer employing this vowel-sound needs no explanation. The continuity and the conduciveness to speed *vis-a-vis* Kesarbai's music are the features to be taken up for discussion a little later. Till at least 1940, the public address systems were not in easy use and the microphones too were not very sophisticated. We come back here to the breadth-low-pitch syndrome. Kesarbai was interested in projecting her voice; she could achieve this only by singing in an undistorted 'aa'. It is an acoustic fact that the perception of pitch is weakened by the perception volume. Taken all in all, it provides us with the total causation of the phenomenon under discussion. It is interesting to remember that she detested the microphone and made it a point to 'forcefully request' the organisers to remove it. The power and the breadth of her vocalisation would have been distorted by a conventional equipment and an unimaginative setting of the double-edged weapon that the microphone is and apparently she was well aware of this.

The Jaipur *gharana* which Kesarbai chiefly represented, stresses through its usage, the significance of *aprachalita raga* as well as complex *raga*-s. In fact, the followers of the *gharana* lay so much emphasis on including such *raga*-s in their performance-repertoire that their insistence has led to creation of a 'specialisation-effect'. Rare *raga*-s and Jaipur have come to be equated with each other. However, as far as Kesarbai's recorded music is concerned, her *repertoire* is not adequately reflected. It is true that from the disc-music, *raga*-s like *nand*, *nat-kaamod*, *maaru-behag*, etc., can be categorised as *aprachalita*, but in *mehfils* I have heard her renditions of *raga*-s like *badhans sarang*, *suhaa-kaanada*, *triveni, khokar, saavani-kalyan, basanti-kedar, hindol-bahar, jaun-bahar, khaṭ, sampoorna-malkauns*, *jayat*, *meerabai ki malhar, poorba* and *megh*. Even this illustrative listing is sufficient to prove the depth and variety of the *aprachalita* component in her repertoire.

However, the more interesting feature was that her approach to even *prachalita raga*-s carried a hint of the *aprachalita*. She conceived and presented them in such a way that they proved more intricate than their familiar faces would otherwise suggest. She achieved the effect most of the times through an introduction of complexity in the phrasing but sometimes she also resorted to the age-old trick of somewhat arbitrarily employing notes conventionally considered weak in these *raga*-s. For example, in *raga jaijaivanti* she used to introduce the *komal gandhar* in a phrase like '*saa re saa ga re*', a phrasing that is not very common. Similarly, in the case of *raga desi* she used to employ both the varieties of the *dhaivat* note in a way that could be considered arbitrary when subjected to musicological scrutiny. The flexibility and the boldness unfolded in such usages are qualities not generally associated with the Jaipur *gharana*. The author still remembers a concert in which she sang *raga poorvi* but phrased the two *madhyama* in such a way as to cause a minor (*raga*) identity-crisis amongst the listeners. Her rendition of the simple looking *Durga* was yet another instance of her approach which exhibited a marked propensity to introduce musical riddles. In her presentation the *pentatonic raga* would acquire another character and would seem full of potentialities as she wove her intricate patterns.

The *Taankriya*—Formation and Execution of *Taan*

Her *taans* too exemplified the characteristic of complexities. Some of the procedures she relied on could be easily identified. For instance, she used to group musical notes in varying numbers, with odd and even numbers sometimes alternating. Another, rather scarcely heard principle of constructing a *taan* was to sustain an intermediate (not the initial or the final) note longer than the others which were kept moving fast. A third specific effect especially associated with the Jaipur *gharana* was a vigorous and weighty execution of a 'double-stranded' *taan*. In this variety of *taan*, the progressions would go as follows: "*Ga Ma, Ga Ma, Ga Pa, Ma Pa; Ma Ni; Pa Ni; Pa Saa, Ni Saa,*" etc. It was of course apparent that much of the complexity of her *taans* was to be traced to the basic, original movement of the *raga* which in this case, when examined structurally was itself a complex entity. In such a *raga* even the slow-tempo *alap*-s were complex. As the *taans* are a retracing of the musical map already etched in the *alap*-phase, the principle of musical consistency could not have possibly allowed her the luxury of simpler *taans*. This, however, was only a partial explanation of the complexity of the *taans*.

She also used some supplementary devices which magnified the intricacy of the original design. For instance, very frequently she utilised a triadic patterning, wherein she initiated and completed a pattern of few notes—the pattern, itself was complex. After initiating the basic pattern, she immediately went on to repeat the same pattern in the two succeeding halves of the scale. Presented in this manner, the pattern was registered thrice within a span of about one and half octave but with different notes. The outcome was a certain magnification of the pattern. Perhaps the triadic design was also necessitated by the original or the intrinsic complex movement of the *aprachalita raga.* This sounds plausible because almost without exception such *raga*-s are examples of '*vakra chalan*', that is, convoluted tonal movement. They cannot proceed straight along the line of the gamut without running the risk of distorting the essential *raga*-identity. In the same context, Kesarbai's *taans* could not be described as fast; yet they created an impression of speed. This could happen because due to the intricate patterning she managed to cover wider tonal spaces. In all probability the breadth of voice she maintained throughout a performance without any tapering-off effect also contributed to the speed-illusion so capably created by her. In other words, the overall effect was of speed because a large musical mass was kept moving continuously. It was as if the medium pace appeared as fast pace on account of the broader singing line.

Discussion of her *taans* can hardly be exhausted easily. At least one more subtlety in her approach needs to be mentioned. During the *taan*-progressions she was wont to make a skillful change of pattern from the one that was being followed to ensure that a listener does not get accustomed to it and begin to expect it with certainty—so inimical to the aesthetic impact. The dangers of initiating a complex pattern and dragging it through the entire *taal*-cycles, are two-fold. Firstly, too regular an appearance of a pattern kills the golden goose of surprise. By itself this is enough to blunt the aesthetic sensibility of the listener. Secondly, a rigid regularity of patterns verges on affecting the listeners in such a way that they begin to perceive the *taan*-patterns as mechanical practice-exercises. Such exercises do not decorate the music that is presented—they tax it.

Incidentally, it is an example of musicological and terminological appropriateness to know that patterns which could decorate music are called '*alankar*' (ornament) and those which are expected to help in attaining technical virtuosity through intensive practice are called *'paltas'* (reversal). However complex the pattern in a *taan* might be, its repetition could be overdone: Kesarbai avoided it by a mid-way change of pattern-types. On numerous occasions, the immaturity of a musician is easily detected through his reluctance to leave a pattern and take up another (without of course violating the law of musical coherence). By unerringly picking up the right moment for introducing a change, Kesarbai eliminated the possibility of parading adherence in place of creative coherence.

And to cap it all, she displayed enough aesthetic flexibility to loosen the shackles or the constraints imposed by the concept of grammatical, musicological correctness, especially in her *taan*-s. She ignored the unbending syntax of phrasing which she so assiduously used to maintain in the *alap*-s and repeatedly introduced and effectively executed 'straight' *taan*-s. This amounted to a movement towards musical climaxes by brushing aside the strict protocol of phrase-succession. In fact, this is a device which the Gwalior *gharana* singers have perfected. (Just as nothing is as eye-catching in cricket as a straight drive past the bowler, similarly, there is hardly anything as ear-filling in music as a straight *taan*.) The climactic effect achievable (only) through such a *taan* could hardly be dispensed with. Therefore, Kesarbai's unerring performance-logic came unhesitatingly into operation. She reasoned that if and when an atmosphere of a *raga* is adequately built up through meticulous and detailed *alap*-s, nothing could damage the edifice even when grammatical fidelity is relegated to the background for some time. The author remembers in this context, the way Pt. Anant Manohar Joshi (a prominent disciple of Pt. Ichalkaranjikar of the Gwalior *gharana*) differentiated between the respective roles of *alap*-s and *taan*-s *vis-a-vis raga*. He said, "*alap*-s shape the individual *raga*-s into their individualities, *taan*-s bring out the unity of all *raga*-s". It was clear that Kesarbai subscribed to the view. In the final analysis, every rendition of a *raga* is a matter of balancing unambiguous projection of the musicological as also the interpretation-aspect, which represents the essential freedom of the creative mind. It is to Kesarbai's credit that she could achieve the rare feat most of the times.

While evaluating any musician's contribution it is necessary to remember that ultimately there is nothing like 'correct or incorrect' music. It is more appropriate to say that 'music is either relevant or irrelevant'. Whether in *alap*-s or in *taan*-s, Kesarbai used to step out of the *raga*-frame and this going across the border was a well-calculated move. The aesthetic justification for the deliberate contravention of 'rules' was not, in reality, far from the dictates of musical commonsense. If a *raga*-frame is to be established properly, it is necessary to loosen the same intermittently. Without the graces of flexibility, a *raga* will become a musical strait-jacket instead of being a mould of suggestive musical guidelines. The content of every musical endeavour is finally determined not only by an artist's particular presentation at a particular point of time but also by what he manages to suggest. Depending on the assimilated training, cultivated temperament and the gradually acquired risk-taking ability of the artist, this loosening of the *raga*-frame can be actualised in various ways. Kesarbai achieved it largely through a preconceived arbitrariness in the matter of conformity to the *raga*-grammar as also through straightening out the contours of the *raga* during the *taan* phase. To anyone who had heard other prominent Jaipur vocalists (such as Shri Gulubhai Jasdanwala, Smt. Mogubai Kurdikar), the individuality of Kesarbai's approach would be easily recognisable.

Her (un-noticed) Eclecticism

A marked feature of her music was her eclecticism. This came out in a personal discussion I had with her some time during 1968-69. She accepted this position, though with great reluctance and in a somewhat round-about manner. In that memorable 'encounter' she questioned me very closely about an article I had published earlier. In it, I had pointed out that even though Kesarbai followed the ideology of the Jaipur *gharana*, she was able to go beyond the confines of the *gharana* much more significantly than a majority of the other vocalists belonging to the Jaipur fold did and it was this touch of rebellion which made her a better musician. I had also argued further that she was able to carry the non-conformist banner so effectively because she displayed an alert absorption of the salient and selective features of other *gharana*-philosophies like Gwalior. I had added that this was apparent in her treatment of *raga*-s like *yaman* as opposed to her treatment of *raga*-s like *nat-kaamod*. She was more imaginative and free in the former and scintillating but disciplined in the latter. Secondly, I had also pointed out that on occasions she presented *alap*-s which were so elaborate and gradual that they could not have been improved even by a direct disciple of the Kirana *gharana*! And finally, I had maintained that unlike many others of the Jaipur *gharana* (with the exceptions of Manji Khan, Pt. Mansoor and Smt. Padmavati Gokhale) she had not shied away from musical forms like *thumri* and *bhajan* and this too had helped in toning down the austerity of her music.

I had then concluded that all these features separated her from the Jaipur hard-core. (In support of the arguments I had referred to specific *mehfil*-s and specific *raga*-s that she had presented as evidence.) Her responses, as they emerged during the discussion, ranged from 'very vocal to the equivocal'. The Gwalior-touch she was not too reluctant to admit; in respect of her occasional, detailed *alap*-s she credited them to the *talim* she had received from Ustad Barkatullah Khan (the well-known *been*-player) and the third point she ignored. But in spite of all those admissions to eclecticism she averred that she had not overstepped the confines of her *gharana*! The musical paradox of a musician's eagerness to leave behind the territory of the initial *gharana* and yet to claim an unswerving loyalty to the same *gharana* holds no mystery. In all probability it is a clannish hangover from the days when the concept of *gharana* was tied to family-fidelities.

The Precision

All the rich content of her music and her abundant powers of presentation would have been of no avail in the absence of that rare quality she displayed in all its glory, precision. The most important manifestation of her preciseness was her conception of the content. On no occasion did she leave behind an impression of tentativeness in the formulation of her musical ideas. One was never compelled to guess or deduce. Her thoughts were spelt out with great clarity. There was no fumbling with words, no half-hearted enunciation of the vowel-sounds, and no excruciating suspense on account of a protracted process of reaching the required pitch-levels. In spite of the complexity of design, there was no obscurity in her music. A very perceivable instance of the quality of precision is the manner in which a musician attains the *sama*-point. In Kesarbai's music this was always a moment to remember. Initially it appeared that she had crammed the entire available temporal space of the *taal*-cycle with music-almost to the last fraction of a second, before she took up the *mukhda*. And yet, she seemed to create additional *taal*-space which no listener could have suspected to be there and add something before she sang the *mukhada*. This required a sort of 'unimaginable' precision and this invariably invested her *sama*-s with extraordinary weight. She never came to the *sama*, she arrived at it regally.

And the Authority …

It was not surprising that the cumulative effect of her music was the sense of immense authority she brought to bear on everything she did. Due to her kind of music-making one instinctively accepted the position that musically she could do no wrong. Udayanaachaarya, one of the ancient Sanskrit grammarians, is believed to have said, "The correct in grammar is what Udayanaachaarya says. The east is where the sun rises!" Kesarbai was imbued with a similar confidence and she communicated it as an assurance to the audience.

To a great extent, this was possible because of the sound structuring of her music. Even in her musically weak moments, her performances did not fall below a certain level, which itself was pitched quite high. There was a guarantee in her music that due to its firm backbone it would never go limp and hence, at least the 'standard' musical fare could be hoped for. This made her an ideal artist for a student, a safe performer for a connoisseur and an admirable phenomenon for a musician.

The year was 1968-69. I had been appointed the first Director of the Bombay University Music Centre. With advisors of the artistic calibre of Shri P. L. Deshpande or Shri Vamanrao Deshpande in the lead, the entire committee decided that the inauguration must be done by Smt. Kesarbai Kerkar's strumming the *tanpura*! So she was to be formally requested and invited. After some discreet preparatory telephoning, it was decided that I should go to her residence at Dadar along with Shri Satyendra Trivedi who was regarded an undisputed knowledgeable in the *thumri*-genre. Due to some reason I alone reached at her place at the appointed time.

She was sitting in an old-style chair that allowed restful positioning of the legs. The room was not brightly lit. I was sitting on a straight-backed chair which was about 10 feet away from her seat. I extended the invitation and then followed a memorable 'dialogue':

"Why do you trouble an old woman like me?"

"Well, blessings can be given only by the seniors, is it not?"

There was absolute silence for some moments!

"Are you the one who writes articles?"

"Yes, sometimes," I said and took a gulp and a deep breath.

"What is your age?"

"My *guru* Pt. Gajananrao Joshi respects you as his guru, so I am like a grandson to you I think!... May I draw my chair near please?"

"Why?"

"It will be easier to talk."

For the first time Smt.Kesarbai looked at me 'neatly' and continued...

"O.K., But why do you not collect information before you write? You also give speeches, is it not? I have heard you in the condolence meeting arranged when Bade Gulam Ali expired."

"In our family, the tradition of music-study consists both of singing as well as speaking and writing on it. I have written after devoting some thought to it and only when I am certain bout it."

Now this direct 'exchange' had some background. In the series of articles on *gharana*-s and artists that I wrote in *Maharashtra* Times, I had included one on Smt. Kesarbai. Her musical greatness and superiority were, to some extent, due to her ability to reach beyond her own *gharana*, was one of my themes in the article. She had immediately written a curt and obviously an 'annoyed' letter to the *Maharashtra Times*, saying "I do not know who this Ranade is, I do not agree with his views and I had not given my photograph to him."

So now she went on, "Do you know when and how much I learnt from Abdul Karim, or Vazebuwa?" She then told me that she was very young and learnt very little from these two. Picking up the thread I then interrupted and started counting specific *mehfils*, in specific locations and her special touches. For example, her detailed *alap* in *raga darbari* in Chabildas High School, *yaman* and *nand* in Laxmibaug Hall and *jaijayvanti* in Talamki Wadi. This seemed to convince her about my credentials! So she changed tracks and began asking embarrassing questions about my *riaz*, and also ordered tea for me! By that time I was emboldened due to her changed tone and demeanour. I asked her opinions about other celebrated musicians. In a characteristic bluntness she responded in one-liners which brought out her keen perception about music and musicians.

"Master Krishnarao?"

"Does lot of acting."

"Vilayat Hussain?"

"Good for *talim*."

"Bhimsen?"

"He does lot of *Riaz*"

"Kumar Gandharva?"

"Look at his gestures."

"Bhaskarbuwa?"

"He was the best of them all."

After discussing the details of the inauguration programme, and while getting up I said, "Our artists are not dependable—they may or may not talk! Otherwise those who write would be keen to discuss with them before writing."

When I moved towards the door, Kesarbai got up to see me off. Then she said, "You are intelligent but write after discussing things with the likes of us."

"That means I would come again", I added.

She had the last word though. Standing there smilingly, she responded, "If my health is Okay, I will see you. Otherwise I will give you some tea and then you will have to go back!"

Once Kesarbai was giving a concert in the Indian Merchants Chamber Hall. She was rendering a *thumri* with great absorption. Suddenly there arrived Smt. Siddheshwatri Devi—the well known exponent of Benaras style *thumri*! Seeing her, Kesarbai rounded off her *thumri*. Then Smt. Siddheshvari protestingly said, "Why did you stop? It was going so well!" Kesarbai looked at her smilingly and exclaimed, "If I had received proper *talim*, I would have sat on your head and sang *thumri*!" Both of them laughed warmly and openly. All of us were wonder-struck—at their skillful appraisal of one another's respective talents!

On the stage Kesarbai moved with great confidence and freedom. Sometimes she was almost playful. In my student days, I could listen to her sitting at a hand's distance. On one occasion she seemed to have some difficulty in climbing on the stage and so Ustad Majid Khan, who was her accompanist in *sarangi* for years, instítinctively extended his hands to help her. Kesarbai then exclaimed with appropriate gestures, "You are not my *saajan* to offer me your hands!"

The Gomantak Maratha Samaj in Mumbai was felicitating her in Sahitya Sangh and I was one of the speakers. Quite recently Smt. Indira Gandhi had won admiration from all due to her courageous stand in the Bangladesh Conflict. I had suggested that Kesarbai's music never drops down below a certain average standard because she had set it so high. I had added that she can do this because the foundation of her music-making was very strong. On the spur of the moment, I also added that two Indian women exemplify what a strong foundation means—Indira Gandhi and Kesarbai! Not only the audience but Kesarbai herself had laughed heartily and I felt I was in seventh heaven!

PT. OMKARNATH THAKUR
(26-6-1897 TO 29-12-1967)

9

Pt. Omkarnath Thakur

(26-6-1897 to 29-12-1967)

A Brief Life-sketch

He was born in Jahaaj (district Khambat, Gujarat) to Gaurishankar (father) and Zaver (mother). Gaurishankar, noticeably well-built and handsome, was serving in the cavalry of the Baroda State. Spiritually inclined, he became a disciple of Aloonibaba, an ascetic. In fact Omkarnath was so named because of Gaurishankar's initiation in *pranavasadhana* (the *pranav mantra* is known as Omkar). Gaurishankar soon retired from the mundane world and went to live in a hut on the banks of the Narmada. Consequently, the family had to fend for itself. With the help of Mr. Shapoor Mancherji Doongaji, a Parsi gentleman from Broach, Omkarnath enrolled in the *Gandharva Maha Vidyalaya*, Bombay, to receive music training (1910-16). He was then apppointed head of the Lahore branch of the Gandharva Maha Vidyalaya (1916) before returning to Broach in 1919. He married Indira, daughter of Mr. Prahladji Bhatt from Surat in 1922 and ran a music-school in the town till 1923. Then he shifted to Bombay and opened a music-school called *Sangit Niketan* in 1934. He acted in a film called *Kabir* (1939) but again went back to Surat where he looked after a music-institution from 1942 to 1950. Pt.Omkarnath was primarily responsible for institut-

Omkarnathji's father had almost become a monk when Omkarnath was a boy. Having settled into his ascetic routine, Gaurishanker once called both his sons to his hut. As a blessing he wanted to pass on some already chewed *paan* to his sons. The elder son refused to eat it, but Omkar accepted it. Then Gaurishanker wrote something with his ring on Omkarnath's tongue and prophesised, "He will earn fame and success in the world."

Does it mean that the *guru*'s blessings may appear in an unpalatable form too!

ing the Faculty of Music in the Benaras Hindu University (1950). He was also Dean of the Faculty till 1957. He represented India in many International Conferences (Florence in 1933, Budapest in 1953, Germany in 1954). Pt. Omkarnathji was awarded *Padmashree* (1955), and many other honours followed. He delivered a lecture-series on *Raga and Rasa* (M.S. University of Baroda, 1950) and *Maha Gujarat ka Sangit Tatva* (University of Bombay, 1962). Six parts of *Sangitanjali* (1938-1962) and *Pranava Bharati* (1956) are his other major scholastic contributions.

His Varied Achievements

Pt. Omkarnath Thakur worked in many areas connected with Hindustani art music. He was a performer, composer, educationist as well as a theoretician. It is obviously difficult to deal with any single aspect of a musician's work in isolation, especially when different aspects come to the forefront in different phases of an active musician's life. For example, a performer who flowers late as a theoretician is likely to explain and justify his own performing strategies and vogue through his own theorising. On the other hand, a theoretician coming to the performing arena later in his life is more likely to change his theoretical stances. Such are the compulsions of actual musical experience realised through the evanescent phenomenon of performance. In evaluating performers, the relative dynamics of diverse performance-related aspects should form an important consideration.

Every artist is likely to pass through three phases in his life. In the first phase his aim is to present music as it was taught to him by his *guru*. His performances during this phase indicate his sense of loyalty in not crossing the periphery of the music taught by his *guru*. In most cases this phase (fortunately) does not last for long. The artist begins to strive to say something of his own, and in the process, one witnesses his struggle to find a new idiom, format, techniques, etc. This phase may last longer. It may also result into a closed stance in which the artist may insist that his music and he as a performer—are the best. The accent is on efficiently marketing oneself and it requires tremendous artistic honesty to move ahead and beyond this self-centred phase. In case of durably great musicians, this phase is also left behind and then the musician earns the honour of being a role-model for others.

Omkarnathji was, by all accounts groomed in the Gwalior *gharana* of Hindustani art music as it was propagated by Pt. Vishnu Digambar Paluskar who, it must be noted, belonged to the Maharashtra branch of the *gharana*. The *gharana*, based originally in North India in the musically magnetic and the erstwhile princely state of Gwalior in Madhya Pradesh represented a comprehensive and coherent musical ideology which formed the basis of many interesting musical deviations and Omkarnath was a major deviationist from the accepted Gwalior patterns of music-making, in both Maharashtra and Gwalior. Perhaps, Omkarnathji's multiplicity of music-fields of operation was directly connected to his musical deviationism. To begin the examination of his contributions from his performance will naturally provide the perspective necessary to assess him because he was nothing if not a 'performer' in all senses of the term and turned in other directions to back his own vision of music.

Evocative Voice and Use

The first striking feature that brings him into relief in comparison with his *gurubhai*-s (i.e. other disciples of his own *guru*), such as Pt. Vinayakrao Patwardhan or Pt. Narayanrao Vyas was Omkarnathji's remarkable voice and its evocative use. His voice was sweet, and more importantly resonant. The most significant aspect of his voice was his ability to change the tonal quality according to the musical requirement. In case of the two other stalwarts mentioned above (and, in fact, in case of many others following the larger Gwalior musical approach), a certain monotonous effect pervaded irrespective of scale-ranges traversed, the musical genre selected or the *raga* elaborated. To maintain an even, open and minimally distorted vowel 'aa' was an ideal mainly and tenaciously pursued, reasons being historical, cultural, aesthetic as well as those attributable to physical and external conditions related to performance. Consequently, there was almost a negligible trace of modulation of voice, an effect well described in Indian musicology as *swarakaaku*.

On the other hand, Omkarnathji sensed the significance of the dimension of timbre as indispensable to the music-making he was interested in, as also the necessity of exploring and exploiting the aspect of quality in voice. This enabled him to generate varied effects in singing. For example, in *neelambari* (*"O mitwa"),* the tender and anguish-filled rendition moves the listener, while the forceful (to the point of being harsh at moments) and vigorous *taan*-patterns in *sughrai ("Mai kantha")* overwhelm. He produces solemnity in *malkanuns ("Peer na jani"*) and conveys a regal poise in *shuddha kalyan*

(*"Bolan lagi"*). While his vocalisms in *shuddha-nata* (*"Karat ho"*) are unmistakably serene and joyful, he is melodramatically emotional in *bhajans* (*"Mat ja mat ja jogi"*) and could introduce a sense of fervour in his rendering of *Vande Maataram*. To an extent these remarks are impressionistic and yet, linking them with specific instances of recorded music in the context of voice quality should enable listeners to test their validity. From his generation it would be difficult to trace another vocalist who used so much variety, purposefulness and skill in employing tonal colour.

He was a very conscious vocalist. Technically speaking, his use of both the lower and upper registers of voice was effective and flawless. Unlike Ustad Abdul Karim Khan who mainly relied on the upper register, or Ustad Faiyaz Khan who concentrated on the lower, Omkarnathji used both the registers. Firstly, this made it possible for him to traverse a range of two and a half octaves without, at any point, sacrificing the musical quality (which is not the case with the other two maestros mentioned). Secondly, Omkarnathji's voice resonates remarkably well. As both the registers were exceptionally well-matched, the flow of music suffered no breaks even in staccato *taans (sughrai)*. Even while executing forceful passages he was able to avoid abrupt cutting-up of words (e.g. *shuddha kalyan* and *shuddha nat*). At all times he was able to create and leave behind tonal shadows even after the progressions had moved ahead or when music was interspersed with minute pauses.

However, an exceptional voice combined with a faultless technique of bringing into play the third (and much neglected) vocal dimension of timbre, would not have sufficed to mark Omkarnathji as significant musician. These features were only contributory to another, but more basic characteristic, namely, his attitude towards 'meaning' in art-songs taken as a class and also to specific words in particular song-texts. This feature introduced yet another qualitative difference. A few facets of his treatment of the song-texts are notable. Firstly, he took care to pronounce words clearly (so much that it is possible to copy the text while listening to him). In fact, in the initial portions of many of recordings he took care to surround individual words with deliberate pauses and thus successfully brought them into an aural relief as complete entities or units. This was obviously intentional because in the later portions of the same recordings he showed a cool disregard for the unity of the same words and dismembered them to facilitate musical elaboration. On such occasions he coolly 'broke' or 'disintegratd' the word-units according to rhythmic and tonal requirements in *bol-taans*. A telling example is from the piece in *shuddha kalyan*, in which the words "*bolan lagi*" are nonchalantly truncated into '*bo bo bo lan lagi!*' A similar unhesitating cutting up of textual units is also observed in *shuddha nata*.

It is deducible that he certainly believed in the efficacy of words as important bases for elaborating musical ideas of all varieties, hence his careful and clear pronunciation. However, once listeners had received them as words, he treated the words as any other raw material used in music-making. Compared to positions adopted by his contemporaries in this respect, Omkarnathji's two-pronged policy itself constitutes a deviation. Unlike him, other vocalists considered words as dispensable or uninhibitedly endeavoured to camouflage them. On the other hand, Omkarnathji regarded them worthy components but not through the entire progression. This surely seems an admirable aesthetic opportunism.

Of course, words also have other roles to play in music. They are potent carriers of emotive power and content and Omkarnathji was well aware of the fact. Mere solicitude for clear pronunciation of words should concern a phonetician more than a musician. For a musician words are useful because they are also evocative. The most poignant illustration of his awareness and use of the evocative power of words is his rendering of *raga neelambari*. In the entire presentation he had pronounced and employed the word '*mitwa*' (beloved) with great emotional charge—he is at once intense and controlled. Sometimes he takes the word on high notes, sometimes repeats it as if he is enchanted with it and sometimes isolates it from the adjacent words—all in order to bring out the persuasive, anguished, cajoling and deeply felt atmosphere that the word is invested with. He is not content with projecting the 'meaning' of the word—and this indubitably adds a dimension to his music-making.

Though not with the same high quality and consistency, he shows a similar awareness of the efficacy of words as music-making units in some other presentations too. For instance the renderings of *malkauns*, *shuddha nata*, *devgiri bilawal* also exemplify his approach. As I have pointed out elsewhere, Ustad Abdul Karim Khan and Ustad Faiyaz Hussain Khan also displayed ability to articulate words of song-texts with discernible emotional charge. However, their tonal colorings lacked in subtlety and in depiction of shades of meanings. For instance, Abdul Karim Khan lent to his entire music a tone of yearning, while Ustad Faiyaz Khan relied on a manly eroticism. Omkarnathji, in comparison, was more mindful of the emotive subtleties and their place in music. This enabled him to project a wider spectrum of feeling-tones through his use of words.

The Element of Craftsmanship

Perhaps, at this stage it would be pertinent to briefly comment on the element of craftsmanship in his music. For this purpose it would help to bear in mind the usual division of early, middle and late years of the human life-span. In Omkarnathji's case,

This was some time after 1933. He was about to leave for Russia when the news of his wife, Indiradevi's death during delivery reached him and he came back. He was so affected that for some time he lost his memory. Many years later, when he was requested to sing *neelambari* in a music conference in Calcutta, he paused and said "You must excuse me ... This was my wife's favourite *raga* and I will break down if I start singing that." A great hush descended on the audience.

craftsmanship was to the fore in the early, and somewhat surprisingly, the late years. But there was a noticeable difference of character between the two manifestations. In the early phase, the element was fully backed by a matching, faultless performing ability, which in the later phase was almost reduced to a shadow of musical intent. In fact, it would be more appropriate to say that while the earlier phase exemplified real craftsmanship or skill, its later version was more like a music-related exhibitionism. The difference between the two is not presence/absence of the requisite physical ability to execute feats of vocalisation. After all, decline of physical powers and musical excellence are not mutually exclusive. What distinguishes one from the other is the way the skill is oriented. A content-oriented skill, for example, is different from a technique-oriented one. In this contest two items, regarded to be important in matters of craftsmanship can be mentioned. They are: execution of fast-paced and complicated *taan*-patterns and, secondly, the quick transitions made from high to low notes and vice versa. An earlier piece, (e.g. *sughrai*) is notable because Omkarnathji did justice to both the vocalisation modes with ease and fluidity. His precision in coming to *sama* proved that he was completing a design and not trying to impress listeners with his vocal abilities. In contrast, this does not take place in a later piece (e.g. *devgiri bilawal*). The loose ends of the musical progression, as also the lack of tight designing become obvious.Without an inherent content-orientation, he, it seems, is compelled to divert listeners' attention by claiming credit for having achieved 'difficult' things on his way to *sama*!

Perhaps one more feature may find place here as an instance of his craftsmanship. There is a convention in Hindustani art music to sing the same compositions as a *bada khayal* as well as a *chhota khayal*. This is however mostly confined to that 'rare' *raga* in which there is a felt paucity of compositions. However, Omkarnathiji had put this to practice in case of a *raga* like *Miyan ki Todi* which is full of a compositional variety and in respect of a *bandish* too welll known ("*Garwa mai san lagi*"). This strategy results in creating interest. In slower tempo he has distributed the word-units in the song-text in a manner differently presented in a faster tempo. "*Jhanzaria jhanke*" (a composition in *raga deskar*), is also a well-known composition and it is treated differently. Obvioulsy the efforts bring out the craft-element.

However, an artist is to be judged by the best he produces. Hence, examined when he was at his best, Omkarnathji's craftsmanship succeeded in elevating him to the 'virtuoso' status. His *taans*, for instance, displayed ample technical variety. For example, he was flawless and impressive in *sattta's* (straight *taans*), *jabdi taans* (i.e. those fast passages executed with jaw-movements), *gamak taan*-s (those in which every component note in a melodic line is given context of the adjacent note) and *taans* of the *tappa-ang* with the unmistakable stringing of *khatkaa*-s (group of stressed and separated notes). His effective vocal range, spanning over two and half octaves, though notable in itself, counted as a technical asset because he traversed the entire compass rapidly, forcefully and yet with resonance. Shrillness, nasality, flatness or a single-reed thinness or huskiness never appeared in his music and hence it always remained aurally satisfying.

His Musical Imagination

Adequate ground has been covered now to pose a question relevant to any evaluative endeavour, especially when it has been already suggested that Omkarnathji remains a major deviationist in Hindustani art music. What kind of musical imagination did he possess? I would submit that a one word response is possible to the question: his musical imagination was 'dramatic'. This descriptive category is obviously drawn from the critical vocabulary of the group of performing arts (dance, drama and music). Dramatic quality, as such would often be expressed through operations of the principle of contrast. Contrasts in music are of various types. They may be tonal (i.e. realised through employment of varied timbre), positional (i.e. those depending on the scalar positions of notes selected) or rhythmic (i.e. those experienced through successions of tempo-variations). In addition, words, gestures *et al* may also be pressed into service to build a whole array of contrastive effects. As may be illustrated from Omkarnathji's disc-music, he could be credited to have explored the principle of contrast generously. We have tonal contrasts (*neelambari*), positional (*shuddha kalyan*), rhythmic (*sughrai*) and *tempi*-based contrasts in almost all pieces.

A special dramatic touch pervasive in his music is describable as the technique of presenting music in which musical content is shaped through phrasing inherent to an act of speech. The strategy which he pursued to accomplish the end could be easily perceived. He selected certain effective/operative words, or phrases formed with them and 'sang' them keeping their speech-orientation intact. For example, in the rendering of the *khayal* in *shuddha nat*, he selects the phrase "*Karat ho*" as a detachable and a speech-mode-based unit and employs it in varied contexts. Similarly he was wont to use the minimal sentence "*Mat ja*" from the famous Meera-*bhajan* in a like manner. It is known that the device of meaningfully distributing words and concurrently to lace them with matching musical phrases is a technique perfected in a type of *thumri*. The use of this device in *khayal* helped Omkarnathji in effectively communicating with the audiences because the semantically directed music supplied listeners with relatively familiar clues in following the progression of musical ideas. Further, the speech-oriented musical phrasing acquired a dramatic quality in his music-making because the contrast between musical and spoken expression became vivid and consequently made listeners aware of an additional dimension: the musico-dramatic.

As I have shown elsewhere, Ustad Faiyaz Husain Khan's music, speech-tone was inducted in music while in case of Omkarnathji, speech-phrasing was pressed into musical service. The process was effectively executed and in Omkarnathji's performances audiences felt it possible to participate in the proceedings. Those who had attended his 'live' concerts would remember how readily he was inclined to launch forth into rhetorical speech-sallies. These were symptomatic of his dramatising proclivities. Unfortunately, in later years, the 'speechifying' was overdone as his creative faculties declined and he was unable to strike a balance between the counteracting forces of the cognate performing arts, namely music and drama. It is worth noticing that in spite of his flexible voice and meaning-oriented music, Omkarnathji's repertoire hardly included *thumri*-s. This, clearly, is an instance of an astute operation of a performer's logic. As he was already blending *thumri*-elements in his *khayal*-singing, independent presentation of *thumri*-s would have, in all probability, resulted into a glaring musical tautology and hence his exclusion of *thumri* from his own active singing repertoire.

It may not be out of place to mention some slightly extra-musical features while discussing the musico-dramatic quality of Omkarnathji's imagination, chiefly because they corroborate conclusions derived from his music. He was a performer among vocalists and a showman among performers. In other words, he unabashedly exploited all kinds of non-musical means to create an atmosphere conducive to an *impressive* music-making. For example, he would ensure spreading of a special carpet over the platform from which he was to perform; he would always be preceded by his accompanists and rather ceremoniously ushered in by his disciples; he would have four *tanpura*-s instead of the usual two and on this backdrop he would make an entry! This was followed by a very elaborate bow to the audience. In fact, all his movements and gestures were just a little exaggerated. Peter Ustinov, the English actor has noted somewhere that the great Laurence Olivier's tone and demeanor would suddenly and radically change even if he was talking to a stage-hand, the moment Olivier became aware that some other person might be watching proceedings! Omkarnathji was not much different. He would not hesitate to use a tremulous voice, to shed tears or to weep, make wide dramatic gestures of hands, etc., if he felt that these would help him in establishing a rapport with the audience. Even in case of his accompanists he acted out his encouragement to them and commented picturesquely on their contribution. It is safe to say that these extra-musical devices formed a part of his total presentation technique. It is only to be regretted that they were overplayed in the less inspired years of his career.

One more manifestation of his musico-dramatic imagination should also be noted. In an otherwise conventional or a routine presentation of the *khayal* in *malkauns* ("*Pag ghungroo baandh Meera naachire*") he employed meaningless syllables as in *nom-tom*. One construction which can be put on the unconventional improvisation is that the syllables were aimed at representing the devotion-filled dancing by Meera. The other possible interpretation is that the attempt was to incorporate a '*Tarana*'-element in his *khayal*-singing. Whatever the explanation, the longish passage certainly creates a contrast rarely used. Though the array of musical genres in Hindustani music includes forms that consist of elements from both *khayal* and *tarana* (e.g. *chaturang*), to include the '*tarana*' element in improvisation because the song-text carries a suggestion of dance (or alternatively to use it for improvisation) is an unusual procedure indicative of Omkarnathji's dramatic inclinations.

Raga-interpretation

Omkarnathji's contribution in respect of Hindustani repertoire had two aspects. Firstly, he composed plentifully. More important however, was the fact that he reinterpreted *raga*-s of Carnatic origin so completely as to remove all traces of their origin and he rendered them in his Hindustani music-making. In addition, the *raga*-s he thus transplanted in the Hindustani fold were mood-oriented. In this context it is essential to remember that during the early decades of the nineteenth century many efforts were being made to standardise music-education. Unfortunately, this was resulting into some sort of regimentation. Thus *raga*-movements were excessively simplified and interpretation was replaced by stereotyped presentation in the name of methodical/systematic singing. Consequently, pedantically dry performances were becoming more general. It is at this juncture that Omkarnathji's renditions of *raga* such as *neelambari, Saraswati* and *Gorakh kalyan* assume significance. These *raga*-s, as he saw them, are mood-oriented because their respective identities do not depend on strict succession and structuring of phrases that follow a rigid sequence. His *neelambari* is an excellent example of a mood-oriented *raga* and Omkarnathji's outlook in the matter. It is therefore instructive to note that his *neelambari* does not include all features associated with *khayal*-singing. For example, a special mention must be made of the near-total absence of *taans*.

As already mentioned Omkarnathji did not sing *thumri* but accepted *thumri*-effects. It is a musico-cultural fact that as a dominant form of Hindustani art music, *khayal* is being increasingly threatened or challenged by *thumri, ghazal*, stage-song and the like throughout the century. There are those who believed in the inherent adequacy of the form—those who valued the *khayal*-vision of combining classicism and individual freedom of the artist. These musicians try to stand by the form and attempt to enhance its appeal. Omkarnathji's contribution was in this direction.

Conclusion

In his music as well as in his communicative techniques, Omkarnathji comes out as a major deviationist. He engaged dangerously in giving undue importance to showmanship in his later years and paid the highest penalty for it by parodying his own musical achievements. But that does not diminish the worth of his accomplishments. His music convinces by its emotional appeal, challenges on account of the craftsmanship and invites fresh thinking into voice-use for an age which allots a lot of merit on the dimension of timbre.

Post-1919 period. Omkarnath was sent to Lahore for sometime to look after the music-teaching institution established by his *guru* Pt.Vishnu Digambar Paluskar in 1901. Omkarnathji soon established himself, through various means we are told. It is reported that people were talking about a lion in the local zoo which frightened visitors through his roars. So Omkarnathiji went to the zoo and outroared the lion in such a way that it then became near-docile.

In 1930-s competition with and victory over other performers was still considered an acceptable act of manly valour. In that year in the Nepal royal court, Pt. Omkarnathji proved very popular. A local musician, Pt. Balaprasad was so infuriated by this outsider's success that he publicly vilified Pt. Vishnu Digambar, Pt. Omkarnathji's *guru* and also added that Balaprasad's servant at home was also called Omkar! Finally, the Nepal court organised a contest of the warring musicians and reportedly Pt. Omkarnathji was declared a winner.

Pt. Omkarnathji sang *Vande Mataram* as a national anthem from the pre-partition and pre-independence days. On the first day of independence his rendering was simultaneously broadcst from all stations of the All India Radio. His singing of *Vande Mataram* had therefore acquired a different stature. Once, on some occasion, he was singing it when he saw that the then Prime Minister was utilising the time to give autographs. Without batting an eyelid Omkarnathji thundered , "Panditji what are you doing! I am singing the National Anthem here!"

In 1948, Surat had no rains and people had nearly lost all hopes. Omkarnathji went to the banks of the Tapti river on three consequtive days and sang. When it rained people were in ecstasies and hailed Omkarnathji!

On December 28, 1967, Pt. Omkarnathji passed away in Bombay. His disciples took his body to Broach, the funeral procession was taken out, all sang the *bhajan "Raghupati Raghav Rajaram"* to the accompaniment of *tanpura* and he was then cremated. When asked why they insisted on this, they said that Pt. Omkarnathji had told them that this was his final wish!

Master Krishnarao Fulambrikar
(20-1-1898 to 20-10-1974)

10

MASTER KRISHNARAO FULAMBRIKAR
(20-1-1898 TO 20-10-1974)

Brief Life-sketch

Krishnarao Ganesh Fulambrikar was born in a village near Alandi, known as a major seat of the *Varkari* devotional sect in Maharashtra. Krishnarao was to earn a place in the musico-cultural history later due to his multi-faceted contribution as a *khayal* singer, actor-singer, music-composer for the Marathi music-drama and as a pioneering music composer for the Hindi and Marathi films.

Krishnarao's father was a priest and financially unstable. He then switched over to the vocation of a money-lender and did well for some time. But soon the business collapsed and when Krishna was about six years of age, he lost his father.

Krishna began his career by joining a well-known drama troupe called *Natyakalapravartak* and played small roles when he was about 11-12 years of age. In one of his plays he had a song beginning with the words "*Himnag pashan*". Krishna did not like the tune taught to him. So he changed it autonomously by borrowing a popular tune from another play and earned the audience's applause. Everybody was pleasantly surprised by his innovativeness and foresaw this as a sign of his versatile imagination and musical courage. His singing was also creating waves and he was able to present a special solo-concert at the age of 13 in *dhule* and impressed all with its success.

He had some early training from Pt. Rambhau Kundgolkar of the Kirana *gharana* but his main *talim* was from Pt. Bhaskarbuwa Bakhale during the years 1910-1922. Pt. Bakhale was a major vocalist who had successfully combined the musical ideologies of both Agra and Jaipur art music. Moreover, he was known for the rare accomplishment of always successfully generating the highest musico-aesthetic effect identified as *rang* (colour) whenever he performed.

Krishna's next step was to join the famous *Gandharva Natak Mandali* in 1918. As an actor-singer, he played many roles under the *Mandali's* banner till 1933. In that year he joined the pioneering film company '*Prabhat*'. In addition he continued giving concerts and also composed music for stage-plays (e.g. *Nandkumar* by V. C. Gurjar in 1925). Till 1941, he composed music for the Marathi and Hindi films produced by the Prabhat Co. in its path-breaking artistic march in the new idiom. His music certainly contributed to the cinematic successes. Between the years 1942-1953, he participatd notably in the movement of reshaping the Marathi music-drama.The movement was launched by a pioneering dramatic troupe called *Natyaniketan* under the leadershiop of the celebrated new dramatist Mr. M.G. Rangnekar. Pt. Krishnarao's musical contribution was acclaimed as a qualitative step forward.

Around 1947, he took up a cause—that of advocating the primacy of *Vande Mataram* as a National Anthem and composed a simple tune for it. In his concerts he often used to sing the complete text of the song at the end. In 1953, he was a part of the delegation of artists sent to China. He frequently commented on the essentially pentatonic Chinese music. Pt. Krishnarao earned honours such as

Natyacharya Vishnudas Bhave Gold Medal (1969), *Padmabhushan* (1971), and *Sangeeet Natak Akademi Award* (1972). In his own compositions he used Krishnadas as the *nom de plume*.

His publications include *Ragasangraha* (7 volumes), *Shaleya Shishu Sangeet* (3 volumes), *and Sangeet Mohan Mal* (notated compositions from stage-plays and films). His racorded music is varied enough to prove his musical versatility and substantiality.

He expired on 20th October, 1974 in Pune.

The present attempt is only to assess his contribution as a Hindustani vocalist.

Some Features of His 'Different' Music

In the pre-independence period more than two generations of the Marathi speaking world were so charmed by his music that it was difficult to find a place for any other music. Firstly, Pt. Bhaskarbuwa, an extremely knowledgeable *gharana*-trained and 'effective' musician had given Krishnaraoji a thorough traditional grooming. Secondly, Krishnaraoji has on his own developed a liking for and an insight in the lighter forms and idiom in Hindustani art music. Thirdly, Krishnarao adapted himself extremely well to the new media that were emerging on the music-making and music-propagation scene. All this has determined the final shape of his music-making and hence he was able to be 'with the times' and still remained a true voice of the tradition. As a cumulative effect of all such factors evaluation of his music becomes a challenging task. To apply the usual criterion of the capacity to fruitfully go beyond the usual framework becomes a tricky business as his *guru*, Pt. Bhaskarbuwa himself was a prime instance of a successful deviationist. Hence the best way is to examine and analyse Master Krishnarao's music in terms of its contribution to the recent past of the Hindustani tradition.

His singing was attractive. This was perhaps the first characteristic that everybody could notice. As in the case of a great play that exudes appeal simulaneously at many levels, Krishnarao's music too could draw heterogeneous audience and the most common effect was a certain joyfulness. One of the factors conducive to this effect was that his music was dynamic and the dynamism was hardly restricted to the outer or surfacial matters. For example, his music could never mean adoption of a medium tempo but saddled with a dragging musical elaboration. The inner tempo of the music was also an example of the dynamism. (In this respect he is similar to Balgandharva—the legendary and a pioneering actor-singer of the Marathi music-drama.) In Krishnarao's music something noticeable was happening all the time. In common language his music was never 'boring'. However it must be remembered that to be dynamic in this sense is not to be hasty. For example, when he was certain that the desirable note has been properly extablished, not a fraction of a second was given more to it. Additionally, his dynamism was achieved with utmost ease and there was no heavy effort involved and hence there was no clumsiness in the entire act of music-making.

In addition *taan* and *bol-taan*, the other two important agents of dynamism were also abundantly in action. His *taan* was clear, easily articulated, complex in construction and did not appear to be an attempted exhibitionism. It was an integral and an inevitable development of the total musical dynamism functioning in his music. It also brought out the quality of his imaginative approach discussed later. *Bol-taan* was an uninterrupted progression with the additional dimension of words delightfully explored. A variety of *bol-taan* that moves without stressing time-divisions and proceeds as if it is not aware of the acccopanying *tala*-circle was perhaps his favourite. All in all he was not fighting with rhythm but was delightfully engaged in playing with it.

That his vocal and conceptual dynamism could prove durable was due to his musical imagination. Though it is difficult to define musical imagination it is possible to roughly refer to what it does. For example, it made his music unpredictable. Unexpected melodic phrases etc. would appear at unexpected junctures and more importantly once having appeared on the scene they struck as musically inevitable and convincing. Or he will take up the *mukhda*, or a cluster of words and keep them before us in context of numerous note-phrases or rhythmic patterns. One would not have thought that the *mukhda* that he had chosen had so many possibilities. He appeared to be a magician in music-making!

The imagination also helped him in aesthetically satisfying presentation of known as well as unknown *raga*-s. His renderings of known *raga*-s impressed by freshness and novelty while those of the rare *raga*-s did not become dry and grave recitation of musical conundrums.The way he solved the posers of rare *raga*-s, his presentations appealed as finding skilful solution to puzzles.

Perhaps this needs some detailed examination. Even when he was dealing with well-known compositions and easily circulating *raga*-s (such as '*Sudhe Bol*' (*Bhoop*) or '*Bajore Mohammadshah*' (*Miyaki todi*) the tempo was medium. This meant that in Krishnarao's singing the places of pauses differed from those featuring in presentations of artists from other *gharana*-s. This led to a different filling up of the *tala*-divisions. Yet another way the imagination worked was when he 'filled' the composition.This act involves taking up different words, embellishing them sparingly but noticeably and thus proceed forward. Sometimes he provided a tonal shadow to some words in order to change their character, but just enough to arouse interest. It should be stressed that to achieve all these and similar other procedures in a medium tempo is not an easy task. In sum the known *raga* became a new entity due to his active musical imagination.

The strategy in dealing with rare *raga*-s was equally interesting. He sang them in such a way that one felt the *raga* concerned is not as complex, intricating and intellectually heavy as people made it. His favourite unknwon *raga*-s were *jaimini-kalyan, prabhat bhairav, khamaj bhatiyar, basant-kedar, devsakh, shiv kalyan* and *jayat kalyan,* etc. It appeared that his key-concept was that each rare *raga* is near or adjacent to some well-known *raga* but it never appears to be so. The next step was to identify a note-cluster in which familiar as well as the unfamiliar was heard. Such phrases are almost signatures of the concerned *raga*. Ensuring that these 'musical signatures' were repeatedly heard he went on to elaborate the *raga*. It is an observation made by performers that if any *raga* remains unknown for too long it creates a disadvantageous resistance in the listeners' mind. These listeners under siege then respect the artist but no admiring love can be elicited.

Accomodative Cheerfulness

A significant characteristic aspect of his singing was accomodative cheerfulness. His music (like that of his *guru*'s) was always full *rang* (colour), a trancendent ultimate and enduring overall quality that impressed listeners even if they may not be aware of it. As is known it is difficult to associate *raga*-music with specific identifiable emotions, yet the musical tempo and ranges explored for elaboration have allowed some broad generalisations. For example, slow tempo and lower octaves = gravity; medium tempo and middle octave = cheerfulness; and fast pace and high notes = anguish, compassion etc., are usually accepted as indicators of music-mood relationship. In other words, cheerfulness, etc., are simultaneously pointers to general post-music effect as well as their use as certain identifiable technical features. I suggest that the regular and an unforced employment of medium tempo and middle octave range generated an overall cheerfulness in Krishnarao's music.

Pronunciation of words had an important role to play in the pervasive presence of cheerfulness in his music. His was not a stressed pronunciation. The pronunciation was not blurred nor was it heavily etched or carved out. Words were not dragged along. No melodic overload or an attempted emotional charge drove them down in the ground. The cumulative effect was conducive to cheerfulness, as discussed above.

> He was rendering a house-concert in Prof. B.R. Dhekney's house in Bombay. Prof. Dhekney was the principal of the Sydenham College and a lover of Hindustani music.The audience consisted of Mr. Wamanrao Deshpande, the pioneering aesthetician of Hindustani art music and Smt. Mogubai Kurdikar, the well-known disciple of Ustad Aladiya Khan of Jaipur *gharana*. Krishnarao began with "*E Madmat*", a composition set in *tala Rupak* and in *raga Marwa* with the on the lower note '*dha*'. Against all expectations, inspite of the *raga*-structure and the placement of *sama,* the music did not have the brooding quality usually associated with this *raga*. This created an interesting situation. It could be seen that quite a few liked the music but they were not able to reconcile with the fact that it was different in some major aspects. As a result, it was difficult to elicit the appreciative responses such as "Vahava, Kya Baat Hai" etc. Krishnarao then sang some stage songs. After the concert was over Shri Vamanrao gave a lift to me and I was then privy to some interesting conversation between him and Smt. Mogubai who was also travelling with us. Among other things Smt. Mogubai suddenly remarked, "But you know, we really do not know how to appreciate music which is not like our's. Our *guru* certainly knew how to do that!"

Incidentally, it must be mentioned that Krishnarao was not only methodically trained in to the intricacies of the *raga*-music but also he knew a large number of *raga*-s and compositions. He was a veritable storehouse of traditional compositions (*bandish*) and he was able to draw on both quantity and quality of the musical riches.Those who heard him only towards the twilight of his performing career may think that he was merely a singer of 'light' or 'popular music' and may also hold that he was popular in Maharashtra only on that account. But this was not so. He knew and remembered all his *bandish*-s. It was unthinkable that he would forget the '*antara*', etc.

On some occasion I was lucky enough to meet him in the convivial surroundings of his daughter Smt.Vina Chitko's house and I could freely talk with him about matters essentially musical. During the course of the conversation I asked him, "You were doing so much touring and concert-singing—then what happened to your *riaz*?"

"For a professional performer a concert is a true *riaz*. Because of the concerts, I used to think all the time about music. The *Riaz* you do at home is really a strudent's *riaz*." He quickly explained.

While discussing various *raga*-s, compositions, etc., he was ready with all the details such as who taught him, the number of *bandish*-s, etc.

To egg him on I said, "We have a variety of *raga devsukh* that consists of both the varieties of '*gandhar*'-notes." My intention was fulfilled. He got curious, asked me to hum it and then went on to reel off many impressive compositions from unknown *raga*-s.

Once, when he was well advanced in age, his Studio concert was arranged by the AIR Bombay for an invited audience. He was accompanied by Amir Bux, a very old talented *sarangi* player from the Staff. Amir Bux used to accompany with his head constantly bowed down, as if to ensure that he was not out-performing the main artist. Krishnarao was singing his favourite *jayat kalyan* but the music was a routine fare with nothing extraordinary happening. In between Krishnarao took a pause to allow the *sarangi* player some scope and Amir Bux produced such substantial music that everybody, including Krishnarao instantly applauded him! Now what happened proved the artist in Krishnarao. He was so inspired and challenged by Amir Bux's music that for a few minutes he produced music of his prime days—at once attractive, full of musical meaning and imaginative. This was 'his' real music. The audience was overjoyed and even Amir Bux looked up in amazement!

I often feel that Krishnarao's music lost its intensity because more often than not he had audience which was satisfied with musical platitudes. During a period of patronage-transition he was keen on pleasing his heterogeneous audience and progressively diluted his *khayal*-music. What used to happen in *Brahmin Sabha Girgaon*, Bombay may be taken as a sample. Almost every year since say, 1947, he gave two/three concerts during the 10-day Ganesh Festival. Here I could attend and listen to his music at close quarters. The audience expected three things from him: that the concert should go on from 10 p.m.to 4 a.m., that he should cut jokes with his accompanists during the concert and finally he should sing:

a) "*Na maro Pichkari*," (*thumri, khamaj*),
b) *Abhang* compositions such as "*Dev mhane*" or "*Krishna majhi mata*" or "*Tujhiye nidhali*",
c) and at the end, before rendering the full text of "*Vande Mataram*" he should also sing "*Sham bajaye tore*"—a film composition set in *Bhairavi*.

In these concerts he used to render two pieces seriously, one at the beginning of the concert and the second immediately after the interval.

On the contrary, I have heard him in other celebrated locales in Bombay (such as Laxmi Baug) where he had presented *prabhat-bhairav*, a variety of *bhatiyar*, the *thumri* "*Tore Binati karat hun*" in *Bhairavi* in such a masterly manner that the audience which was full of musicians, used to become thoughtful.

He was certainly an extrovert and would mix many non-musical acts when he was about to perform or even when he was performing. For example, in the said *Brahmin Sabha* concerts he would arrive, get seated and start fumbling in his coat-pockets audibly muttering all the while "Buwa," (i.e. his *guru* Bhaskarbuwa). Then his accompanist would point to him that Bhaskarbuwa's portrait was on the wall in front. He would look relieved and ceremoniously offer *Namaskar* with closed eyes. As this happened every time it appeared to be an act that would attract the attention of the audience.

However, what was more incongruous was what he said while making music. Once he was rendering a stage song "*Jate he aji Shakuntala*" set in a pathos filled *jogia*. In Indian households and connected lore, a recently married daughter's going away to her husband's house has created much moving poetry and song-corpus. Krishnarao was singing soulfully and everybody was absorbed in the rich music. A grand-fatherly old man siting in front was touched and moved to tears and tookout his handkerchief to wipe away the tears when Krishnarao, taking a pause in his melodic weaving loudly said, "Why? All this is play-acting, you know!". Was he not involved in the music-making, I still ask myself!

Even when one listens to his eariler recordings, when he was in his prime, one hears the same dynamic music-making and creations of an ever-moving musical imagination. Does that mean some types of musical content was inaccessible to him? Whatever he achieved was remarkable, but was he not really equipped to accomplish more? Admittedly, it is a nagging feeling.

USTAD BADE GHULAM ALI KHAN
(1902 TO 23-4-1968)

11

Ustad Bade Ghulam Ali Khan

(1902 to 23-4-1968)

Ustad Bade Ghulam Ali Khan hailed from Kasoor in Punjab and received training chiefly from Kale Khan (uncle). It has been reported that initially he earned his living as a *sarangi*-player. Obviously this must have helped him in being one of the most nuance-filled tuneful musicians of the recent past. He is regarded today as the main exponent of the Patiala *gharana* which has a special place in the Hindustani music world on account of its appealing presentations of *khayal* and *thumri-dadra* of a distinctive flavour. Ustad Bade Ghulam Ali migrated to India after 1948. He had good knowledge of folk-musics of Kashmir, Sindh and the Punjab regions and this was subtly reflected in his music-making.

Ustad—A Janus Faced Musician!

It must be stated at the outset that what is attempted here is not an analysis of his singing in conferences attended by the indiscriminate hundreds.The reason for this seemingly high-brow distinction is that in the Conferences the Ustad never sang the same music as he did in more intimate or traditionally arranged *mehfils*. It will certainly be dificult to find another musician who would serve nearly opposite musical fares in public performances and intimate *mehfils*! In the public performances he would dilute everything in his music. Due to his unique vocal resources and also profiting by the different images of his *thumri* and *bhajan* singing he had successfully created, in the conferences he would sing to elicit stock-responses and stop there. Often I used to feel that on such occasions the great vocalist in him must be standing aloof and watching the whole fun closely. On the other hand, in his early concerts, or in his *mehfils* in the School of Indian Music run by Prof. Deodher, or while singing on the occasion of Ustad Faiyaz Khan's death anniversary, he would and could put everything he knew to test. Then his music was sweet but disturbing on account of its emotional depth and intensity. This was the essential Ustad Bade Ghulam Ali to be studied and evaluated in the context of Hindustani music-making in the very recent past.

Unique Voice and the Merit of *Prasad* in His Singing

I heard him for the first time in a Bombay concert in 1948. He opened with *raga kedar* and within seconds touched the *mandra madhyama* with such clarity, strength and sweetness that the audience burst into a spontaneous and overwhelming applause. To anybody familiar with the *mehfil*-protocol, the uncommonness of this event would be apparent. During the initial phases of any *mehfil*, praise is more polite than deserving and more gestural than vocal. This is not because the audience is hostile or a reluctant listener, but because the warming-up period required by the artist is usually considerable. Not so in case of this Ustad.

His music was never restricted by the limits of his voice. Listeners were never compelled to imagine what he had in his musical mind because his own singing realised his ideas—precisely and in toto. Ustad Bade Ghulam Ali Khan had a unique voice which could boast of a very wide range, effortless production, all-round sweetness, extreme flexibility and ease of movement in all tempi. Consequently his music flowed with an exceptional and unmatched lucidity. Perhaps in the final analysis, the quality sought to be described here is better explained by a term from Sanskrit poetics, *Prasaad.* Mentioned as one of the major qualities of style, it means clarity in addition to serenity or calmness. This is the quality that enables us to have an unobstructed experience of art-work (e.g. a poem). This was what happened in Ustad's vocalisation due to his voice. The voice was so transparent that the musical design came through as it was originally conceived. It was not the musician that was seen but music which was directly experienced. The veil of a faulty voice-production was totally absent in his musical endeavours. (It was not necessary to lift it with warming-up procedures.)

Emotive Pronunciation and Intonation

The welcome and near total absence of musical obscurity in Ustad's music came to fruition in many ways. For instance, Ustad's enunciation of words was very clear. In addition, his approach to pronunciation was marked by an element of leisure. The formulation of the vowel-sounds and consonants could be completed with unhurried attentiveness. Even the joint-consonants of the words were not glossed over (e.g., the words *"premki"* in the *sohoni thumri; "tatsat"* in the *bhajan "Hari Om tatsat"*; and the word *"swaami"* in the *khayal* in *raga malkouns*). What was more amazing was his ability to maintain the same quality even when words were pitched on high notes. Generally speaking, vowel-sounds tend to become indistinct on higher notes in case of many vocalists because the voices are operating under strain. The fact that Ustad could maintain the phonetic outlines of the vowel-sounds unaffected at all levels indicated an extraordinarily well-coordinated voice-production. The quality was equally evident in his *tarana*-singing. The grouping together of unusual, prosaic and often unintelligible consonants in the *tarana*-syllables has often compelled vocalists to sound forced, harsh and consequently utterly unmusical. However, Ustad could maintain his 'sing-at-ease' quality along with a firm shaping of the phonetic units in singing the *tarana* due to his rare voice-qualities. Therefore the edges of the words were never lost or rounded off in his singing. Words were carefully chiseled into their individual shapes—unblunted and yet produced without strain.

Another important manifestation of the *prasaad*-quality in his singing was the care he bestowed on the tonal values of individual notes, almost treating them as full-fledged musical entities. Nobody of course denies that all component notes of melodic expressions like *alap, taan*, etc., are significant individual entities. But a careful or an alert listening of various musicians (including many instrumentalists) frequently reveals the fact that in most cases only those notes regarded structurally important, are given their full values. For instance, it might be seen that very often the initial or the final note of a melodic phrase receives the due attention and (therefore) its full musical value while the others arc only endowed with approximate values. In particular, most of the musicians tend to do so in *taan*-s where the attempt is to impress the listeners with speed. In such cases note-values are often merely suggested. Employment of *gamak* too displays a similar approach.

Ustad's vocalisation was free from these defects. In his music, the values of the individual notes remained intact irrespective of the length and tempo of the *taan*-s as also of the proportion of *gamak.* He was never 'slippery' in *taan*-s and never remained merely sonorous in *gamak*-s. The melodic line was always clear, the component-notes unfailingly received their full values and the termination-points never remained abrupt dots. This was all the more creditable because in the Patiala *gharana* (which he so ably represented) fast and intricate *taans* are accorded a special status and weightage.

The Intricate *Taan*-patterns

His slow-tempo elaboration i.e. *alap* were not intricate. In this phase he moved gracefully, confidently, tunefully and note-by-note. Intricacy made its presence felt in the *taans*. Speed was of course given a place of pride. As is usual with vocalists who enjoy a light and flexible voice, the Ustad excelled in *sattaa taan*-s (i.e. straight-moving). The distinctive feature of his *taan*-s, however, was a consistent use of a speedy movement of short, spiralling patterns spanning the entire range of vocalisation. While *satta taan* impressed due to its power and evoked surprise due to its miraculous and instantaneous shortening of the tonal space, the spiralling variety featuring in Ustad's singing registered two achievements: it created greater awareness of the tonal space and accentuated the intricacy of the design involved. The spatiality of the tonal gamut was accentuated because the octave note or any other terminal note was gradually approached into the spiralling design. The intricacy of the design was also brought into relief because the very nature of a spiral involves repetition. The chances of the clear perception of complexity of design rose considerably as the core-design was repeated on progressively higher pitch-levels. The total effect was of a flashy or dazzling musical surprise.

The Impress of *Tappa*

It was here that a very salient characteristic of the Patiatla *gharana* came to the forefront: the influence of the *tappa,* a distinctive genre in Hindustani art music. The form is flashy in its overall design, intricate in intent, fast in movement, and light in touch. It therefore excels in producing an impact of an aural dazzle rather than an effect of any sustained musical power. The Punjab region and its folk-music is reputedly the home of this form and it was not surprising that Ustad should have incorporated major features of *tappa* in his *taan*. Significantly, he did not sing *tappa* independently. It is obvious that singing *tappa*-compositions independently would have amounted to musical repetition as the *tappa*-oriented *taan*-s were already enjoying a major scope in his *khayal*-singing. The *tappa*-oriented sections in his music were prominent in the *chhota khayal.* This placement of the *tappa*-oriented musical expressions was in a way inevitable because to fill up the large *tala*-spaces of the *bada-khayal* with the fast *tappa*-patterns would have been both difficult and unaesthetic. Ustad's *chhota-khayal*-s in *todi* (*"Bhor bhai"*), *malkauns* (*"Aaye pi more mandarwaa"*) are good instances of how frameworks—themselves originally set in fast tempo—could facilitate an effective emergence of fast and intricate *taan*-patterns.

And His Incomparable *Thumri*-s

Repertoire-wise, Ustad was also known for his singing of *thumri*-s. In fact, in the opinion of many, his place as a *thumri*-singer was to be considered higher than his ranking as a *khayal*-singer. Though tenable, the argument creates an interesting situation.

It seems that actually in Ustad's case three musical genres exerted mutual influences in his repertoire. Curiously, it was the genre not included in his active repertoire, i.e. *tappa*-s that deeply impressed both *khayal* and *thumri* in his music. His *thumri*-s borrowed the flashy element, from the *tappa*. It was arresting to note that in spite of the strong, musicological convention in favour of eschewing *taan*-s and intricacy from the *thumri* in the interest of sustained and unimpaired emotional appeal, Ustad succeeded in combining both flashiness and emotionality in his *thumri*-s. A little more explanation of his contribution to *thumri*-singing is therefore in place.

When he appeared on the Indian musical scene as a major musician in the late forties, the two well-established *gharana*-s in *thumri*-singing were the Benaras and the Lucknow *gharana*-s. (The two other minor variations were exemplified by the Agra and the Kirana musicians: the former consolidated the manly-erotic type and the latter *khayal*-oriented.). In brief, it may be stated that the Benaras *gharana* with its high seriousness and poise and the Lucknow *gharana* with its minute delicateness and *ghazal*-orientation, had created types that were in danger of becoming too rigid. The sets of the *thumri*-texts in circulation, the procedures of presentation and even the norms to be followed by the accompanists were about to degenerate into musical stereotypes. Under these circumstances, a new interpretation appeared to be difficult if not impossible. The *impasse* had to be met with musical ingenuity and towards this end the Ustad intuitively chose the option of impressing his *thumri* with the *tappa*-orientation. He was an ideal artist to attempt such a task because his voice was well-equipped to do so. Any laboured introduction of the *tappa*-features in the thumri would have made it impossible to keep the spell of the words intact. As Ustad could interweave the complex, abrupt and fast *tappa*-patterns in his *thumri*-s effortlessly, the evocative power of the words was not adversely affected. Naturally his *thumri*-compositions were themselves set in a faster tempo and their texts were also different. In both these respects his *thumri*-s therefore acquired an independent identity, making them distinguishable from both the other major *gharana*-s mentioned earlier. Perhaps Ustad himself too might have felt that his contribution to *thumri*-singing could be considered original and ostensibly to extend the scope of the genre he sang a *thumri* even in a *raga* like *sohini.* The suggestion is that he was more inclined to treat *thumri* as a legitimate and pervasive point of view of looking at all musical material instead of merely regarding it as a member of the hierarchy of musical genres considered 'lighter'.

Referring back to the mutual influencing act among the three forms, it can be concluded that while the *tappa* influenced both *khayal* and *thumri* in Ustad's music, the *thumri* too influenced his *khayal* to an extent. The *tappa* remained unsung but as shown earlier, not without a noticeable representation. It surely cast effective and long musical shadows.

The *Raga* Repertoire etc.

Ustad never made any claims to being a 'learned' musician. He repeatedly stated that he really knew only a few *raga*-s. This was also borne out by his rather limited effective repertoire. His emphasis was on the *prachalita* and mood-oriented *raga*-s. Most of his 'potent' *raga*-s have fortunately been recorded. Apart from these *prachalita raag*-s the author has heard him present *shukla-bilawal, khat* (Punjab *ang*) and *gunji kaanada*—but it was obvious that they were second-class citizens in his realm. He was also reported to have known about fifteen varieties of *pahadi*—a folk-melody used conspicuously for 'lighter' compositions (and etymologically connected with the music of the people living in the mountains, i.e., *pahad* in Hindi). A recording of his entire folk-repertoire would have certainly thrown better light on his creative process. It seemed that though he knew a number of traditional song-texts of Hindustaani art music he did not have them in plenty or perhaps many of them left him cold. The deduction follows from the fact that he composed under the *nom de plume* 'Sabrang' and also from the fact that he presented the same compositions again and again. One salutary effect was that the listeners could become familiar with his music in a limited number of exposures. Instead of 'novelty' he had therefore to bank on originality in music.

This is important and warrants some attention. By the fifties, standardisation of music-education had been well under way. The mass-media had already established its hold on the lay listener of music. During the period, musicians were therefore trying to attract and hold fast to audience through various stratagems.

One exception to his favourite 'sutra'—Emphasise the known "was perhaps provided by his own creation of a *raga* called *Kohari Kalyan*. The *raga* moves as in *Bhoop* in the first half of the octave and as *raga kalavati* in the upper half. It is obviously based on a sweet folk tune called *Kohari* from Rajasthan. The Ustad regarded my fourth *guru* Prof. B.R. Deodher (popularly known as Deodhermaster) as his own brother. He had taught the *raga* to Deodherji who once sang it from the Bombay station of AIR and the performance was very well appreciated. Deodherji came back home to see the Ustad, to welcome him and congratulate him. Not only that, he said "Bhai, you have sung it so well today that now the *raga* belongs to you—I will never sing it!" Apart from Deodherji's qualitatively rich music-making this is also an instance of the Ustad's nobleness of character.

One of the easiest devices they employed was to puzzle and dazzle the listener into musical captivity. These ends were sought to be achieved through musical acrobatics and through emphasising one's knowledge of *aprachalita raga*-s. Ustad did not follow this easy road to recognition and insisted on *creating new music from the known*, in matters of *raga, tala* and compositions alike. In fact he never seemed to address himself to the connoisseur. His unspoken faith was: if you can move the musical common-man then the learned will also be moved.

The *Sargam*, *Swaramandal,* etc.

He had also grasped one more truth about the common man: a common man likes music which fills his 'ears'. Ustad relied on continuous sweetness to carry out the task. The same logic created space for another effective feature of his presentations—this was the way he sang *sargam* i.e. the note-names. In brief he can be stated to treat the note-names as if they were meaningful words. He would utter them in a persuasive, cajoling manner eliciting meanings from them. In view of the premium he placed on continuity he, while uttering, say the note 'Ga', would carry the pronunciation of 'Ga' till the next note 'Ma' is in command and so onwards. Thus what one heard were two seperate notes which were not in effect seperated. (Of course if the voice would not have reached the desired note correctly that would have created a conflict situation for the listener.) This same desire for continuity was also responsible for the way in which his '*swarmandal*' seemed to contribute to his performance. It helped him in creating and maintaining a kind of ever present musical aura. It provided to all listeners an unbroken, subdued but a rich circle of sound matching his voice more than a bowed string-instrument (e.g. *sarangi*) could have hoped for.

At that time, Shri Soli Batliwala, a known lover of arts had founded an institute called Bhulabhai Memorial Institute in Beach Candy in Bombay where he provided all kinds of facilities to artists to carry on their respective creative activities. Once in a performance there, the Ustad was rendering Marwa in a slow tempo, in a ruminative introvert manner and compete self-absorption. One after the other, the musical progressions followed according to their own imperatives, (nothing and nobody seemed to matter for the Ustad as the music flowed through him). There I felt that I understood why the Ustad always talked of sea-waves when referring to music-making!

In Sum...

He used to remark that music should be like playing, dancing or like rhythmic movements of the sea-waves. The impressionistic attitude reflected in such remarks was also perhaps symptomatic of his deeper desire: to de-ritualise music and in a way to make it less serious and more enjoyable. Perhaps he did not want to be serious about music all the time. His music certainly held a mirror to his views.

Prof. B.R. Deodher
(19-9-1901 to 10-3-1990)

12

Prof. B.R. Deodher

(19-9-1901 to 10-3-1990)

Brief Life-sketch and His Wide-based Education

Prof. B.R. Deodher was born on 11th September 1901 in Miraj, a small princely state in the neighbourhood of other musically important States such as Kolhapur and Ichalkaranji in Southern Maharashtra in a Shastri (i.e. a priestly) family. He showed liking for music from the childhood and his early music-training was from Pt. Nilkanthbuwa Jangam during 1910-11. Deodher came under the direct influence of Pt.Vishnu Digambar Paluskar when he joined the *Gandharva Maha Vidyalaya* in Bombay in June, 1918. But, as Deodher stated later, he could not get much direct training from Panditji though he absorbed discipline, missionary zeal, wide musical perspective, organisational skill, progressive attitude and a spirit of nationalism from him. Deodher obtained a degree in music from the *Mahavidyalaya* in 1922.

The story of his academic education had more twists and turns. Deodher had left the school in 1921 to take part in the Non-cooperation Movement. During the same eventful period of 1920-21, Pt. Vishnu Digambar gave him a scholarship to learn the *piano* and Western music from Prof. Scrinzi, who was a leading teacher in Western music and a respected critic of Western music in *The Times of India*. Prof. Scrinzi was to open Deodher's 'ears' in many respects. For example, apart from explaining to Deodher the elements of harmony, he also took him to Italian Opera performances in 1924 and this was Deodher's introduction to the science of Voice-culture. Scrinzi analysed the Hindustani singers' voices in a scientific manner. At about the same time, Deodher happened to read Pt. Bhatkhande's first volume of *Hindustani Sangeet Padhhati*, and his eyes were opened too! It is symptomatic that it took him so long to reach Pt. Bhatkhande, though later he began meeting Pt. Bhatkhande more often when the latter used to take walks on the Choupaty sands. In fact Deodher became a frequent visitor at Pt. Bhatkhande's Walkeshwar residence. Due to his earnest musical inquisitiveness Deodher finally gained Bhatkhande's trust. So much so that in 1929 he succeeded in bringing both the Vishnu-s i.e. Pt.Vishnu Digambar Paluskar and Pt.Vishnu Narayan Bhatkhande together at a function in his own school. Till Pt. Bhatkhande's death, Deodher met him often and on various occasions. He gratefully received advice on how to listen to music, whom to listen, how to collect compositions and systematise them, etc.

Prof. Scrinzi also goaded Deodher to return to the academic training and Deodher passed his Matric examination in 1923. At the behest of Prof. Scrinzi and Pt. Vishnu Digambar, Deodher decided to continue his academic education. He enrolled in the University of Bombay from which he graduated with History and Economics in 1930, i.e. at the age of 29.

However, as per his tendency, Deodher was simultaneously knocking at many doors. Deodher tried composing music for films in the Silent era (1926). Reportedly his interest continued till about 1933. Unfortunately no music from these films survives. It is symptomatic that Deodher's training in Western music came to an end in 1925 as Prof. Scrinzi concluded that Deodher was admittedly not given to harmonic thinking which is different from melodic construction of the tonal material as per the rules laid down. Sensing the slippery situation and returning to his first love, Deodher opened his own music-teaching institute, The Deodher School of Music in 1925. The same year he left learning Western music but not the Western liberal views he imbibed from Prof. Scrinzi and the tradition he represented. As it transpired later his interest in voice-studies also remained undiminished.

Towards Documentation and Voice-culture —His Life-work

With some hindsight it now appears that while carrying out his varied activities Deodher was gradually moving towards his life-work. With concentration on vocal music, this consisted of collecting *raga*-compositions from different sources, methodically interpreting them, gathering information about musicians and the lore associated with them. His efforts combined the knowledge stored in oral tradition with the scholastic. He was able to bridge the 19th century and the 'uneducated' (not illiterate) artists with the later period dominated by the British-educated followers of musical trditions in the country. In a way his work rejuvenated the old tradition.

Various factors contributed to the quality of his efforts. In 1941 he shifted the school to the Opera House area and that created a separate identity for the man and the institution.

Then, though he had known and met Ustad Sindhi Khan in the *Vidyalaya* when Deodher was a student, he could establish his own, independent channel of communication with the Ustad from 1942 onwards. Now he heard the Ustad informally as well as formally, discussed musical matters with him in confidence as well as with confidence and finally, also learnt from him. More importantly what the Ustad passed on to Deodher was not only compositions (*bandish*) in various *raga*-s but a different lyrical and emotive idiom of music-making based on these and other such *bandish*. This entirely changed Deodher's musical vision.

By 1944 he also had 'connected' with Ustad Bade Ghulam Ali Khan of the Patiala *gharana*. The Ustad almost became a brother to Deodher. It is important to note that both these musicians—Ustad Sindhi Khan and Ustad Bade Ghulam Ali Khan—projected music which exuded appeal, content and technique completely distinguished from what the other well-established *gharana*-s in Maharashtra had been propagating and what Deodher had actually learnt.

Prof. Deodher—As an Editor and a Writer

Further, Deodher also began editing *Sangeet Kala Vihar* from 1948. He shouldered the responsibility for over 25 years. One major task of an editor is obviously to make others write. It is therefore to be noted that till 1973 he published nearly 17 series of articles on various aspects of music written by various authors. They related to diverse fields such as history, aesthetics, accoustics, musicology, and also included translations of rare works on music. This body of about 177 articles proves interesting even today.

He also interviewed about 50 'traditional' musicians or verbalised accounts provided by these musicians. This turned out to be one of the most important features of the magazine. The artists belonged to different *gharana*-s, hailed from different regions, and spoke different languages, but Deodher could make them all articulate. The way this material is presented, brought alive one historical era of Hindustani music which had almost vanished or was on the verge of disappearing. With a slight slant he also wrote *Kalakaaronke Kisse*. These were small anecdotes /stories throwing a different light on the temperament, attitudes and unknown shades of musicians' personalities.

It is clear that Deodher was able to win the confidence of the musicians because he himself was knowledgeable and secondly, because they could sense in him a sincere desire to present them in the best possible perspective, irrespective of their academic illiteracy or unevenness of their professional success. When most of the uneducated traditional musicians had developed an inferiority complex in face of the modern age, he succeeded in documenting their accomplishments and note their place in the history of music and culture with perceptible honesty.

In addition to his credit are: a biography of Pt. Vishnu Digambar Paluskar, five volumes of *Ragabodh* (consisting of information on *raga* and compositions in them), and a pioneering book on voice-culture as applied to Hindustani vocal music. The last one was a product of his amazing work on voice-culture done at the ripe age of 60. He went to New York to scientifically learn voice culture from Prof. Engum in 1959. In 1962, he also recorded in English an introduction to Hindustani *raga, tala* and singing for the Smithsonian Institute. In view of the new medium and the different target audience this effort would rank as one of the pioneering ventures. From 1933 onwards he had toured many countires to represent India in international conferences and seminars. The visits included World Music Conference, Italy (1933), Manila for the Saarc conference on music (1955), and to East Europe (1958) as a member of Cultural Delegation.

His work as Dean of the music faculties in Banasthali and Benaras Universities was also a contribution to music-education at higher levels.

A Vocalist and a Teacher

Expectably, due to his eclectic attitude his singing and teaching also provided instances of deviations from the conventional ways.

Obviously he was not a performer who gave repeated stage-presentaions. But his broadcasts and the recordings done at various places provide interesting and concrete evidence of his enriched concept of music-making. Listening to him for the first time makes it clear that his voice was not a naturally 'good' voice. However, it is soon perceived that he has cultivated the voice for a careful and tuneful presentation. Neither in the articulation nor in the intonation are there signs of undue and unpleasant-sounding force. The text of the *bandish* is treated with respect and feeling. The melodic elaborations are not very extensive but they are convincing as far as the specific character of the *raga* is concerend. *Taan* is not fast and sparingly used but the patterning is imaginative, intelligent and different from the usual. Comparatively speaking he was not in his element in the *bol-taan* and it does not appear that he relished or enjoyed 'playing' with the rhythm aspect. The same is true about the *sargam*-phase in his renderings. His singing repertoire is rich and consists of known as well as many unknown *raga*-s. His is not a singing of a concert-performer but of a learned musician who is offering sound and correct demonstrations of the numerous facets that Hindustani art music can display. His singing lacks the fluidity of imagination and the practised ease of execution of a performer.

But for a musician he was an exciting teacher. His decisions as to what to teach, whom and how—prove his standing as a *guru*. He could teach a trained Western musician such as Mr. Walter Kaufman. With equal ease he could pass on knowledge of Indian art music to an Indian composer such as Vanraj Bhatia who was however nurtured as a Western musician. Finally, he could lead a prodigy like Pt. Kumar Gandharva into the high artistic mysteries of Hindustani art music through unorthodox but successful methods, ensuring that the teaching does not become stultifying for the genius he was nurturing.

I first approached him to acquire training in voice-culture. He explained to me that the science cannot be taught in isolation and it involves learning music from him. When I asked my first *guru* Pt. Gajananraoji's permission to do so, Pt. Gajananraoji unhesitatingly told me to proceed. He added that Pt. Deodher is a very knowledgeable musician. This was in 1969-70 when I had taken charge of the University Music Centre (Bombay) as its first Director. By then I had received training in Hindustani art music for over twenty years (I had started my *talim* in 1948). I was writing on music in prestigious magazines, periodicals, etc., composing music for plays and participating in various music-related activities. As Prof. Deodher later told me often, since his return from America after taking training in voice-culture I was the first musician who expressly requested him to teach voice-culture. I had read avidly on the subject as I wanted to frame a relevant syllabus in voice-culture for the University course. Pt. Deodher's teaching was comprehensive. He was ready to respond to all kinds of queries and would unhesitatingly admit if he did not know enough about any particular aspect of the discipline. As he was teaching it in the context of Hindustani *raga* music in circulation each training session was also a discussion about the *raga* or composition selected. As soon as a *raga* was decided upon he would take out his notebooks of notations which were methodical and systematic to the core. He used to hum what he had learnt in the selected *raga*, then ask me what I already knew in the *raga* and then it was mutually decided what should be taken up. After carefully listening to the song-corpus he had put forward I used to select what I wanted him to teach me. I often used to tell him that I chose a composition in which I could sense his 'touch', as that made the composition especially attractive. He could see the implied meaning of my remark, smilingly he would have his pinch of snuff and we proceeded. It was his usual practice to ask me to sing any compositon which I had learnt from him at any time—obviously to test my capacity to learn and assimilate. Every composition in his notebook carried details about 'who, when and where' taught it to Pt. Deodher. Very often more than one version of the same composition would also be found along with the version he had finalised. He used to finalise after taking into consideration textual as well as musical aspects. In this enlightened manner I learnt from him nearly 300 *bandish*-s.

What I learnt from this *talim* and the way it was imparted was not only new but it also made whatever I had already acquired newly significant! In fact it gave me a new musical vision to make sense of the totality of Hindustani art music. In some cases I deliberately chose to learn the Deodher version of compositions I had already learned—as they had become so lyrically new due to the Sindhi Khan touch passed on through Pt. Deodher. For example, the version of the composition in *lalit-pancham* ("*Udat vandan*") which I had learnt in the Agra as well as the Jaipur way was entirely transformed in the Pt. Deodher version. Same was true in case of *raga* such as *savani kalyan*, *sarparda bilawal*, etc. Sometimes I feel that Pt. Deodher specially aimed at collecting different versions or variants of whatever codified expressions of rare *raga* or compositions Pt. Bhatkhande had already managed to collect. Alternatively he also looked for what was not collected, documented and codified. In a sense this was a task of carrying on Pt. Bhatkhande's work a step further. It is difficult to imagine how he acquired so rare a corpus whithout a sharp and insistent focus because Hindustani traditional musicians are and were never known for allowing an easy access to their knowledge. Along with the compositions and the *raga*-lore, Pt. Deodher always pointed out that music need not be presented as if it is dragged down by

Here is an excellent example of the *guru-shishya parampara* I am referring to. Once he taught me a composition which carried no obvious marks of the *tala* in which it could be presented. I therefore asked him, "In which *tala* have I to set it ?" He smiled, had his quota of snuff and as if peering into the past said, "I had asked this question about this same composition to Ustad Sindhi Khan and his response to it—I will pass on to you as it happens in the true *guru-shishya* tradition. Ustad Sindhi Khan looked at me piercingly and asked me, "Who are you to set it in a *tala*? It is already in a *tala*, find out that *tala* it is in and follow what this composition is trying to tell you to do!" Is it not true to say that this is an aphorism in aesthetics?

Once my wife and I had gone to a party at the Max Mueller Bhavan. Pt. Deodher was of course there. Beer was flowing but as per the protocol I could not and did not avail of it because my *guru* was present. Hence I was discussing things with him rather seriously! He always had interesting informational and music-related tid-bits about so many things. He asked me whether I knew to whom the place in which the party was being held originally belonged. When I replied in the negative he said, "This bungalow belonged to that music-loving, reformist and aristocratic lady Atiya Begum Faizee Rehman." The answer of course opened up a new interest.I began looking around with added curiosity. Meanwhile Pt. Deodher picked a mug of beer from the waiter and offered it to me telling my wife, "As I am Ashok's *guru* I intend to teach him everything I know!"

There are very few who present a *drut* composition in the rare *raga Lalit pancham*. Pt. Deodher came to know that a senior music-teacher in a Bombay municipal school knows one beautiful composition in the *raga*. Pt. Deodher's immediate plan of action consisted of respectfully inviting the person concerend to all functions in the School. The teacher, an experienced old-timer in the field of music perhaps 'read' Pt. Deodher's mind and once asked him , "I am happy that you have started inviting me to the programs you arrange so systematicaly, but tell me what you want from me?" Pt. Deodher was a little embarrassed but then talked to the teacher with candor and explained to him his intense desire to learn the specific *drut* composition to complete the repertoire. The teacher was glad to teach him. The teacher continued to receive the invitations. Pt. Deodher gratefully digested the composition in his repertoire representing the beauties of the Hindustani *raga* riches.The said *tarana* "*Tirkid tak dhom dhagin dha*" is indeed a landmark compositon.

Once Pt. Kumar Gandharva, the child prodigy who had been Pt. Deodher's most illustrious disciple, had come to my home in Bandra. I was showing him one of my old *tanpura*-s. He was attentively playing it and carefully testing its tone. After that he suddenly sat down and removed some creases from the carpet I had spread in a *baithak* style. He looked at me, winked and smilingly said, "Do not forget we are all Pt. Deodher's disciples , he would not have tolerated this sort of… …!" True, Pt. Deodher was a stickler for punctuality, protocol, orderliness, neatness and such other things related to music-making. For him keeping the notebook of notation and properly stretching the carpet in a music-hall were both important.

Pt. Deodher renewed and earnest quest in voice-culture began late in his career. He purchased a large mirror and sitting in front of it he began his exercises of properly opening the mouth, checking the tongue position, producing the vowels pharyngeally etc., often in view of his visitors too! Most of his contemporaries ridiculed him and he was fully aware of the ignorant points of wisdom they poured forth behind his back! However he once told me that only Ustad Amir Khan, after listening to Pt. Deodher's broadcast came immediately to Pt. Deodher's house and complimented him. He said, "Let them say what they like, but there is a definite improvement in your voice and congratulations!"

raga-norms, *tala* or rhythmic moulds. That words can be evocatively uttered without getting overtly emotional about them was another insight he offered. He also emphasised that it is not mandatory for a musician to include all ways of melodic elaboration such as *alap*, *bol-alap*, *bol-tan* and *taan* in every presentation. He also said that a musician should not excplore a *raga* as if he is carrying out an exercise—but should move like waves on water. Very often he would say in response to my question, "I had asked the same question to Ustad Sindhi Khan and I will give you the answer he gave me—because we are followers of the *guru-shishya parampara*!" He did not have to do this deliberately because this was an inevitable part of this *talim*.

When Pt. Deodher alias Deodher-master passed away on 10th March 1990, he had left behind a legacy of pioneering and rich work directly connected to the performing reality of Hindustani music.This was an instance of theoretical work which was not 'bookish' in the pejorative sense.

Pt. Jagannath Buwa Purohit
(12-3-1904 to 20-10-1968)

13

Pt. Jagannath Buwa Purohit

(12-3-1904 to 20-10-1968)

Brief Life-sketch

Pt. Jagannath Buwa Purohit was born in Hyderabad and spent the childhood in great difficulties. He received his early training from Muhammad Ali (Sikandrabad), Shabbo Khan (who hailed from the well-known Tanrakshan *gharana*) and Gulam Mohammad Talwandiwale (Lahore). The training he received from the last mentioned *guru* was however in Kolhapur. His ultimate grooming which he regarded as the prime shaping influence on his music was from Ustad Vilayat Hussain Khan (Agra). Jagannathbuwa heard the Agra Ustad in 1924 and since then, an especially close relationship sprang up between the *guru-shishya*. Jagannathbuwa also had good *talim* in *tabla* from Ustad Ahemadjan Thirakwa. In 1940 he toured some foreign countries as an assistant to Pt. Govindrao Tembe—a pioneering composer, writer and harmonium player. Reportedly, he seemed to have temporarily settled down in Kolhapur around 1945, but shifted to Bombay—the main seat of his achievements—around 1952. He was a renowned composer and teacher and composed under the name Gunidas. The galaxy of renowned musicians who learnt from him suggests that he was venerated as a *guru* for receiving advanced training. His disciples included Pt. Ram Marathe, Pt. Yeshwant Joshi, Smt. Manik Verma, Pt. C.R. Vyas and Shri G.N. Joshi. Shri Bhai Gaitonde is known to have received training in *tabla* from Pt. Jagannathbuwa.

His Music

It may not be an exaggeration to say that no major place in Maharashtra is without at least one disciple of Pt. Jagannathbuwa. Apart from these disciples many more vocalists enjoy singing his well-known compositions. However, if one raises the question: "How many sing his *gayaki* (vocalism and musical ideology), the response is not very positive. The main reason is that there is almost no remarkable artist in his followers who has been entirely or mainly trained by him alone. Most who turned to him were well-trained singers groomed earlier by some other *guru*. As a consequence, it is difficult to evaluate his contribution as a *guru*. It is therefore more fruitful to analyse his music and if necessary, try to trace some features of his art in others' music-making.

One major feature of his art was that he had re-moulded the music-making as practised in the Agra *gharana* in a marked way. He has not entirely rejected the Agra mode but in a significant way deviated from it. However, as hinted earlier his followers have been more influenced by the varied richness of his singing repertoire and his own compositions with the name Gunidas included in the text.

A Rather Economical Melodic Elaboration

He seemed to remain content with a limited melodic elaboration in his renderings of *raga*. The Agra '*nom-tom*' was also nearly absent in his music-making. Further, he did not indulge in the phase known generally as '*khayal bharana*'. This phase normally consists of filling up the framework of the original *khayal* composition with phrases and clusters of notes after the *khayal* has been presented in the initial stages. In his performances one never felt that he was unfolding the *raga* step-by-step or spreading it in great details. It was more a matter of quick, skillful and attractive brush-strokes employed to etch a *raga*-outline. To effectively attract attention to the major melodic centres in a *raga* and authoritatively introduce some selected *alap* of a *raga* these were his favoured strategies. The overall tempo of his music was inclined towards medium tempo and that also precluded a more detailed treatment of the *raga*-framework. But the choice of the basic tempo of music-making is of course the accepted prerogative of the concerned musician. In sum, either because he was not a frequent concert-performer or because he mostly performed in the presence of knowledgeable musicians, he did not render any *raga* in great detail.

The earlier reference to the similarity of his singing to brush-strokes also suggests the copious use of accented or stressed phrasing in his singing. Music which is not inclined towards detailed melodic elaborations is inherently antipathetic to sequentially pay attention to all important notes in a raga. Such music naturally moves towards a prominent use of rhythm-determined patterning of notes. When one remembers that the Agra way of music-making in itself favours the rhythm-oriented phrasing, this may not come as a surprise. Thus recognising the importance of *tala* as a generative rhythmic pattern becomes a major shaping force. During all the phrases of music-making, to remain aware of the *tala* and make others conscious of it, is an article of faith for the Agra *gharana*. Throughout music-making, the artists of this *gharana* maintain a relationship between *tala*-divisions and the flow of musical ideas. As a corollary, the accentuated music-making accords increasing importance to words and syllables, but as sound-patterns. Words of the song-text become more active. This is the reason why his singing gave such an important role to *bol-taan*. He knew *tabla* well and consequently he would get engrossed in the phase of the *bol-taan*. As he relied less on *alap, taan* also became less natural. The upshot was that in his music *bol-taan* became the major way of leading music to climaxes. Expectably, in his singing the *bol-taan* often consisted of nearly 'prosaic' though energetic utterances of words.

A very notable feature of his vocalisation was his renunciation of the Agra intonation, which was one enveloped with the vowel-sound 'a' (as in 'fat'). Even in the absence of *alap* this feature became obvious in his pronunciation of words. In fact frequently he appeared to turn to the pronunciation as meaningful linguistic units of the spoken variety. It is possible that he imbibed this practice because he had looked carefully at Hindi and Braj, as he himself was a conscious composer.

Rare but Evocative *Raga*

He certainly had a rich repertoire of *raga*-s and in his concerts he preferred to present rare *raga*. However, it is to be noted that the said rare *raga*-s were not merely pedantic or intellectually conceived entities but they were mostly also highly evocative configurations. His own compositions in these *raga*-s also display similar qualities and numerous artists therefore sang them with relish. His own renderings were characterised by brevity and appeal. It is indeed difficult to create this appeal in the absence of *alap* and *taan*, but he achieved this feat more often than not. The *raga*-s, such as *jogkans, shivmat bhairav, ahir bhairav, swanandi, jaun-bhairav* and his compositions in them are pointers to his love of rare *raga*-s and the qualitative richness of his composing abilities.

Peer Parai

As is truly said the proof of the pudding is in the eating of it and to sense his mastery discussed above one would do well to sing his compositions! But the second best alternative is to discuss one of his compositions in a rare *raga*. We have an apt example in the recording of Smt. Manik Varma of "*Peer parai*"—a *chhota khayal* in *raga jogkaun-s* set in a pacey *teen-tala*.

That the composition is a *chhota khayal* indicates its rendition after a *bada khayal* has already been presented and it had already carried out its responsibility of a detailed decoding of the *raga* concerned. This means that the criteria used to evaluate the *bada khayal* are not to be applied to analyse and rate a composition identified as a *chhota khayal*. In other words, a faithful or the least distorted indication of the major features of a *raga* is a task a *chhota khayal* is supposd to carry out. In the composition under discussion the three major distinctive features of *raga jogkauns* namely, an interplay of two varieties of note *gandhar*, well-placed use of the phrase (*Dha-ni-sa*) in the upper half of the octave to point to the other component *raga kauns*, and the bridging function of the note *Pancham* are well established. In this context the arrangement of the text-lines in the composition is worth-examining. The composition begins from the note *komal dha*, and the melodic line after touching the note *Pancham* settles on the fundamental note 'sa' after introducing the phrase of two varieties of *Gandhar* note. In other words, in the very first line one major melodic movement of the *raga* is well introduced. The second line begins from the note 'sa' (i.e. from the note on which the first line has ended), goes quickly to the lower octave, then porceeds straight to the *komal gandhar* of the higher octave before coming down to settle on the note *Pancham*. Three things are to be remembered about the second line: (1) As it ends on the note *pancham* which joins the two *raga*-s there is a useful blend. The two halves of the scale are not felt as separate entities. (2) As the first line is the refrain of the song, it naturally re-appears after the second line is completed. The first line, it is noticed, begins on the note *komal dha* and hence the ending of the second line on the earlier note, i.e. *pancham* provides a kind of musical coherence. The first line can be picked up after the second without a jerky feeling. (3) The melodic contour of the second line is also interesting. It covers a vast tonal range (i.e. the half of the lower octave, full middle octave and one fourth of the higher octave) in a straight movememt and thus a delightfully contrastive relationship is realised between the convoluted first line and arrow-like progression of the second line. Truly speaking both lines became more effective due to their mutual contrast.

The *sthayi* i.e. the first half of the composition consists of only two lines and that may appear to create a rather abrupt ending. However, there are two grounds for the overall shortness of such compositions. Rare *raga*-s are usually convoluted in movement and thus have limited possibilities of easy expansion and secondly fast compositions such as the *chhota khayal* work with the assumption that the *bada khayal* which usually prcedes it has already taken care of the elaboration.

It is generally observed that the *sthayi* (i.e. first half of the *khayal* composition) and the *antara* (i.e. the second half of a *khayal* composition) are located in different halves of the octave. Apart from avoiding repetition this norm also helps in bringing into view the total field of a *raga*. In "*Peer parai*" the *antara* begins with the ascending phrase *ma-dha-ni-sa*,touches the mid-located note 'ma' in the higher octave and settles the line on the *komal 'dha'* of the middle octave. The next line i.e. the last line of the compositon begins on the middle '*sa*' and comes back to note *Pancham* after touching the higher '*sa*'. Thus ends the *antara*. The second line of the *antara* is interesting. The earlier line has ended on the *komal 'dha'* of the middle octave and this is followed by the last line which executes a sweeping downward movement to come to the middle '*sa*' note. This is somewhat new and also surprising. In no time one realises that this is to be considered as a melodic pattern. It is a replica of the first line of the composition, thus establishing a noticeable symmetry. What sounded unexpected turns out to be a reappearance of the earliest known and an artistic plus is experienced.

Bandish needs to be understood as a well-realised seed-form. In every musical manifestation the ultimate aim is to realise a form. In fact all art activity sets the realisation of form as its final goal because that signals the success of the entire venture. In music the form is realised on two levels. A particular, completed and artistic activity in its totality is what we call the work of art. But it is preceded by a self-sufficient unit containing all potential expansions or elaborations and hence it should be identified as a seed-form. For example, presentation of a *raga* by an artist is the proposed final form while composition in genres such as *bada khayal* is the seed-form. Therefore, it is obvious that the realisation of the final form is dependent on a successful realisation of the seed-form. A composition which is capable of providing the required fundamental framework for the necessary artistic elaboration is identified as *bandish*, otherwise it is merely called a *cheez* (literally meaning 'a thing'). This is the reason why a *bandish* can be described as self-sufficicent. Thus inescapably *bandish* is a music-making component of utmost importance though in itself it is inadequate for the attainment of the final intended form. When we describe a presentation of a *khayal* as successful we are indicating that the potentials of the seed-form are fully realised. When a genre of *chhota khayal* is performed one more step in the attainment of the complete, final form is taken (as it is conceptually taking over the task of attaining form in *raga Jog-kauns* from a *bada khayal* that precedes the *chhota khayal*). When this *bandish* is also fully explored the ultimate form becomes a reality and we can then conclude that the *raga* is successfully attained. (One may reach further in case the presentation is a part of a full musical concert. The singing /presenting of this *raga* should create expectancy for the next and so on, till the last item is artistically satisfying. This certainly means there can be an infinite progression in music-making.) Following Vishwanath, a well-known Sanskrit writer on *Sahityashastra* (loosely meaning poetics or aesthetics of literature) one may say that if a *bandish* is a *vakya* (sentence) then a full concert is a *mahavakya* (a great sentence).

Why "*Peer parai*" can be identified as a *bandish*? Firstly, it is attractive in the melodic as well as the rhythmic aspects. The melodic framework is inherently precise and brings out the major features of the *raga* to the fore. As the *mukhda* is in the middle octave one can move upwards as well as downwards from it and elaboration gets a wide scope. The tempo is moderately fast and this too facilitates expansion and exploration of musical ideas. Even though the *raga* is rare and convoluted in movements the *bandish* is not so, and this encourages bringing in variety in the overall musical design. The *bandish* enables focusing on each single line as a take-off for elaboration as each line makes a meaningful statement about the *raga*.

The rhythmic aspect also attracts attention. The inherent tempo is quick. This is corroboratd by the fact that the *bandish*

Pt. Jagannath Buwa Purohit and my first *guru* Pt. Gajananrao Joshi belonged to the same age-group. Both have come up after a long struggle before they came to be recognised as vocalists and *gurus*. As both were based for a while in Kolhapur they knew about each other's intense musical work. They later chose to settle in Bombay. They used to be busy in concerts and giving *talim* to numerous singers who had already made a mark and who were hoping to receive advanced training. There might have been a hidden spirit of competition between the two. Once Pt. Gajananbuwa was returning from a *talim* and walking down the bridge at Dadar when he met Pt. Jagannath Buwa who used to stay nearby. After initial greetings Pt. Jagannathbuwa insisted that Pt. Gajananbuwa accompanies him to Jaganthbuwa's house. After reaching there Pt.Jagannathbuwa himself cooked some '*shira*' (a sweet preparation of wheat) for Pt. Gajananbuwa, served him with great affection and exclaimed with admiration, "Buwa I know how you have struggled and made a great name for yourself in singing as well as through artistic playing of *violin*, without anybody's help." This was of course a great praise from a great praiseworthy musician and, who would not like it? When finally Gajananraoji reached home we were almost sick with worry as nobody knew where he was. When he narrated what has happened we were elated and moved by Pt. Jagannathbuwa's simplicity and artistic honesty. One felt it was very apt that he assumed the *nom de plume* Gunidas in his compositons—Gunidas means 'a slave of the meritorious'.

fails to deliver if presented in a slow tempo. It's text is not long and does not add up to a compulsory item of recitation.

Jagannathbuwa's compositons are not *cheez* but *bandish* as discussed earlier. His compositions invoke marvels of imagination and therefore he is to be admired as a composer. Such men extend boundaries of music and hence need to be considered in the right perspective.

SMT. HEERABAI BADODEKAR
(29-5-1905 TO 20-11-1989)

14

Smt. Heerabai Badodekar
(29-5-1905 to 20-11-1989)

The Kirana *Gharana*

In Uttar Pradesh, near Saharanpur there is a small village called Kirana. During the times of Mughal Emperor Jehangir some flood-hit artists were rehabilitated in it. Many of them were players of *been* and *sarangi*. This fact is deliberately mentioned here because some features of the artist discussed and the *gharana* she represented are related to it. *Kirana gharana* is regarded important in Hindustani *khayal* music today. Achievements of Ustad Abdul Karim Khan and his nephew Ustad Abdul Wahid Khan have ensured it a prominent place among other *gharana*-s in Hindustani music. On the foundations built by them many others have raised their own respective performing structures. The *gharana* has contributed in spreading appreciation of Hindustani *raga* music among audiences that are varied as well as wide-spread.

To understand the Kirana musical ideology and to assess its contribution to Hindustani music, the best way is to analyse the performing quality of its major followers. A reasonably sufficient samples thus analysed is equivalent to writing a chapter in the history of the said *gharana*. The best possible way to understand the nature of an individual artist's art is to take account of the following: a brief life-history, some analysis of the recorded music within a specific context if any, some technical information of the *raga* the artist has rendered to help identifying his concept behind the effort and finally to put down an assessment on these basis. It is necessary that care is taken to avoid the slippery adjectival profusion in praising/criticising the artist as well as dry academism while engaged in this exciting venture! The great artist whose work is to be discussed in this manner is Smt. Heerabai Barodekar.

Brief Life-sketch

In the year 1905, in Miraj (South Maharashtra) a girl was declared nearly srill-born on birth and was therefore kept away unattended! Fortunately it was as if God prompted somebody to think otherwise and make the necessary attempts to revive the flickering flame of life and the girl lived to become known as Heerabai Badodekar. She was destined to carve out a musical niche for herself on account of her sweet voice, varied singing and cultured presentations that created a socio-cultural prototype of female singers who performed in public from the concert stage in times when this was not easy.

She received her early training from her mother Tarabai, who was a musician in her own right. Tarabai soon managed to get *talim* for Heerabai from Ustad Wahid Khan, who was Ustad Abdul Karim Khan's brother. Though there was a small stint of training from Ustad Mohammad Khan of Agra *gharana*, Heerabai's main musical grooming was under Ustad Wahid Khan from about 1918. Even though the training lasted only for about four years, Heerabai was quick to learn and was absorbing music from all quarters with great intensity. Tarabai separated from Ustad Abdul Karim Khan in 1922 and as if to declare her own independent identity she herself, son Suresh, Krishna and the youngest daughter Saraswati carried the surname Mane, while daughters Heerabai and Kamalabai carried surname of Tarabai's pre-marital family, i.e. Badodekar.

When Heerabai began receiving *talim* what was the atmosphere in the world of music? Some events would indicate the quality of those times. Pt. Vishnu Digambar Paluskar had already began propagating music-education by formulating a syllabus and by founding *Gandharva Maha Vidyalaya*. In addition was his vogue of arranging annual music-conferences and establishing *Ramadhaaraashram* in Nasik. Mr. K.B. Deval had brought out his famous book on Indian Musical Scales and microtonal intervals and Ustad Abdul Karim Khan was actively associated with this venture. Pt. Bhatkhande arranged the All India Music Conference in Delhi. In this conference, Atiya Begum Faizee Rehman put forward a resolution suggesting the establishment of a University of Music. The resolution was not carried because the expected expenditure was nearly Rs. One lakh! Ustad Allauddin Khan had accepted patronage from the Mahiyar Court and taking some orphans under his wings he had formed an orchestra. A significant feature of this orchestra was the use of new instruments. For example, one instrument was called *nal-tarang* and consisted of metal pipes made from gun-metal and thrown away as scrap. In Maharashtra, which was Heerabai's main area of operation, *Balwant Sangeet Mandali* had begun putting up performances of the well-known music-drama *Manapaman* with Master Deenanath's aggressive music and dazzling singing in the lead.

In 1921, in the music conference organised by Pt. Vishnu Digambar Paluskar, Heerabai (age 16 years) made her debut with a rendition of *raga Patdeep* and made such an impact that the *raga* and Heerabai's name became a linked entity! In the same conference Pt. Vishnu Digambar Paluskar had also arranged a *piano*-concert of Western music by Prof. Scrinzy. During this same year Pt. Vishnu Digambar awarded two scholarships, one to B.R. Deodher to learn Western music from Prof. Scrinzy and the other to Dhundiraj Paluskar to learn *violin* from a Bombay-based Italian musician. He also sang a *bhajan* to quieten a restless crowd in one of Mahatma Gandhi's public meetings. Smt. Siddheshwari Devi (at the age of 18) made her debut in a music conference at Calcutta and sang so well that Ustad Faiyaz Khan refused to perform immediately after her concert and exclaimed, "This young artist is going to be the Empress of *thumri* after Gauharjan". *Lalitkala* and *Gandharva Natak Mandali* put up a combined show of *Manapaman* to collect funds for the Swarajya Fund. All these seemingly unrelated events are noted here to bring to notice some of the evolving features of the Indian performing culture.

In sum, Female artists and activists were coming to the fore. Women's socio-cultural perestige was certainly on the rise. Their contribution was being taken seriously. For all musicians some kind of institutionalisation of music training was becoming an important support. Music was fast moving away from merely being an item of entertainment. Moreover, it was making its presence felt in more and more life-areas. Women artists such as Smt. Heerabai made these processes well-entrenched through their performace-quality, bearing and non-aggressive image.

Expectably Heerabai's performing career consisted of giving music-concerts and teaching music in the school of music her mother, Tarabai had opened. In 1933 she cut her first gramophone disc in which she rendered *raga Durga* and a *bhajan*. The new medium enabled her to reach a very wide public and also proved her mastery of the new medium as she displayed extreme skill in creating effective and appealing music with unfailing certainty even in renderings of short duration. Such was the expertise she gained that in her life-span she cut around 175 discs. In addition to the impressive number what she recorded is important because of the width of the repertoire. In a significant coincidence the *Ravi Kiran Mandal,* a voluntary association of poets coming together to declare allegiance to a new kind of poetry, identified as lyric poetry had also recently come into effective existence in these same years when Smt Heerabai was making the 'song' musically more alive. Leaving behind the vogue of evocative reading or purposeful recitation the *Ravi Kiran Mandal* poets were moving towards the song-phase and Heerabai proved an appropriate vehicle. *Gramophone* discs and broadcasting were the media which launhed the genre to sky-high heights.

Following the procedure adopted earlier some art-related events can be noted to see the relevance of Heerabai's music-making in the changing cultural atmosphere. For example, in this same year Ganpatrao Bodas, the renowned stage-actor began participating in drama-performances accepting honorarium on per-performance basis. This meant abandoning the established mould of acting only under the banner of a particular dramatic troupe in its productions. The majestic *Gandharva Maha Vidyalaya* in Bomnay had to be auctioned off. The Government imposed the Entertainment tax. The lessons of these events are to be understood properly. This meant that the patronage was changing rapidly. Each emerging mass medium was demanding music suitable to its own structure and technology but the common feature was short but sweet music, more variety of voices as well as genres and finally music in regional languages. That Heerabai's efforts fitted the bill in every respect becomes obvious.

It was on this background that Heerabai had begun organising her own ticketed public concerts from 1924. This step at once spoke of courage as well as self-confidence. Anybody saying something new or different is likely to find the existing institutional and organisational infrastructure resistant to receive it. Apart from overcoming this difficulty the artists concerned have also to shoulder the responsibility of creating and training one's own audience. Heerabai was precisely doing this. New media, new forms of music, new platforms all found a place in her performing strategy. It is interesting that the first *Keertana* Convention was organised in Pune in 1928. The same year Das Ganu, a celebrated saint ventured to sing a *lavani* in his *keertan*. Pt. Vishnu Digambar organised a convention of music-teachers. Cheaper Gramophones of Japanese make, costing about Rs. 15 arrived in the market. As mentioned earlier, Heerabai was in the forefront of making music for and through diverse media. She was also braodcasting from nearly 40 stations of All India Radio.

Before the twenties were completed two 'dramatic' events took place. The legendary Balgandharva, who had created history through his singing heroines in the Marathi music-drama presided over the prestigious annual Theatre Convention. He spoke favourably about women from 'respectable' houses/families taking more active part in the prevailing theatre. The doctrine of Realism was acquiring influence in arts and it was argued that female-characters in drama could become artistically convincing only if females played the concerned roles. It is on this background that Heerabai stepped on the Marathi stage as a singing actress. (Her first role was that of Subhadra—playing which Balgandharva himself had made history!) Once more sweet, appealing singing and restrained acting made her popular. It must be remembered that she was making her mark in music-drama when the traditional music-drama and the music-making conventions associated with it were on the wane and a new musico-theatric sensibility was gradually assuming shape and acquiring influence.

In the context of Heerabai's stage-music two factors need to be considered. It is true that the traditional stage-music sounded appealing in her singing but the style and the content could not move out of the Balgandharva mould. The accent thus remained on presenting old, stylised music through a new voice. Thus listening to her songs from plays such as *Saubhadra, Vidyaharan* means that one listens to effective music but the content is the same. On the other hand, her singing in plays such as *Yugantar, Jagti Jyot* or *Saubhagyalaxmi* appears to make new musical points but the music-making was hampered by stylised and old-style plays. One feels that she ws trying to sing something different (and not only differently) but could not get the plays needed for that path-breaking venture. In theatre-history the new music-drama with Mr. Rangnekar and such other protagonists of the new theatre had not arrived and by the time it established itself Heerabai had changed the channel of her music-making.

As noted earlier, Heerabai was in the lyric-singing movement which was an upshot of new musico-literary thinking in the post-1930 Maharashtra. '*Bhavgeet*'—a term indicating a direct literary response to the English term Lyric was making an entry but as Mr. J.L. Ranade, one of the major pioneering artists in the concerned movement used to say, before the *bhavgeet* came to its normally understood form, the attempt to soulfully sing the new lyric poetry passed through a phase best described as *bhav-pada*. This format was perhaps the bridge between the earlier *natyapada*-singing and the later *bhavgeet*-rendering. Thus the poetry for this genre was not imbued with theatrical sensibility and made poetic statements. The music that accompanied the *bhav-pada* allowed scope for elaboration of musical ideas—*a la natyapada*. This was the variety in which Heerabai excelled. She was singing songs and thus went far beyond mere evocative recitation of poetry and yet she had moved away from the musico-theatric mode of making music, i.e. *natya-pada*. Due to her musicianship she could sing these *bhavpada*-s in music-concerts as legitimate genre-items. The appeal was certainly different. *Thumri* and *bhajan* were the two other forms she used to present with notable success. But her *thumri*-s lacked the 'bite'-the semi-erotic suggestivity that characterises *Thumri* as a form, whatever the *gharana* might be. She was not given to the appeal of the '*gajra*' in a *kothi*-situation or of the *shama* in the *mushaira* ambience, her appeal was similar to the *samai* in a temple.

This way she continued to create music till 1965. In between she also created a record of a sort by becoming the first female

> We used to stay in Girgaum, a middle class locality in Mumbai. The hall in the *Marwari Vidyalaya* nearby was a regular venue for music-making. On the occasion of somebody's marriage many musicians including Ustad Vilayat Hussain had come. After the music-making was over it was nearing early morning and my *guru* Pt. Gajananrao Joshi persuaded many, including Heerabai, to come to our house for a cup of tea though my mother had gone away to her native place. The moment Heerabai sensed the situation, she quickly got up and unhesitatingly moved towards our small kitchen to prepare tea for all of us.
>
> In Girgaum, our immediate neighbour was Mr. Sadashiv Anant Shukla, a well-known lyricist, playwright of music-dramas and also a script-writer in Marathi. His first music-drama was titled '*Saubhagyalaxmi*'. He was so poor that at night he used to sleep on the foot-steps of a coal-merchant in the locality. The first performance of the play was scheduled and on the previous night he dreamed that Laxmi, the Goddess of Wealth blessed him and truly his fortunes changed dramatically after the first performance. However, he used to say that Heerabai sang *Asar Pasara* in his other play titled *Sadhwi Meerabai* and since then his fortunes changed for better.

singer to perform in the celebrated Harballabh Mela in Jullandhar in 1941. She passed away in 1989 with at least two generations of music-lovers affectionately rememberig her and her music.

Patdeep

In view of the exposition of Heerabai's art so far it would be helpful to discuss in some technical detail, selected examples of Heerabai's recorded music. The *raga patdeep* she has sung is a good beginning.

The *raga* is a new addition made to the Hindustani *raga*-corpus in circulation during the late nineteenth century. There are many *raga*-s such as *bhim*, *palasi*, *pradeepki, dhani, komal bhimpalasi* and of course *patdeep* which are clear deviations from the *raga bhimpalas*. All of them hold their own respective attractions but *patdeep* certainly offers a wider scope. The major feature which makes it dramatically different from *bhimpalas* is the replacement of *komal nishad* in *bhimpalas* with *shuddha nishad*. The *raga* does not allow much *meend* and consequently the internal tempo remains medium and it is also elaborated mainly in the middle octave. Though it is not an expansive *raga* yet it is not too brief. Yet another characteristic touch is that the note *nishad* is employed after isolating it a little in the phrases woven. Even otherwise the note creates expectation bordering on anxiety. As the meaning of the term *nishad* itself suggests the appropriate image of an archer who is about to shoot his arrow. Even in the Western system of music it is significantly described as a 'leading note' because of its capacity to suggest the next note, the octave i.e. the '*sa*'. Hence it is not surprising that the note constitutes the high-point of *patdeep*. The inherent feeling is of expectancy, anxiety and some emotional disturbance. As if to corroborate the fact, the tradition has allotted it the time-span of evening, when the sun has almost set but the moon has yet to appear. The *raga* is not confined to any season, thus reiterating its all-time validity.

To use the contemporary idiom, *patdeep* was Heerabai's brand-name. With her sweet appealing voice and transparent renderings she contributed to the popularity of the *raga*. It is also symptomatic that she was famous for her extra and sure evocative intonation of the note high '*Sa*'. That Patdeep should allow a special role to the movement from note *nishad* to '*Sa*' is much more than a happy coincidence.

The *khayal "Piya nahi aaye"* which she renders is nothing extraordinay as far as the textual content goes. The *chhota khayal* is presented with alertness. After etching the general melodic contours Heerabai explores the region around the note *shuddha nishad* and creates multiple contextual clues. And then she moves to the *high 'sa'*! The moment seems to light up the entire musical proceedings—such is the power and sweetness of her voice. Usually *high 'sa'* is a testing-note for many vocalists who earn the prize but only with much labour. When this is remembered, the value of Heerabai's mastery in this respect will come home. Of course, there are *bol-taan* and *taan* etc. but what lingers in mind is the quietly disturbing *nishad* and the *high 'sa'* which seems to resolve all conflicts. Heerabai has also sang a stage song in *yugantar* ("*Adheer man baaware*") with equal effectivenss in the same *raga*. It shows that her prowess was an abiding achievement.

Vrindavani Sarang

Some *raga*-names in Hindustani music easily go beyond declaring the name of the *raga*. Such names have a special relationship with certain locations and thus gain in evocative power. The *raga* under discussin is an example. The name *Vrindavan* reminds one of the innocent, beautiful and fun-loving village maidens in a pastoral culture and along with the playful, music-creating Krishna, the creator of joy in childhood as well as in youth. There is no evidcene that the *raga* is performed more frequently in Vrindavan, the famed seat of Krishna-*leela*. However, throughout the country, for generations, innumerable devotional, folk and women's songs (including lullabies) are rendered in a way that they unfailingly remind us of this *raga*—the *Vrindavani Sarang*.

The somewhat limited '*meend*' in the *raga* requires a skill and the interplay between the two varieties of the note *nishad* is also a challenge to imagination as well as tunefulness. The *raga* has adequate scope for *alap*, *taan* and all kinds of elaborations. The *raga* explores all octave-spaces and the internal tempo is not demanding. The cumulative effect is that most performers are likely to feel at ease in it. The *raga* is allotted the noon-time and there is no special relationship with any season. Notes 'Re' and 'Pa' are the respectively *vadi* and *samvadi* notes .Interestingly the name of the *raga* similar to it in the South Indian system of art music is also *Vrindavani Sarang*.

Heerabai's presentation of this *raga* is worth-remembering on many counts. The composition set in *tala Jhaptala* is short but joyful. Secondly, even though the composition text is not traditional it successfully brings together most of the Krishna-related themes and thus evokes multiple emotions.The content is expectably easy to understand: "Krishna—handsome as Cupid is delightfully sportive in the Madhuban. Let such deity become engraved in your mind." Thirdly, the rendering emphasises all the plus-points in Heerabai's art. For example, as the composition begins from the note *shuddha nishad* we are immediately in the field of forces Heerabai explores so effectively. Her *tara shadja* never fails in being tuneful, sensuous as well as an agent of resolution of tensions. Heerabai sings with admirable ease. She knows her strong-points and her experienced artistry enables her to be in control.

Madhu Madhura

There is a special propriety in discussing this record. This composition is based on the famous *thumri* of the Benaras *gharana* "*Chhab dikhla ja*". The composition reaches the *tala shadja* almost immediately on inception. What more does Heerabai need! With notable ease she goes on weaving the melodic patterns. And even though the elaboration is inclusive of *khatka, murki*, *taan* and other embellishments associated with the genre, the enveloping feeling is of melodious continuousness. As is known, the Benares-style *thumri* is dignified in movement almost paralleling the *khayal* and yet it is full of joy. Its relationship with *tala* appears simple but requires skill. Heerabai enjoys all this. She is also able to attract listeners'attention to important individual words and decorative tonal clusters. All this ensures that the music communicates easily. One feels the permeating presence of the music and not the singer.

Apart from realising her musical ideas Heerabai had to shoulder the responsibility of establishing an acceptable prototype of a modern female vocalist in Maharashtra so that other aspirants to the stage find it easier to make a performing career. Without diluting her music she achieved it and this could not have been easy.

Pt. Mallikarjun Mansoor
(31-12-1910 to 12-9-1992)

15

Pt. Mallikarjun Mansoor

(31-12-1910 to 12-9-1992)

Brief Life-sketch and *Talim*

Pt. Mallikarjun Mansoor was born in a place called Mansoor (Dist. Dharwad, Karnataka) on a no-moon day and also when the *Mula* constellation was in the ascendency. As a consequence the birth of this child was considered inauspicious and ominous! So the parents went to the *Math* nearby with the intention of dedicating the child to the God. Fortunately the monk in charge of the *Math* was compasssionate and was able to understand Neelamma's (i.e. Mansoor's mother's) feelings. So he allowed the child to be kept with the mother. Reportedly throughout his life Mansoor bore the hurt of being rejected by everybody except the mother.

Actually Pt. Mallikarjun Mansoor was not Mansoor! The family originally hailed from another village Pecchapur and its surname was Erihakkal. 'Eri' meant black and 'Hakkal' meant a field from which the ripe grain had been removed. So the great singer under discussion did not have a helpful surname!

Whatever that may be, his father Bhimrayappa was the village-elder and he was fond of music and theatre. He was specially fascinated by *Dodatta*—a folk drama in the region. Mallikarjun's elder brother Basavraj was a stage actor in a company called

Vishvagunadarsh run by one Mr. Vamanrao Master. Mallikarjun also joined the Company. He was married very early with Gangamma (who expired in 1985). Pandoba—the harmonium-teacher in the company and Sangbasappa—taught music to Mallikarjun in the company. While Basavraj enacted roles of kings etc., Mallikarjun took over the roles of singing characters. Reportedly Mallikarjun's roles such as Prahlad (*Bhakta Prahlad*), Vijay (*Krishnaleela*), Narada (*Mahanand*), Bajirao (*Swarajyalaxmi*) and Vidyaranya (*Varapradan*) were popular. But Mallikarjun decided to take to learning music more seriously. Therefore, leaving the company (in 1922) he went to learn from Pt. Neelkanthbuwa Mirajkar (nee Alurmath), who was trained in the Gwalior tradition of Hindustani music and had settled in Miraj. At the age of 11, Mallikarjun had thus clearly indicated his choice. Having continued the *talim* till 1929 he returned to the drama company but to participate in and compose music for the play *Veer Abhimanyu*. His role of Shakuni and his songs in *raga des* and *kamod* became a rage.

About the same time he gave his debut-concert. Once again Mallikarjun decided to concentrate on music and left the drama troupe but only to join another called *Vaanivilas Natak Mandali* because the Company agreed to pay for Mallikarjun's continued training in music under Pt. Neelkanthbuwa. While in this Company Mallikarjun's roles of Dilawarkhan (*Kittor Rudramma*) and Madhwacharya (*Varapradan*) created waves. In 1933 he cut his first gramophone disc, rendering *raga adana* and *gaudmalhar*. Indicating his popularity and ability to make music he performed on all the ten days of the Ganapati Festival in 1934. Obviously his musical stamina and the acquisition of adequate musical material were put to test and he proved his high stature in no uncertain terms. Unfortunately, his *guru* Pt. Neelkanthbuwa expired in the same year and for a long time Mallikarjun grieved the loss.

It is safe to deduce that by 1935, Pt. Mallikarjun Mansoor had definitely arrived as a renowned vocalist. He continued to record, perform and soon began his *talim* from Ustad Manji Khan, son of the famous Ustad Alladiya Khan who had brought Jaipur *gharana* to recognition. It is helpful to note that Ustad Manji Khan sang Jaipur but with a difference. Pt. Mallikarjun performed in the landmark music festival organised in Shikarpur (Sindh). In 1937, he gave three consecutive concerts in Pune which created a kind of record of meritorious music-making. While he was thus creating a special niche for himself as a music-maker, he lost his mother in an accident and (as noted eariler due to his deep and special bonds with her) it took him a while to come to terms with this loss. To make things worse, Ustad Manji Khan also died and nothing could have unsettled Mansoor more at this juncture. In 1945, he composed music for two films—*Subhadra* and *Chandrahas*—but more important was his decision to continue music-training from Ustad Bhoorji Khan, the second son of Ustad Alladiya Khan who was based in Kolhapur and obvioulsy Mallikarjun was seeking some kind of continuity of musical vision in his training. As he often mentioned later in this year, while taking a walk near a lake in Halgeri (near Dharwad, Karnataka), Mallikarjun suddenly had a revelatory realisation about how to really improvise and create in music. After this miracle his music could hardly remain recitation or presentation of the known or well-practised. Artist Mansoor was born at that moment and new explorations and creations became his goals. Around 1950, he suddenly began composing music for the traditional devotional compositions in Kannada which are known as *Vachana*. He continued to perform, receive honours and earn plaudits from knowledgeables and the 'simple', till he died on 12th September 1992.

Voice and Intonation

The most distinctive feature of his music (one may say the Mansoor-touch) was felt in his voice and intonation. To describe generally, one would say that his voice was thin, light and inclined towards high pitch. However, some subtle aspects need to be noted. The voice was thin but did not sound bodyless. It was a product of rigourous practice as brought out in his forceful employment of *gamak* in all octaves. His intonation was mostly effortless and yet frequently one senses a breathiness that certainly suggests a deliberate application of strength. One can also detect in the initial phrasing of both *alap* and *taan* a presence of the 'H' sound (which, on account of its greater requirement of breath-power is aptly described as *Mahaprana* in the Indian tradition). A slight tapering off of vocalisation is also felt in both *alap* and *taan*. Both these vocal effects may indicate that necessities of the *raga*-music he wanted to present must have introduced some intonation peculiarities in his voice. A corroboration is found in his lyric (song) singing, in which these touches are nearly absent. However, on the whole it is the Mansoor-tone which is clearly omnipresent in his music. As in case of many traditional musicians from his era there was an unmistakable uniformity in his singing tone that bestowed a unique and uniform identity on his music-making. His singing was marked by a sustained vocalising quality and hence the music never suffered from unwanted breaks. The intial vocal stress/ accentuation also did not jar too much because his voice was thin. The same kind of intonation in a broad voice would have, in all likelihood proved inimical to effective music. In all probabiity this accentuation was a side-effect of his predilection to generate rhythm-oriented music.

In his vocalisation there was also a pervasive resonance. In other words, his singing did not suffer from 'flatness'of voice.

In addition, it is generally found that after a stable intonation of notes such as *gandhar, pancham* and *tala shadja,* he subtly brought about volume-changes i.e. intensity of projection, thereby making the resonance more perceivable. Sometimes a slight nasalisation is also felt. As is known to all vocalists, nasalisation endows the projected voice with a pointed quality. This also means that he had avoided employing the undistorted vowel 'A' especially when vocal movement was involved. It is discernible that he loved the doubled melodic phrasing such as 'ga ma, ga ma', 'ma pa, ma pa'. It is to be noted that while embellishment such as *khatka* and *murki* bring a decorative element in music, the doubling of note referred to makes music more volatile or mobile. The doubling does not have a surfacial appeal but it generates a kind of intellectual, structural appeal consisting also of a musical poise. This way of tonal movement is inevitably found in abundance in the Jaipur way.

I remember some seniors palusibly suggesting that the kind of resonance Mansoor carried so thoroughly was due to the Ustad Rahimat Khan (Gwalior *gharana*) influence which Mansoor imbibed via Ustad Manji Khan. The way Ustad Rahimat Khan generated this effect was through leaving behind a shadow of the note and while doing so fade out or blur the acoustic shape of the concerned original vowel such as 'A' or 'ee'. This enables a singer not only to maintain a continuity of projection but also to add some tonal colour. It may be that this way of making the phrasal termination less distinct arouses more curiosity among the receivers of music. It is true that no abrupt ending of a phrase nor a sculpted clarity of sound can lead to perceivable suggestivity.

Repertoire and 'Singing'

Mansoor of course sang *raga* and compositions that dominate the Jaipur-Atarauli repertoire. Thus, well-known *raga*-s, such as *todi, multani, yaman, jaijaiwanti*—as well as *nayaki kaanada*, *kafi kaanada*, *bihagda, khokar* and varieties of *Bilawal* were also frequently heard in his music. His preferred tempo was around the medium, nearly irrespective of the *raga*. He obviously regarded tempo more seminal to his music than *tala* and hence he hardly performed in rara *tala*. Unlike some of his fellow-singers in the *gharana* he used to render both *sthayi* and *antara* while presenting a *raga* .In fact even when exploring the *raga* in the *alap*-phase he was accustomed to repeatedly sing the *sthayi*. Most probably this was intended to keep in constant view the *raga*-map he was following in his elaborations. This surely benefited the listeners and in the end it worked as a device of aesthetic efficacy. Frequently he employed the strategy of keeping the *mukhda* in double the tempo of the *tala*-circle and this would slightly lessen the rigidity of the tala-frame projected (e.g. listen to his "*Piya banjara*" or "*Mero piya*"). Very rarely the accompanists were heard to fill a whole cycle with their contribution in the final music-making. The emphasis on rare *raga* and repeated reference to his own concept of the *raga* through the *sthayi* rendition certainly appeared to be deliberate strategies.

Expectably, in keeping with the *gharana* vogue his *taan*-s were complex and wide in range. The medium tempo of the *tala*, double melodic weave in general, inherent fast pace and finally because they were in definite relationship with the overall tempo (i.e. double, triple of it) his *taan*-s were felt to be multi-layered. However, dazzling speed and straight surprising movement were not their chief characteristics. On most occasions he placed a small but clearly composed cluster of notes immediately after the *sama* as the intial design and then followed it up with similar or changed phrasing; thus determining the logic of the *taan*–phase. A very major consequence of his total approach was that the listener was not allowed a breather in his music. In fact the element of pause did not seem to have much value in the entire effort.

As a part of the centenary celebrations we had organised a series of concerts in memory of Pt.Vishnu Digambar Paluskar in the famed Convocation Hall of the University of Bombay. One evening we had Pt. Mallikarjun Mansoor's concert. He sang, *multani, yaman, khokar* etc. with his characteristic zest and sweetness. Expectably more than half of the audience consisted of practising, well-known musicians of various *gharana*. His *khokar*, leaning more towards *khamaj* had intrigued some but his mellifluous *yaman* had enchanted everybody. Later, whenever we met he used to ask me in his special Marathi spoken in double-fast tempo "Ashok, on that occasion in the University, the *yaman* was good no!" And as was his wont, he extened his palm immediately for a confirming clap! For a great musician he was simple, smiling and guileless!

Once a meeting was convened by Mr. Keshav Kothari, the Secretary of the Central Sangeet Natak Academy to discuss and deliberate on the idea of establishing a Central Institution for teaching music conceived on a wide basis. Acharya Brihaspati, Pt. Mallikarjun Mansoor, Shri P. L. Deshpande and I were the members. Acharya Brihaspati was a renowned musicologist with an overall aggressive personality. While discussing he said that many vocalists, including those coming from Maharashtra, were careless about the textual as well as the grammatical aspects of music. His statements and the aggressive and dismissive tone were jarring and Pt. Mansoor suddenly felt so aggrieved that he started singing one compositon after the other—challenging Acharya Brihaspati to show what was lacking in them. Acharya Brihaspati for once got flustered and very confused. Pt. Mansoor went on proving the quality and correctness of the musical traditions in Maharashtra. We all enjoyed his music and also felt nearly unable to conceal our silent laughter. The Acharya realised the weakness of his blanket generalisation and the meeting had to be immediately adjourned for lunch.

Once we met and discussion as usual centred on music. One of my questions addressed to him was, "How to ensure that one's music lasts even during the old age?" He did not have to think for a second. Partially holding up the first phalanx of the middle finger of his right palm he exclaimed, "Lower the singing pitch slightly, only this much!"

When I used to discuss music with great 'traditional' musicians in my Television series entitled *Pratibha and Pratima* Pt.Krishnarao Pandit, Pt. Mansoor and such other seniors all used to be full of candor, and open to technical discussions. Not only that, they were honest to the piont of accepting their faults.

On one occasion I had invited Pt. Mansoor to my house in Bandra for lucnh. Simple, vegetarian food was served and received without making any fuss! Sensing his simplicity and liking for traditional ways, my wife serving him the last item, i.e. rice and curd and asked him whether he would like to have some fresh cream with it. Not only did he smile and accept the offer but his entire face lit up. So simple was he.

Pt. Gajananrao Joshi
(30-1-1911 to 28-6-1987)

16

Pt. Gajananrao Joshi

(30-1-1911 to 28-6-1987)

Brief Life-sketch and *Talim*

Pt. Gajananrao Joshi was born on a 'no-moon' day in Mumbai on 30th January, 1911 to Shri Antubuwa and Indirabai. Pt. Antubuwa often used to say that the day was inauspicious and these off-hand remarks left a life-long shadow on Gajanan's mind. His pet-name was Ram. Expectably Ram's first *guru* was his father, Pt. Antubuwa. Unfortunately, Smt. Indirabai died early and Antubuwa was disturbed and nearly lost interest in mundane ambitions and interests. He began roaming over various places in Maharashtra till he settled down in the small princely state of Oundh (Satara District). Gajanan's later training was under many illustrious *guru*-s of different *gharana*-s. Gajanan came to learn from Pt. Vazebuwa (Gwalior), Ustad Bhurji Khan (Jaipur) and finally from Ustad Vilayatkhan (Agra) at various stages of his musical development.

Around 1923, Gajananbuwa began playing the *violin* under the orders of Pantpratinidhi (*Raja*) of the Oundh State. Gajananbuwa was in way compelled to develop a technique and a style of playing this challenging instrument because he was asked to accompany the *Raja* in the latter's *keertana*-performances. Obviously he succeeded in the difficult task of honing adequate performing skills and by 1928 he began broadcasting vocal as well as instrumental music (i.e. violin). He was in the orchestra set up for the first and pioneering Prabhat film '*Ayodhyecha Raja*' in 1930s. Married in 1933, Gajanan's important music-learning stints which interspersed his performing career form an interesting chronology: from Pt. Vazebuwa, from Ustad Bhurji *Khan* in 1945 and Ustad Vilayat Hussain Khan around 1963. During the years 1953-68 he worked as Music-advisor on the All India Radio. The main awards he received were Central Sangeet Natak Akademy (1972), I.T.C. (1982) and Tansen Sanman (Gwalior 1985).

Pt. Gajananbuwa—Artist and *Guru*

As an artist in vocal as well as instrumental music and as a *guru* in both these music-making avenues, two features appear to be noteworthy. Firstly, in spite of the fact that he hailed from an established family of art–musicians who specialised in vocal music he took to a foreign and rarely studied instrument such as *violin*, developed the necessary method of studying it, a technique and an idiom of playing it and a style of presenting its music with professional competence. Secondly, as far as Hindustani art music is concerned he did a pioneering job of establishing the *violin* as a music-making agent. A feature placed in the same context must find a separate mention. Whether as a vocalist or as an instrumentalist he always sang or played what he thought fit, irrespective of the audience or its reactions and responses. A question may be asked: was he more popular as a violinist than as a vocalist? The answer may vary but one thing is certain that his music content remained the same in both his roles. Like many traditional performing Indian instrumentalists he claimed with some insistence that he played his vocal music in his instrumental music-making. Similar, if not identical musical motivation undoubtedly remained with him as a steady shaping influence throughout his life.

In his career Pt. Gajananbuwa was a steadfast follower of the Gwalior musical ideology. Yet one could say that very early he was listening to the other musical ideologies in circulation and had carefully noted what musically significant components they had which were different from the Gwalior repertoire. To understand, digest and finally to translate such features in one's own vocalism was of course a laborious process. However, if the influences penetrate deep in one's mind, they unfailingly play a role in shaping the performing personality. It is true that Pt. Gajananbuwa first imbibed the essentials of the Gwalior *gharana* but one must note that the Maharashtra version of the Gwalior *gharana* was rather simple. In fact it was often derisively referred to as '*Hardasi*' i.e. as sung by *keertan*-practitioners who are semi or un-trained in the complexities of the art music. Compared to the Maharashtra version the Gwalior version of the same *gharana* was more complex, *tappa*-influenced and 'art'-oriented. In all probability, Pt. Gajananbuwa was attracted by this version and hence he did not leave the Gwalior ideology but tried to expand or widen its periphery. His attraction for Gwalior and his (repeated) moves away from it remained a determining principle of his music-making.

If looking outside Gwalior though remaining in it was his first developmental strategy, the second was to approach Pt. Vazebuwa for further training. During the same period when he was modifying his focus, he was also appreciatively and 'firmly taking in' Balgandharva and Master Krishnarao. (This argument is developed further while discussing his violin-music.) As a person settled in the Pune-Mumbai belt he must have heard other *gharana*-s too. But when in a formative stage a learner-achiever tends to follow something which is different, likeable but also familiar and accessible to personal efforts. Consequently Pt. Gajananbuwa, who was keen on deviating from the simple Gwalior-version current in Maharashtra and searching for more imaginative, complex and new music-making turned to Pt. Vazebuwa as well as artists such as Balgandharva and Master Krishnarao. In addition was the fact that the more significant music-making properties in Pt. Vazebuwa's music were not dependent on the gift of a good voice. The music rested on a kind of intellectualism and thought-inspired complexity. This argument was also corroborated later because the musical attractions in Pt. Gajananbuwa's next two *guru*-s' music namely, Ustad Bhurji Khan's and Ustad Vilayat Hussain Khan's were also not dependent on sweet voice, etc. Pt. Gajananbuwa moved to Pt. Vazebuwa for imbibing complexities and related elements in music and to Balgandharva, Master Krishnarao for imaginative, lyrical approach to musical material. The latter elements were reflected in his *violin*-music. This is what made his music tri-coloured!

Pt. Vazebuwa, Ustad Bhurji Khan and Ustad Vilayat Hussain Khan—And Their Music

Some analysis of the resultant spectrum due to his later *guru*-s can be attempted.

Pt. Gajananbuwa sang in the Gwalior-preferred medium tempo but the elaboration was not simple in design as in the Maharashtra branch of the *gharana*. The 'A' vowel in *alap*-s and *taan*-s is not undistorted, often it is distorted to 'ya' and there is no ease in intonation. There is a hint of aggressiveness in all vocalisation. These features are traceable to his own voice-qualities and to the Pt. Vazebuwa touch. As far as the complexity of design is concerned, Pt. Vazebuwa's influence definitely worked. Pt. Gajananbuwa frequently told us that Pt. Vazebuwa taught him how to unravel the mysteries of rare *raga*-s. In the Gwalior *gharana* quite a few rare or *aprachalita* (i.e. not in easy circulation) *raga*-s are taught though they are not rendered too often. The rare *ragas* that received the most preferred treatment were, for example, *Bhairav-bahar*, *Malgunji* and *Bageshri kaanada* in the repertoire. During the same period when Pt. Gajananbuwa was performing, Pt. Vazebuwa brought into circulation *bhatiyar*, varieties of *kaanada, khat* and a host of other rare *ragas*. However, he had no effective followers and secondly, his method of solving rare *raga*-s made his renderings more unpredictable and the listeners found the Jaipur or Agra versions more accessible. On this background Pt. Gajananbuwa's turning to Pt. Vazebuwa would appear artistically inevitable.

He turned to the Jaipur-way because of the widening gap between what he wanted to sing and what he knew well. He used to say," I heard Kesarbai in 1943 in a concert in Laxmi Baug but could not understand her. So I heard her till I understood her music. But then, that music would not fit in my performing competence, so I decided to learn in that *gharana*." As hinted earlier Pt. Vazabuwa's approach produced music which was unpredictable and in a way created doubts about the realisation of the intended form in music. On the other hand, Jaipur mode was accomodatively well-structured, i.e. all phases of the music-making were thoroughly mapped or pre-planned. In addition, Smt. Kesarbai's presentations were so clear in design and emphatic in presentation that precision, definiteness and certainty were easily felt as the prime features. The term 'Method' was thus roundly proved. In the final analysis, Pt. Gajananbuwa's learning from Ustad Bhurji Khan was thus a *fait accompli*. For accomplishing this he had to leave Pune (where he was well-settled with his family after marriage) lock, stock and barrel and shift to Kolhapur but he did not flinch in his resolve and followed his inner urge. So methodical was he in imbibing the Jaipur vision that while singing *khayal*-s rooted in that *gharana,* he did not include even a single phrase which did not belong to that *gharana*. This speaks for the intensity of his resolve and the hard-won craftsmanship.

After having groomed himself in the Jaipur-*gharana* on his volition, why did he turn to Agra *gharana*? In this context too voice-quality and a penchant for rhythm-work can be put forward as the basic motivating factors. But there is one more reason. He also developed a liking for having more varied *raga*-frames to enable him putting forward a different musical content. It is also possible that this was viewed as a compensation for the lack of appeal in the voice. Making a comprehensive attempt to enrich his musical armoury he thought of more *raga*-s and aggressive rhythm-work as suitable additions to be made. Considering the fact that he turned to learn the Agra *gharana* repertoire quite late in his life it indicates how intense can be artistic hunger for someone like him. He stands as a representative example—because when he began learning from Ustad Vilayat Khan he was already well-established in every worldly way.

Thus he had in his repertoire *raga*-s and compositions from three *gharana*-s. He did not wish and therefore did not mix or merge the different *gharana* idioms but consciously presented them as contributions from the respective *gharana*-s. He did not perform anyhing unless he had received adequate *talim* for it. Apart from "*Najar di bahaar*" in *bhairavi* he did not sing any other *tappa*. He sang a variety of *tarana* compositions with greater frequency but speed was not the essence. He did not have *Dhrupad-dhamar* in the repertoire and though he had some meritorious compositions in the genres *Khayal-numa* and *Sargamgeet*, their inclusion in the performing menu was rare. *Thumri* and *Natyageet* were attractive and permanent fixtures in his *violin*-music, but were not active members of his vocal repertoire nor were they a part of his teaching-schedules. In sum, his singing was perceptibly *Khayal*-centred.

One point needs to be stressed. In moving from *guru* to *guru* with deliberation and design, Pt. Gajananbuwa never turned to the new unless the previously learned music was adequately under his control. As a consequence he could and often would present the different *gharana*-s distinctly and with surety. Secondly, the main thrust was towards the vocalism of the concerned *gharana*, its musical philosophy and not merely to perform attractive compositions from the *gharana*-specific repertoire. New *ragas* or new compositions were not objects to be showed off; they were largely symptomatic of a new musical ideology he was enamoured of.

His *Violin*-music

That the overall musical content in his vocal as well as *violin*-music was the same has already been mentioned. The discussion that follows is a continuation from that basic trait.

He was undeniably a pioneer in the task of establishing a close performing relationship between Hindustani art music and the *violin*. Others may have played Hindustani art music on the instrument before he arrived on the scene or done so during the same period he was active, but to stabilise the instrument on the concert stage was a different function and in that campaign, Pt. Gajananbuwa was in the forefront. When he took up the *violin* in Oundh on the orders of the ruling Prince he had no definite, accessible, indigenous tradition of handling the instrument as well as pressing it into service to create music of the kind he was expected to produce. This must be the reason why he decided to somehow accomodate in the instrumental idiom he formulated, the maximum amount of vocal music he already knew well. The pros and cons of this strategy are worth noting.

Firstly, his *violin*-music seemed to have more body, it establishd a weighty presence. The main difference was felt in the melodic elaboration, i.e. in the *alap*-phase which appeared more fully articulated than in the music of somebody who approached the *violin* as a *violin* and not a vehicle for vocal music. Picking up of *raga*-nuances, or sometimes creating phrasing that reflects tonal movements associated with words i.e. textual units are telling examples. This happened even though he never played the vocal *bandish* itself on the instrument. If one follws the Southern system of fingering (e.g. playing with one finger) one is able to execute richer *gamak*-s. However, while discussing his *violin*-music it is better to keep the Southern context away as most of the north Indians were not employing the Southern technique when the pioneers in Hindustani music-world were at work on the *violin*.

The decision to follow the way of vocal music and that too on the background of his training in Gwalior *khayal* music also automatically brought in some other features. Thus his playing was more aggressive. He employed *tala*-s such as *jhumra, tilwada* as in *khayal* music but did not play the *bandish* he usually sang in vocal music-making. His method was to compose a *Mukhda* and then elaborate the related *raga*-map. As a consequence, as he was not using word-based compositional frameworks as the basis of his *raga*-rendering, his *violin*-music also moved away from the *khayal*. *Bol-taan*, *bol-lay* or *bol*-based elaborations were excluded and that also meant more freedom in both melodic expansions and rhythmic complexities—including the scope given to *tihai* (which were not very frequent in his vocal music). On the other hand, other string-instruments such as *sitar, sarod* which followed a method generally described as *gatkari* style had developed a phase called *jhala* in the rhythm-work which Pt. Gajananbuwa did not use because the model of his *violin*-music was *khayal*. This is how his approach to and performance of *violin*-music can be construed.

Obviously, the strategy had some drawbacks. Due to his vocal-music model he used to tune the instrument in a vocalists fundamental pitch and that meant the intrinsic bright tone of the instrument was lost to him and to his music. I do not think that he paid any attention to the tone of this instrument as a result of its specific acoustic properties and structural properties. His instrument sounded low-energy and somewhat masked. His bow-work also was rather rough. Just as he formulated the total import of his vocal music irrespective of his own voice-quality or the lack of it, similarly he shaped his instrumental music without much caring for the innate tonal qualities of the instrument. If the same artist is involved in evolving vocal and instrumental music these entities are bound to affect one another unless one is on one's guard.

In the art music expressed through the *violin,* vocal music of the Gwalior *gharana* provided the map but for the 'light'er(!) music he followed with love and admiration the idiom and music formulated by Balgandharva, Master Krishnarao and to some extent Pt. Govindrao Tembe. When he played landmark stage songs such as "*Yadu mani sadana*" or "*Narwar Krishnasamaan*" the playing style and the imagination were clearly traceable to the Balgandharva-vogue. In addition, whenever he played *raga*-s such as *kafi, pilu, khamaj* and compositional maps in them this same musical vision determined his expression. What was apparent was that his renderings never sounded as imitations. They were instances of music-making when another, lyrical and delicate kind of music-making imagination had taken over. In those moments he was obviously permeated with a musical philosophy which was lying dormant when he played *khayal*-music. I had often wondered if he had come under the influence of northern musical traditons other than the *khayal*, and especially the meaningfully varied *thumri-dadra* traditions in the north, what could have emerged?

Whether in vocal or instrumental music he was extremely tuneful, his *tala*-sense was unerringly sure, his *raga*-knowledge was based on firm footing and his presentations were methodical.

I have not discussed the features separately as these and such other aspects can be assumed in case of a traditional artist for whom music was a family-tradition. Perhaps on account of his voice he was more inclined towards rhythm-work and this can be mentioned as a general characteristic. The penchant for rhythm-work was emphasised in the *bol-taan* and *taan* phases of his performance. It must be noted that the patterning in his rhythm-work, including *tihai*-s were never pre-composed (as it is in case of many instrumentalists). His rather aggressive rhythm-work was improvised in the true sense of the term. He uncomplainingly accepted the risk involved. As has been suggested, he was attracted towards those artists and *gharana*-s that allowed predominance to the rhythm aspect. But when his voice was in the required ease and mood he emphasised the emotive utterance of Ustad Rahimat Khan and presented that mode of music-making very effectively. This was not music which focussed on the conventional emotionality of love-sentiment, pathos, devotion, etc. It was a kind of transcendental 'felt' music for which *tala, raga* etc. were mere vehicles! Sometimes I have felt convinced that this was the music which he really wanted and intended to put forward. When that was not possible he followed the alternative tracks he had so carefully trod on.

He never tried to synthesise the *gharana*-idioms he knew. In his *violin*-music he never attempted to exploit the tonal colour and make different instrumental music. As an artist he was admired as well as criticised. His presentations were seldom described in ecstatic terms. And yet, even today numerous serious students of music find his music engrossing. The reason was that many students of music come to the conclusion that what he actually presented held promise of a much greater and qualitative music. If his music was dry to some and scholarly and intellectual for others, it was full of higher import for a significant minority. Obviously there is a category of such musicians and he ranked high in it.

As a Teacher

Most of Indian musicians avoid the responsibility to speak or write on music or they take to the slippery route of mystifying and talk glibly about rigorous *talim* or *riaz*, music practised in solitude (preferably near the Himalayas!), or finally and emotionally refer to the *guru*'s favour or Divine blessings! Under such obscuring circumstances beliefs about, answers to or positions on questions related to the essential, fundamental or basic musical principles and music-related behaviour are to be deduced from the actual practice of artists, *gurus* and disciples. Pt. Gajananbuwa's teaching method or procedures are to be thus decoded from his music and then evaluated.

Firstly, he firmly believed that having a familial tradition in music is of great importance. In practical terms this meant that if music ran in the family, certain significant features were taken for granted. For example, he would assume that a serious student of music with a familial musical tradition would know the standard locations of the scale and notes, he would be able to read the circularity of the *tala*-pattern and the role of its subdivisions. He would also be aware of the simple or primary method of elaborating a *raga*, and the general musical specialities of various major *gharana*-s. As a consequence of these and other such assumptions, he never taught music 'step-by-step'. For instance, *alap, bol-taan* and *taan* did not feature in his teaching-order in a sequence, the broad, general and larger impression or map of music was to be received and understood first and other details were to follow subsequently. This belief was not restricted to those who were his disciples from the beginning. Even to those who came to him after learning from other authorities, this procedure was hardly changed. For every learner, Pt. Gajananbuwa's logical sequence remained nearly the same.

Obviously one cannot always expect to get students who already had a good background training. To them he would teach simpler items but the aim was only to make deep impressions of how he explored or employed the basic principles of music-making. Actually '*sanskara*' would be the appropriate term for the strategy he followed. There would be certain prescriptions or prescriptive acts but the ultimate goal was to lead the learner to the larger map to be explored. If a student has been brought up in another *gharana*, the assumptions and procedures would undergo some minor modifications. For example, the *talim* became more direct and action(i.e. singing)-oriented. However, one could see that there was no radical shift in the desired final impact. One of his favourite guidelines was: "Be with me". That would mean one's presence whenever he was teaching other students of all sorts. While listening to his *talim* to others, one needed to be specially alert. Attending such non-participating sessions was often a process that was very time-consuming. The realisation that one has learnt many things while listening in this way used to dawn on disciples much later. This unconscious learning had a place in his firm teaching-learning logic.

Yet another feature of his pedagogy was the preferred insistance that one should not continue academic education while learning music. Like many other traditional musicians he swore by the belief that music requires a twenty-four hours involvement of the learner. For an absolutely new but definitely talented student (who wanted to learn from 'Sa Re Ga Ma' as they say) '*sanskar*' was the top priority and there was some change in the teaching material. *Drut, chhota khayal* in *raga*-s such as *bhoop, yaman, todi, bihag* etc. were taught to him along with the *tala* and simpler *bada khayal* were taught without *tala*. A few *alap* were also taught but care was taken to keep them simple in design and they were taught without *tala*. This kind of teaching continued for about three years or so and to sing all the compositions one after the other was a part of the teaching-learning process.

Tala was not of course ignored. To recite *tala*-s such as *tilwada*, *jhumra, ada choutal, ektala, jhaptal* with the relevant hand-claps and finger-counting was the first step. This was followed by the instruction to play the *tala* on *baya* (the left, bass drum from the *tabla*-set employed in *khayal* music). The third step consisted of learning by heart the *kayda, gat* and *tihai* compositions in *tala Tritala* and recite them while keeping the *tala* by hand-claps, etc. He used to describe these as *bandish* in *tala* and also insisted that the recitation must be done with involvement and interest in the artistic patterning involved. Very often after coming from a concert tour, he would take out a piece of paper on which he has written down some new *kayada* or *gat* learnt from somebody he had met. With immediate effect this would be included in the reciting repertoire of the *tala* study-procedures laid down. He used to emphasise that the poetry of *tabla* compositions consisted in the quality of the syllables, their individual weight, the pattern resulting from their interplay with the *tala*-divisions and added that unless this is appreciated and imbibed, it is difficult to be creative in the rhythm-aspect of music-making. He used to distinguish between comprehension of the *tala*-principle and the understanding of a particular tala. Repeated use of the same *tala* may be adequate to understand that *tala,* but to comprehend the *tala*-principle it is mandatory that one gets acquainted with the creative expression of the *tala* and its language. This was the reasoning for his insistence on the non-playing study of *tabla* by an aspiring disciple. If possible he also advocated some serious learning in *tabla*-playing with the representative genres learnt systematically.

Coming back to the *raga*-singing, once an adequate number of representative compositions (without *tala*) had been learnt Pt. Gajananbuwa introduced the disciple to the actual performing arena. The disciple was asked to sing or play with Pt. Gajananbuwa who instructed the disciple, "Do not sing or play what I have sung or played. Produce something which has relevance after that and something which you can properly put forth". Obviously this was easily said than done and the situation became nightmarish for a disciple. The second *sutra* only made the music-making opportunity more challenging. He used to say that even if the *raga* taken up on the earlier day was to be explored again, "Do not sing yesterday's *yaman*. See how things are going today and sing accordingly." The second part of this *sutra* was almost a slap in the disciple's face. Pt. Gajananbuwa would exclaim, "I took a fast *taan*—which you knew you cannot take yet. Then why did you try it? Did it not occur to you that you could have achieved a similar effect through a small *bol-taan*? When would you start using your brain while singing?" His training sessions were replete with satire, sarcasm, stinging comparisons and similes aimed at the disciple. The constant aim was to develop an all-round alert awareness of music in the disciple.

Due to similarity of musical visions involved, the whole teaching strategy described so far was in use even when he taught *violin*-music to somebody. So it was not a strange sight to see that the disciple would be playing while Pt. Gajananbuwa would be singing in a training session. He was not an advocate for practising intricate *paltas* (melodic exercises with different basic patterns involving different arrangements of scalar notes). Straight-*taan* was to be repeatedly practised, all *taan*-s as well as the *shuddha* notes were to be practised in slow tempo for long durations and a final checking of the tunefulness of the fundamental note subsequent to completion of a *taan* etc., were his favourite prescriptions. He himself did all that for hours.

His Philosophy of Teaching—An Evaluation

On this background it is possible to attempt an evaluation of his teaching in general.

In his approach, a definite but unchanging sequence of *alap* did not have a place. Instead, learning the genre (*khayal*), the elaboration-phase (*alap, boltan* etc) and idiom (e.g. according to the Gwalior, Jaipur or Agra *gharana*) determined the content of his *talim*. All these features emerged during the *talim* and they were to be so absorbed by the disciple. Obviously this afforded more freedom but also proved more challenging and difficult.

His was a far cry from the step-by-step approach normally identified as methodical and its absence unnerved a disciple, at least in the initial stages. The disciple realised that he cannot do better than tunefully, and correctly recite seminal compositions in different *raga*-s. Though this seemed rather anti-climactic in some respects, it is also true that after some more *talim* the learner would and could begin singing or playing on his own, then correctly recite *alap, taan, bol-taan* and *tihai,* etc. Needless to say this amounts to a qualitative achievement.

The same is true about the other *sutra* dinned into a disciple's ear, "Do not imitate me but try to follw me". This meant that now the disciple has to assume the responsibility of creating according to his lights and face the consequences. Pt. Gajannabuwa never told us "sing this". His instruction was to take something that could follow what he had already put forward. If the disciple remained hesitant or tentative Pt. Gajananbuwa would himself launch into music-making. For a while the disciple would be thus dragged along in a humbled state of mind. The implication was: music-making is a flowing activity, there is no time to feed anybody and an artist in a creative flight cannot afford interruption as that would virtually mean cessation of the activity, however temporary. That a disciple must understand to interpret the complete map relevant at that moment was the firm belief involved.

The sure-fire strategies such as practising impressive *taan* or constructing and practising complex *tihai*-s had no place in his *talim*-procedures. As a cumulative effect a disciple was expected to simultaneously get an idea of the essentially dynamic, cohesive and unpredictable quality of music-making and performance.

The system appears to lay a special premium on the family-tradition and exclusive and isolated concentration on music. In my opinion Pt. Gajananbuwa's insistence on learning only music and nothing else was unjustifiably rigid. That it can be musically beneficial to have an understanding, creative vision and interpretative insight in other fields he did not seem to realise and accept.

To advocate mutual exclusiveness of music-studies and other pursuits because performing ability is more demanding, was also one of his claims not really borne out by facts and history. Is it not true that Western musicians are also often knowledgeable in other disciplines and yet they are not hampered in their performing quest of music? Music occupation for 24 hours is a metaphorical description and should be treated as that. It is truer to say that while doing music one must be completely in it.

Pt. Gajananbuwa learnt from different *gharana*-s and kept the idioms separate. This cannot and should not be carried too far except in the initial stages of comprehending the distictive featrures of a particualr *gharana*. For an artist the ideal should be to bring about a genuine musical synthesis in a flexible performing approach.

Looking closely at his musical ideals and ideology it is certain that Ustad Rahimat Khan's approach, intonation and patterning combined with Balgandharva's lyrical imagination and effortless putting forward of music were the ultimate determinants of Pt. Gajananbuwa's musical vision. It is notewaorthy that none of these views carry an academic or pedantic baggage. Both do not emphasise the rhythm as a harsh reality in music to be put forward with adequate if not overwhelming aggression. And yet his own active performance was more aggressive and stressful. This meant the disciple had to unravel the mystery of his *guru's* projected music and his implict of implied music. This certainly was a difficult proposition. In addition Pt.Gajananbuwa as a *guru* was also likely to change the orientation of his music without notice. That the disciple had to develop his sensibility to a high level of sensitivity could be considered a drawback in a teaching situation.

Transcending his personal limitations and hostile circumstanes in critical stages of his life, Pt. Gajananbuwa moved with courage and persistence towards a pioneering task of a national stature. This is an attempt to understand his greatness by temporarily stepping out of the time-flow, a task fit for a real philosopher than a keen disciple.

Guruvarya Gajananbuwa—From Close Quarters!

I was in Pt. Guruvarya Gajananbuwa's (henceforth referred to as Buwa) contact at least for 24 years from 1947 (when I was about 10 years old). Obviously I saw him through two viewpoints—from a child's eyes and through a more adult vision during the later years. I saw his struggles as a professional musician, as a student of music and as a family-man. I was a silent witness to his successes and failures. But if I am asked what is the deepest impact I carry, —it becomes difficult to identify and there are reasons for that.

Pt. Gajananbuwa was always candid about what he knew and what he did not. Once when he had been to Mysore, Ustad Faiyaz Khan expressed his desire to listen to Pt. Gajananbuwa's vocal music and also said that he wanted to listen to *raga shuddh kalyan*. Pt. Gajananbuwa sang *raga yaman*. After the concert was over, the Ustad said, "But I wanted to hear your *shuddha kalyan.*" Pt. Gajananbuwa after a moment's silence said, "I have not learnt it. Mostly I have *talim* of simple *raga.*" On the next two days too Ustad asked Pt. Gajananbuwa to sing and he listened to his music with appreciation. On the third day he called Pt.Gajananbuwa, offered him *Paan* and smilingly said, "I liked your music but I have a question: How is it that you have Ustad Rahimat Khan's music in your singing?" Then Pt.Gajananbuwa explained to him how his father, Pt. Antubuwa had accompanied and closley followed Ustad Rahimat Khan in an indirect kind of *talim* situation. Ustad Faiyaz Khan was immensely pleased and then narrated to Pt. Gajananbuwa how his own father had taken Faiyaz Khan to Prof. Chatre's Circus to listen to Ustad Rahimat Khan and how that music has secured a permanent place in his psyche.

Firstly, because I am one of those who learnt music from him from the beginning—right from 'sa–re–ga–ma' as they say. Secondly, as the *talim* was in the traditional *guru-shishya parampara* I was like a son to him. And finally, much later he was on the teaching-staff of the University Music Centre, Bombay where I was appointed the first Director. This multi-layered relationship creates a virtual web of thoughts and feelings in my mind whenever his name is mentioned.

He was a close friend of my father. I, wearing half pant and canvas shoes used to join Buwa when he took his jogging-exercises on the Chowpaty Girgaum. I used to feel very important and virtuous then! Playing the *tanpura* I have sat behind him with trepidation. I have seen and heard his *riaz* (self-study) as well as the *talim* he imparted to others. Impressions from this period are deep but somewhat blurred because I was young and was almost fond of collecting all kinds of mental images of the world, outer and inner, without subjecting them to scrutiny, without trying to make sense of them and without attempting any motive-analysis.It is no use squandering adjectival wealth in trying to describe the memories further. What I have in mind is to try to describe how Buwa appeared to me when he emerged from various conflict-situations he faced. In a way this writing is a private act of communication done publicly.

In my memory he was a great artist who used to stay with us since my father was like a brother to him. Initially he used to come from Pune, carrying his *violin* case, wearing a warm blue coat, a muffler protecting his throat and carrying a big blue trunk. After that a stage came when he used to stay for two weeks in Bombay, gave *talim* to various people, gave concerts and went back to Kolhapur where the family was then based. We used to stay in Samarth Sadan, Banam Hall Lane, Girgaon, a chawl with middle class tenants. We had two rooms and a number of Buwa's tutions were given in our house. While learning from him I would be playing *tanpura* or *baya* sitting in front of him or by his side. When not actively involved in the *talim*, I would be in the gallery or on the metal cot in the same room he was teaching somebody, trying to read or study. Buwa was not fond of anybody carrying on academic study. Progressively his *alap* became more and more complicated, or the rhythm work more and more complex.

Unconsciously I would be trying to keep the *tala* and musically the situation became too hot. It became imperative for me to descend from my academic heights and accept the musical entanglement. And the battle would continue.

Buwa really meant war/conflict in more senses than one. He was always engaged in a private battle. He woke up and the battle on the health front was on. He used to take *triphala* powder, an Ayurvedic preparation mentioned in ancient text for its digestive properties and more importantly as conducive to improvement in voice. The next attack on the same front was to go on the Chowpaty for jogging. Once when we have reached the Charni Road Garden, the point from which we began running, he told me, "Go and bring some pointed stone or something like it." I was of course intrigued, but "there is not to question why!" I could only get a small piece of a broken tile used otherwise for covering the roof of old style dwellings. He took it, went to a '*Vata Vriksha*', stroked the bark till a white gum like substance oozed out. Then he licked it and told me to do the same. This was in compliance with a tip passed on to him on the earlier day by a *sadhu* he met somewhere on the street! Later this practice was (fortunately!) discontinued on the advice of our family physician who was an acknowledged authority on Ayurveda. In his childhood due to some illness one of Buwa's leg was injured and as a consequence it remained and looked weak. Due to his fighting spirit though, he took advantage of this. He was ready on one foot to do anything to improve his health and voice. (And he tried to put his best foot forward in any situation)! He used to measure healthiness in terms of the number of *Surya-Namasakar* one could execute without break. As is known, the Prince of Oundh of that period was praised as well as ridiculed because of his zealousness in promoting *Surya-Namaskar* as the best exercise for all, at all times. Nobody but Buwa could have surpassed him in this enthusiasm!

It might be that the delicateness of his health, or loss of her mother at an early age which turned his father into a wanderer, caused the sense of insecurity that Buwa felt—war-cries, battle-spirit and facing conflicts of one sort or the other remained a constant feature of Buwa's life. This might have kindled in him a permanent combativeness which was also reflected in his music! For example, when the Prince of Oundh suddenly ordered Buwa at a young age to take up the *violin*, it could not have been anything different than being asked to read a book in an unknown language. The natural inclination to enjoy and play with friends, music in the head and an unfamiliar instrument in hands—was this not a battle-situation? Fretless instruments are faithless! They do not seem to trust the player! These recalcitrant music-makers behave as if they have a mind of their own! They appear to produce sounds which they want to and not those which the player intends to! Thus Buwa, without any methodical guidance, model or proved technique to help him began the battle "royal". Through tenacity of purpose and abundant musical calibre he achieved the pioneering task of establishing the instrument as concert-stage music-maker.

In singing, Buwa had to wage two wars—one for his voice and the second against the conventional unyielding pride for one's own *gharana*. With no parental security, supervision and authoritative guidance he passed through some addictions too and that spoilt the voice and health further. But that did not deter him from undertaking rigorous and punishing practising schedules. As some of his contemporaries later described, to fight against the recurring pain in the stomach and head, he would tie scarfs around them but continued with his *riaz*! He had a small place to live in and children would be around, he would close the doors and continue with his music. He had repeated quarrels with his father and ran away to fend for himself but that did not stop his independent and unconventional music-studies. This went on for years.

What victory did he score after these struggles? Buwa used to say, "I gained the capacity to sing something which a true musician would appreciate." The general public found his music 'dry', yet he was respected, and many who knew music well were impressed, provoked and influenced by his music. I am inevitably reminded of what his father, Baba (Pt. Antubuwa Joshi) once said to him. Once, after the famous annual *Shivanand Festival* in Oundh was over, Buwa, Baba and other seniors were having their lunch. As per the protocol, on the first day Buwa had presented vocal music. Baba said, "Gajabuwa, on that day you sang well! Whatever may be your great achievements in fiddle-music, after all you are a vocalist's son. If you had not become a good singer I would have felt something is lacking!" Those were the times when no father was given to sing his son's undeserved praises! Hence, Baba's 'certificate' meant truly a great honour!

The second music-related war that Buwa waged was more complicated, delicate and touched on sensitive issues. No traditional musician in India would be found to praise the other *gharana* or the qualities it projected with easy sincerity. Learning from other *gharana* would also require unusual intensity, courage and conviction. It is to Buwa's credit that there was almost no time-lag between his value-decision about the desirability of learning from a different *gharana* and the actual steps he took towards this ideal! He was not tentative in taking value-decisions pertaining to music and never hesitated to follow up on the decisions arrived at. Pt. Ramkrishnabuwa Vaze, Ustad Bhurji Khan and lastly Ustad Vilayat Hussain—for all of them he had equal respect and also equal interest in the musical ideas they respectively represented. He turned to Pt. Vazebuwa because he was in the Gwalior general mould but could also boast of more complexity and a store of rare *raga*-s. It was not the number of *raga*-s that mattered for Buwa but the mode of making music. Hence, when Baba once asked him in a somewhat ascerbic manner, "Gajabuwa, tell me what did you exactly learn from Pt. Vazebuwa?" Buwa calmly and immediately replied, "I learnt from him how to solve the puzzles that rare *raga*-s are." When Buwa left Pune for Kolhapur to learn from Ustad Bhurji Khan he had rupees 500 in a bank, wife and four kids to look after. And uppermost was the worry about how to set up a new earning routine. But every time I heard him practising what Ustad Bhurji Khan had taught him, it appeared he had no worry about anything else in the world. Once he was convinced about the musical validity of a move to new *guru,* he acted on it and never thought twice about declaring his reasoning publicly.

When he decided to enrich his repertoire and musical knowledge in the Jaipur-mode he had first thought of learning from Smt. Kesarbai Kerkar. I still remember the day when he was readying himself to go to meet her. Before stepping out for any important work he would stand in front of the small, framed photos of Shri Datta and Shivaji Maharaj, close his eyes, fold his palms to utter a prayer and reiterate Shivanand Swami Maharaj's name. I had never seen him so tense and excited as I saw him on that day. Not even for the high-profile *Jugalbandi*-s with Pt. Ravi Shankar, or Ustad Vilayat Khan or concerts with Ustad Thirakwa, not even severe familial crisis or his best friend's misfortunes had touched him so! The tension about Smt. Kesarbai's response weighed on his mind as nothing else had. This is because he wanted to gain a new vision and not merely new data. (This was perhaps the reason why Smt. Kesarbai issued a '*firman*' to all organisers that Pt. Gajananbuwa was not to be allowed an entry to her concerts!) Buwa always declared firmly that he was a *gharana*-follower and not a composition-collector!

His battle-proneness was also reflected in his direct, satirical and sardonic remarks made while teaching. For example, he would nonchalantly declare in a *talim* to whoever was the unhappy recipient, "You are a conch-shell, you can never learn music!" Such pearls of comments and advice were a constant feature of his *talim*. I still remember two of those showered on me, "Ashok, that *tanpura* is better when kept in that corner than when it is in your hands." The other was, "Ashok, do not worry. This is *Kaliyug* and anybody, even you can become a musician." Once he had also ruminatively added, "Ashok, I am comparatively cool-headed now. And in addition, you are not my son but a friend's son. Otherwise by this time I would have thrown this *baya* at your head a thousand times!" As he himself used to play the *theka* on a *baya* while teaching me, I was convinced about the multiple uses of musical instruments in a traditional *guru's* hands! The music-related remarks were also accompanied by remarks or suggestions about how to behave in other walks of life. These ranged from sagacious to salacious! When such rallies were in progress, female disciples would not know where to look and males how not to smile or laugh depending on the degree of directness of the idiom employed! Sometimes my father, always a silent perceiver would remonstrate with Buwa later. But Buwa would say, "I do not have anything except music in my mind when I say this. And you know what I say reaches them effectively!"

Perhaps this same unreasoning directness also led him to his extreme faith in *Swami Maharaj* and other *sadhus* and also to his faith in the role occult played in life. Astrologers, folk-medicine men, miracles and their place in the world, all found a firm place in his life. When Mr. Appa B. Pant was the Indian ambassador in South Africa he proposed that Buwa should visit that country as there was a sizeable number of Indians there who would appreciate Buwa's music. This could have been Buwa's first foreign tour! All preparations were made. New clothes were stitched, lengthy correspondence was made to decide on the concert-schedule etc. And suddenly Buwa got the idea that for such an important undertaking he should get *Swami Maharaj*'s permission. It was ritualistically sought and because the response was in the negative Buwa unhesitantly cancelled the entire tour! Call it superstition or deep faith, it guided Buwa's life except in genuinely musical decisions, where his love for music was an undimmed light always!

Pt. Bhimsen Joshi
(b. 14-2-1922)

17

Pt. Bhimsen Joshi
(b. 14-2-1922)

Kirana and Pt. Bhimsen

Due to many socio-cultural factors it became necessary to re-organise the Hindustani art music during the 19th century. Artists themselves participated in this process and the phenomenon known as *gharana* came into being. If one looks back, the historical transition in the musical ideas concerned broadly moved through stages identifiable as *sampradaya, bani* and *gharana* and each concept contributed to the reorganisation of the *raga* music as the main content of the music-making behaviour. Like other *gharana*-s, Kirana was also a product of this process.

Pt. Bhimsen is a prominent protagonist of the *gharana* today. Let us throw some light on his achievements.

His Achievements

In brief, like his *guru* Pt. Sawai Gandharva he also has crossed the supposed boundaries of his own *gharana*. His voice is not one could easily associate with this *gharana*. It is broad, virile, manly and two-registered. His *alap* often fits the *gharana*-format but the *taan*-phase displays more complexity. The overall attempt in this phase is to dazzle by agility and length. Devotional music forms an unalienable component of his music and it follows the Balgandharva pattern or approach. The overall outlook in music-making is not that of an introvert but one more inclined to extroversion *a la* Ustad Faiyaz Khan. In his performances conscious strategies are followed to bring the audience to submission. First fill their ears and then feed them with music—seems to be the first *sutra* of his incontrovertible musical logic. He is a democratic musician who sees to it that his music reaches everybody.

A Brief Life-sketch

Bhimsen Gururaj Joshi was born on the *Rathasaptami* day. He was named after his grandfather who used to give musico-religious discources with a *tanpura* in his own hands. Obviously Bhimsen's naming was not a sheer coincidence! Though his father sent Bhimsen to a priest to learn *Amarkosh* and such other *sastric* stuff Bhimsen could care only for music. Even music heard from a distance, listening to gramophone records was enough to take him away from everything else. Ultimately he was sent to Janappa Kurtkoti—a practising disciple of Inyatkhan. But somehow Bhimsen was not happy with the arrangement. He took the royal road of running away from home! Singing the two-three odd songs he knew, he travelled by rail without ticket, breathed the prison-air for some days on that account but finally reached Gwalior. In *Madhav Sangeet Vidyalaya* he learnt a little from Pt. Rajabhaiya, then reached Jalandhar and had guidance from Pt. Mangatram—a blind *dhrupad* practitioner. After that for some days he sought guidance from Ustad Mushtaq Hussain. However the time had not arrived to reach the destined *guru* Pt. Sawai Gandharva. He had first heard Pt. Sawai Gandharva in 1930 and Bhimsen's *talim* from him began ultimately from 1935. An added factor influencing his learning music was the ups and downs of the *guru-shishya parampara*. The point is that Bhimsen is a vocalist who sings much more than he has actually learnt! He has imbibed many musical impressions from numerous artists that appealed to him and with *riaz* he has added layers to all that he had learnt. When Pt. Sawai Gandharva's sixty-first birth-day was celebrated Bhimsen sang so well that his *guru* appreciated him as a performer and almost formally accepted him as a true disciple. This was Bhimsen's graduation to stardom one may say. How many concerts has he given so far? To find an answer a full research project may have to be launched—as very often he has given three concerts in a single day!

Voice, Vocalism and Main Features of His Music

The most striking feature of his music is its ability to appeal to knowledgeables as well as to those who are musically innocent! Every stratum of the heterogenous audience gets something from his music. This may perhaps be compared to a good dramatic performance. In a way every musician (nay artist) craves to achieve this wide-based appeal. To say that my art is only for the cognocenti really amounts to a weak apologetic stance a musician adopts in self-defence. How does Bhimsen perform his magic?

The first distinctive feature that made this possible is of course his voice and the way he used it. Befitting the name of the character in *Mahabharata* namely Bhima, his voice has strength and sonority. Generally, volume of a voice is not a dimension which can compete with pitch and timbre in contributing to the ultimate musical effect. Humans do not have much tolerance-level in the context of volume. As a consequence, not much artistry is possible by sheer dynamic changes. Is it not significant that disco and such other musical expressions are held objectionable in many cultures because of their loudness? And yet it cannot be denied that the contrastive use of thin/delicate and loud/voluminous projections catches attention easily, immediately and of many. There are very few musicians like Pt. Bhimsen who employ this strategy so effectively. Even the uninformed and heterogenous audiences are attracted by this exploration of the volume-dimension.

However, a technical detail needs to be mentioned. The contrastive use of thick-thin etc. cannot be merely described as effective change in vocal volume. Technically speaking, Pt. Bhimsen uses both the registers of voice. This is why at the lower level his voice generates effects of solidity, richness while at the upper levels it becomes bright, thin and adept in quickly moving to upper levels. In his fast *taan* one does not experience volume. Their effectiveness is due to the pointed brightness of the upper register. It is beneficial to remember here that Roshan Ara Begum, a senior artist of the same *gharana* was an example of a similar but qualitatively better balancing of the registers in her music-making. The *taan*-s need a discussion a little later—only their reliance on a certain kind of vocalisation was to be noted at this juncture.

Selection of *Raga*-s and Their Presentation

It is true that Pt. Bhimsen's repertoire is wider than the normal Kirana vogue. He knows that to have a new and different *raga*-frame is comparable to getting a new role to play. It amounts to getting an opportunity of telling a new story. He often selects *raga*-s such as *poorva kalyan, ahir bhairav* and *maru behag* but irrespective of *raga* the Kirana strategy of elaborating *raga* methodically, in a step- by-step manner is pursued. *Alap* in which elaboration is centred on each note and the pace of the tonal movement is kept slow and are easily perceivable. Often this makes his performance highly predictable.Obviously the method cannot be applied to *raga* such as *adana* or *shankara* as these *raga*-s enjoy inherent tempo which is inclined to be recognisably fast.

Yet another principle that appears to rule his *raga*-choice or preference is to focus on *raga*-s with intrinsic mood or evocative power. What factors make a *raga* mood-evocative is of course a question to be discussed in Musical Aesthetics and at great length. However, it is easily accepted for example, that *raga yaman* is more evocative than *raga nata-bilawal*, or *raga*-s such as *patmanjari* or *triveni* are not likely to be evocative. It is significant that Indian musicological literature since 12th century has recorded that mathematically more than 35,000 *raga*-frames are possible and yet the defining characteristic of *raga* handed down specifically mentions the feature of entertaining, recreational capacity of a scalar arrangement of 12 notes as the criterion. One may say that in the performing practice of artists such as Pt. Bhimsen, this definition is well reflected. If one decides to sing/present only such *raga*-s that have the innate evocative capacity, then the number of actively circulated *raga*-s is drastically reduced. Pt. Bhimsen has always maintained that in his *gharana* they lay store by the *raga* described as '*aam raga*'. Rare *raga*-s are likely to generate an intellectual appeal and a pleasure but that can happen for a few and for a short while. To bring in something new, attractive and reliable, Pt. Bhimsen has decided to look elsewhere than grammatical novelty and this decision seems to have backing from his audience.

Emphasis on *Alap* and Scope for *Taan*

A step-by-step elaboration of *raga* would necessarily mean giving importance to the melodic aspect of music-making. To do this, words are conducive not only as meaningful units but as vehicles that carry the melodic load. Each word as a sound-pattern is basically a combination of vowels and consonants. Consonants require lesser breath than the vowels and hence the importnace of words of the song-text. This is the reason why so many of vocalists rely on *bol-alap*, a strategy in which melodic elaboration is realized through combining word-contours with melodic clusters. The Kirana way actually consists of two technical stratregies pressed into service. Firstly, the words are treated as sound patterns and not necessarily as patterns of meanings. Secondly, in this *gharana* all articulation is enveloped in the vowel "O". Now this is a vowel which perhaps enjoys the maximum inherent resonance and hence the Kirana projection of words and melodic units (with the superimposition of the "O") sounds fuller, rounded and ear-filling. Thus it becomes possible to produce a tone that can leave a tonal shadow behind and bestow on the musical progression a unique power of making a suastained impact. In sum, selection of *raga*, presentation of musical ideas and the vocal tone produced—all aim at providing a resonant continuity of an important perceptual effect.

Obvioulsy Pt. Bhimsen realised the need to do something un-Kirana like to create a niche for his music. For that purpose he employed two strategies: A *taan*-phase in which the emergent patterns were different from the usual Kirana music. Secondly, he also extended his genre-repertoire beyond the usual Kirana pail.

The *Taan*

He keeps the *taans* perceptibly fast and the phase is notably isolated from his *alap*-work. They are complex and long, and as tempo is not changed in the *khayal* his *taan*-s appear more fast—this is how his *taan* can generally be described. Ustad Abdul Karim Khan, the main founder-protagonist of the Kirana music also wanted to include fast *taan*-s in his music-making but due to his specific vocal technique and approach to music, his *taans* never appeared efffortless and clear in patterning. Pt. Bhimsen has achieved more success in this respect. (Roshan Ara Begum, the senior Kirana artist who unfortunately could not reach wider public was still more successful in her *taan*-presentations. She could in addition also be almost lyrical in this phase of music as becomes apparent from her recordings!) Pt. Bhimsen has frequently admitted that he owes the complexity in his *taan* to the musical influence of the Jaipur artist Smt. Kesarbai Kerkar. However, it is perhaps truer to say that the initial stressing of the *taan*-notes and designs that rely on repetition of the same note being the chief features of his *taan*—he also owes a debt to the Agra way in this respect. In addition is the pervasive effect of vocalisation permeated with the dramatic contrast-effect produced by his employment of two registers as mentioned earlier. No voice can remain unchanged from *alap* to *taan* and the roundness, resonance perceived in the lower octaves and *alap* can hardly be maintained in *taan* and in higher octaves. As a consequence voices invariably sound different in fast pace and on high notes. But in case of Pt. Bhimsen, this change is too radical. His voice in *taan* almost sounds half-articulated and thin. It also distorts the tonal values of the individual notes in the *taan*. Too often only the initial and the last notes are actually heard and the audience is compelled to deduce or infer the component notes in between the *taan*. His *taan* do not emerge from his *alap*-work. It moves away from that a great deal and in many respects. However, the effectiveness of the speed, strength and dramatic quality of the *taan* cannot be missed. The road he takes is not convincing but it must be admitted that he reaches his destination.

Pt. Bhimsen does not seem to be keen on contributing something new through the aspects of *tala* and rhythm-patterns as such. There is consequently no special accent on phases such as *bol-laya, bol-taan* or *tihai*. Not that these are completely eschewed, but there is nothing ear-catching even though he normally includes them in his performances. For example, employment of rare *tala*, compositions in such or compositions displaying rhythmic complexities do not get a place of pride in his music-making. Of course this is not to suggest that to be methodical in music means a mandatory inclusion of such features and without them the stature of the musician suffers a setback on that count. It is ultimately the prerogative of the artist to concentrate on whatever musical aspect he chooses to explore at his own risk. The ability to create music of quality is the ultimate goal in the final analysis. If that is reached everything else becomes insignificant.

Performance of Other Genres

To consider Pt. Bhimsen Joshi in the concert-setting indicates that we must attempt consideration of non-*khayal* genres which he presents with so much appeal. The category of Indian religious music consists of a sub-variety identified as devotional music. Pt. Bhimsen excels in it in addition to the stage-music from the tradition of the Marathi music drama. Pt. Bhimsen certainly owes some of his musical appeal to these 'non-classical' forms of vocal music.

Firstly, a significant proportion of his concert-music is earmarked for rendering these non-classical forms. Earlier his devotional music was largely dependent on compositions popularised by late Balgandharva, the legendary actor-singer on the Marathi stage. Later he launched a programme called *Santvaani* in which he sang *abhang* compositions of the Marathi saint-poets. They became so popular that they became an unalienable components of his public music-making. However in features like the lilt, tone and the involvement in his singing he nearly stuck to the Balgandharva-mode. The kind of compositions that heavily circulated in the category of Marathi devotional music employ a *tala* called *dhumali*. It has an inherent tempo and design of time-divisions that (like similar other *tala* current in different regional continuities of the Indian devotional music) are easily accessible to all. More importantly, due to numerous socio-cultural factors, the *tala* projects pulses which succeed in casting a somewhat hypnotic spell over the listeners irrespective of their knowledge of music. Balgandharva created a prototype of rendering compositions set in this *tala* which were a combination of straight, soft and sophisticated musical statements that struck a balance between repetition and new elaboration in the melodic as well as the rhythmic aspect of the genre. Apart from following on this tested and successsful pattern Pt. Bhimsen's specially composed items explore a larger variety of *raga*-s for the tunes and in addition is not shy of using his body-language in suggesting the emotional thrust of the rendered compositions. Balgandharva was in a way handicapped because the context of his music-making was mostly provided by the female roles he was playing which naturally conditioned his singing and everything pertaining to it (including the body-language). As a consequence Pt. Bhimsen's performances prove to be an efficient mixture of involved music-making with a marked extrovert appeal that accomodates audience of all sorts. Further, Pt. Bhimsen also succeeds in maintaining the 'classical vocalist's touch' in his singing and that also sets his renditions apart. When it is remembered that Smt. Lata Mangeshkar also has brought out an album of *Abhang* compositons which carry an impress of another genre of popular music, mamely the *bhavgeet,* it will become clear that if the devotional corpus in the tradition passes through various categories of music and processes according to its own norms, the activity does not become inauthentic and hence objectionable in itself. The muscial legitimacy of the effort will have to be judged by the criteria related to the category. What Lata has presented is a completely precomposed, orchestrated

While I was heading the University Music Centre (Bombay) we had arranged concerts to celebrate the centenary of Pt.Vishnu Digambar Paluskar in the famed Convocation Hall. Pt. Bhimsen Joshi's was the inaugural concert. At that time much was talked about his habitual and untimely alchohol consumption. Hence I was a bit worried and kept him constant company. He must have noticed my extraordinary sense of hospitality! He sang and the concert was a great success. The *raga*-s *multani* and *yaman* which he presented are still fresh in many listeners'memories. After the concert we went out of the Hall and sat on a bench in the garden. Pt. Bhimsen then turned to me and asked (rather pointedly I thought), "So how was it: Hope it was upto the prestige of the University—You must have noticed I did not take anything, only gave everything!" Then he laughed heartily and joyfully.

and recorded body of devotional music suited to the mass media and her singing is also accordingly mapped. As a consequence versions of Marathi devotional music presented respectively by Balgandharva, Pt. Bhimsen and Lata will need to be differently evaluated and commented upon. What we have analysed here is an art-musician's version in which he has certainly extended boundaries of the traditional Marathi devotional singing.

Compared to his devotional music, Pt. Bhimsen's stage music does not add anything new to the musical heritage. He sings songs made famous by his *guru's guru* i.e. Ustad Abdul Karim Khan (e.g. "*De hata sharanagata*", or "*Ugich ka kanta*") and makes them musically attractive through the use of his usual armoury namely, sonorous voice, tuneful rendering and impressive articulation. It is known that he has also sung effectively and efficiently for advertising jingles and as a playback for at least 19 films. But these are to be taken as side-products of his singing craftsmanship.

Pt. Bhimsen Joshi has continuously produced abundant music till very recent times, but has not looked beyond the boundaries of his own musical culture. The continuity and self-absorbed quality of his music places his achievement high on the musico-cultural scale.

Pt. Kumar Gandharva
(8-4-1924 to 12-1-1992)

18

Pt. Kumar Gandharva

(8-4-1924 to 12-1-1992)

A Brief Life-sketch

Shivaputra Sidramappa Komkali was born in Sulebhavi (Belgaon) in Karnataka. This region, situated in the southern part of India is musically significant because serious and meritorious studies of both Hindustani and Carnatic art musical systems are carried out there and so, in a way Shivaputra's locale was symptomatic of the spirit of musical synthesis. Shivaputra's father was fond of music and Ustad Abdul Karim Khan was his favourite artist. Shivaputra earned immediate name as a child prodigy because at the tender age of 6 he began singing 'like' Ustad Abdul Karim Khan! What was notable was that this was not mere imitation—it was a qualitative performance with mature musicianship evident throughout. In 1936 (his age 12) Shivaputra gave a concert in Bombay and everybody began talking about him. At this juncture Sidramappa took a wise decision of taking the boy to Prof. B.R. Deodher. Professor Deodher—as he was called—was a disciple of Pt. Vishnu Digambar Paluskar. A widely known and respected musicologist Deodher-Master was especially famous for his penchant for collecting musical compositions and influences from various sources and systematising them. He has been selective as well as accomodative and this enabled him to 'teach' Shivaputra, a child prodigy for about 10-12 years in a unique way. His was not a routine *talim*. He would make Shivaputra listen to various musicians, analyse and discuss their music and then teach him relevant compositions. In addition, Shivapurra gave concerts and listened to wide-ranging music with a new vision. Thus Shivaputra developed into Pt. Kumar Gandharva and was so acknowledged. In 1947, Pt. Kumar Gandharva married Smt. Bhanumati Kauns, a sophisticated, art-loving lady with a musical ability of a different sort. Unfortunately Pt. Kumar Gandharva contracted tuberculosis of the lungs and was out of public action and view for about seven years. This was at the time when this malady was considered incurable. He retired to Devas to carry on the fight—a period in which he was entirely given to introspection because he was not allowed even to touch the *tanpura*! Till about 1952 he was almost bed-ridden.

However, a fighter that he was, with Bhanumati's active involvement he carried out what can be described as performing researches into the rich folk music of Malwa region he was located in. His researches enabled him to explore problems such as origin and spread of musical traditions, the process of emergence of new *raga*-s, the role of *tala* in different kinds of music, etc. Most importantly he was able to formulate his own musical idiom and a way of presentation closely and exclusively identifiable with him. Thus his musical personality grew unimaginably and qualitatively.

When in 1954 he returned to the concert stage the eager and anxious audience heard music which was entirely different from what they had expected. Even when he presented known genres, *raga*-s and compositions, the music was unfamiliar to many and as a result ecstatic responses as well as confused critical murmurs were heard about the Kumar-music.

From 1962 to 1983 he received many prestigeous awards and honours. When he died on 11th January 1992 he had successfully created a wide following for his musical ideas and ensured a high place for himself as a composer, performer as well as a performer-thinker.

What and Where was the Difference?

Firstly, his *raga*-elaboration was more lyrical and evocative in a different way. Concentration on creating a *raga*-mood, secondary importance accorded to the grammatical correctness of the *raga* and nearly doing away with the rigidly sequential character of musical phases stood out as significant features. The overall elaboration did not follow the step-by-step method. The movement towards musical climaxes did not tread the path marked by sequence of phases known as *alap, bol-alap, bol-taan* and *taan*. This made his music unpredictable but it was also characterised by an intense evocative urge to make music. The *raga*-s Pt. Kumar created himself were based on folk-tunes. In such *raga*-s individual notes had unconventional pitch-values and the intervals employed also generated different *raga*-images. The usage also appeared to set aside the traditional musical logic. Such *raga*-s have been musicologically described as *dhun-raga*-s i.e. *raga*-s based on a melodic phrase or two. Pt. Kumar's *bhajan*-compositions identified as *nirguni,* surely added to the usual set of devotional compositions rendered from a concert stage.

He highly preferred the medium tempo. His voice was pointedly tuneful, thin and quick-moving in short bursts. Pt. Kumar's voice and intonation were clearly able to unerringly pick up rhythmic and melodic nuances. His performance also exuded a pervasive self-confidence. He later published an anthology of some self-created and some traditional *raga*-s and compositions he composed. The anthology, with 136 compositions in which 57 traditional and 11 new *raga*-s find place, also confirms his views about the close emotive relationship of the textual and musical ideas. Till about 1979 he conceived, composed and presented 11 thematic programmes and they too were a testimony to his inventive urge and the resulting interesting music.

Pt. Kumar's Musical Framework

I would like to describe Pt. Kumar's musical framework as an eclectic one bent on assimilating varied musical essences. As others have been inclined to describe him and his music as an exclamation mark or an intriguing question mark, my reference to a binding/confining phenomenon like a framework may appear ridiculous or even objectionable. As the artist whose music does not ostensibly fit in any of the existing *gharana*-s or one, whose *guru*-lineage cannot be traced easily, he has surely generated a following which takes an unthinking pride in his being entirely different or unique. In my opinion it is a mistake to consider uniqueness or a total difference as adequate criteria for assessing anybody's achievement. His artistry is not so artificial (i.e. man-made) as to have no connections whatsoever with the Hindustani musical tradition in a larger perspective. A live art is to be judged by equally live criteria.

Gwalior, Jaipur, Kirana, Pt. Omkarnath, Evocative Quality, etc.

The premise is that Pt. Kumar's artistry is an inevitable result of a developmental dialectic of art music traditions circulating in Maharashtra. This artistry is not a product of fossilised tendencies but belongs to a living tradition. The artistry strikes many as radically different because it consists of relevant and performing musical components evolving a structure different from that usually practised or heard. For example the formal elements of his art can be listed briefly as: it obviously included the musical flow of the Gwalior, pointed tunefulness of the Kirana, inclination to a convoluted presentation by registering responses to rhythmic nuances *a la* Jaipur, evocative intonation in *raga*-music (like Pt. Omkarnath) and emotive articulation in non-*raga* items or genres usually known as 'light music'. It must be stated that these and similar other components existed independently, in different ways and in differing proportions, even before Pt. Kumar came on the scene. However they were not combined in a manner similar to the Kumar-way. Thus it is possible to state that Pt. Kumar is the only one who had deviated from the current tradition with courage. Prior to him, Pt. Bhaskarbuwa and Pt. Vazebuwa had also deviated and thus Pt. Kumar was not doing anything unprecedented. This is the background on which the nature of his deviation and the agents or features of his deviation are not to be construed.

Pt. Kumar's music follwed the Gwalior-tradition in the way it kept the music flowing and by adopting medium tempo to serve the purpose in this respect. Of course it is not sufficient merely to select a tempo. One should have a positive relationship with it. The Gwalior *gharana* achieves this feat through the strategy of progressions that deliberately choose to avoid recognising the *tala*-divisions or by moving around them except when they represent major division-points such as *sama* and *khali*. (In contrast the Jaipur keeps track of even the half-beats.) The Gwalior melodic movements are therefore more unimpeded and that too through entire presentations. Pt. Kumar had opted for this strategy.

However there is a twist to the situation. Though the choice of medium tempo is conducing to the flowing quality of the Gwalior-music it is also equally aided by the choice of '*aam*' *raga* and a *tala* which is in wide circulation. Here Pt. Kumar deviated as he favoured intricate tonal patterns in elaborating *raga*-s, both usual and unusual. In doing this he seemed to incline towards the Jaipur way of relating music to *tala*-movement. Obviously, this made his music more complex. Yet his music did not become 'intellectually conceived' because (due to the Kirana and Pt. Omkarnath's influences that have permeated his approach) he never abandoned the evocative tone in vocalisations. The Kirana avoids employing the undistorted vowel "Aa" for voice-projection and constantly tries to keep the tone resonant and the intonation pointed. However, the enveloping "O" vowel approach of the Kirana is hardly conducive in any other phase of musical elaboration except the *alap*. Pt. Kumar was heard to employ the joint-vowels "Ya" and "Ye" frequently in his singing. He must have done so to achieve the pointed tonal projection. (Their inclusion in the *taan*-phase however needs a separate discussion.) It is perceived that Pt. Kumar never employed "Aa" for the low as well as high notes. (To some extent he changed the stragtegy in his presentation of Balgandharva music.) In other words the limited Kirana influence served him (as described) in melodic elaboration—adding to the Gwalior and Jaipur colours located in specific undertakings mentioned earlier.

However, the 'original/conventional' Kirana type of evocative quality was confined to notes. It left the articulation of words, relationship to rhythm untouched and in fact sometimes a rather blurring of the precise *raga*-boundaries was also perceived. This is where Pt. Omkarnath's strategies came to Pt. Kumar's rescue. Pt. Omkarnath's evocative approach was more accomodative as it included consideration of 'meaningful' pronunciation of key-words and a more flexible employment of vocal-techniques. Apart from following Pt. Omkarnath's trail of an overall evocative tone accompanied by flexible vocal techniques, Pt. Kumar also explored words as sound patterns. This became noticeable when words from dialects or language such as Rajasthani (e.g. "the" "*mhare*" or consonant such as "na"(ण) in Indian languages—were pronounced. As otherwise most of the Hindustani compositions are in Braj, this emphatic employment of somewhat unusual consonants in other dialects added a distinctive tonal colour. In fact combined with music, their 'meanigfulness' became underlined.

Due to his principle of evocative employment of words Pt. Kumar's music relied heavily on the phase of '*bol-alap*'. Selecting clusters of words from the text and embellishing them to elaborate the musical idea is a favoured strategy of what is known as *Sugam Sangeet*, in which genres such as *thumri*, *bhajan* etc. predominate. This was a feature ever-present in Pt. Kumar's singing. Even when he rendered a genre of music known as *tarana* (which is mostly composed of meanigless syllables such as *taan*, *dere, dir dir*) he liked to treat them as if they were 'meaningful' in the usual sense of the term. On such occasions he appeared to bestow emotional shades on these units.

The *Tappa*-influenced *Khayal*

Analysed methodically, the specific components which made Kumar's music or the act of combining them were not new features in Maharashtra and also in many other regions. Under the circumstances where and what is the difference between other musical achievers and Pt. Kumar? As he was a prominent *khayal*-singer it is appropriate to examine the matter further in respect of *khayal*-music.

I am of the opinion that his *khayal*-rendering was influenced by *tappa*, a genre that enjoys some distinctive features in Hindustani art music. Briefly enumerating the essential features of *tappa* and noting their appearance in Pt. Kumar's music should prove helpful in making the argument clearer.

Essentially, *tappa* is bright singing/playing. Instead of proceeding note by note, sequentially and in an unhurried manner as in *khayal*, *tappa* prefers to select a few tonal clusters, embellish them in an intricate manner and move swiftly forward to another tonal cluster for a similar exploration. In other words, selective and highly localised patterning, a swift pace that is repeatedly interrupted and an overall fast progression makes the *tappa*.

Along with the delicate and yet forceful types of embellishments *tappa* also relies on a special feature, the decorative element. Known as *khatka*, *murki* etc. these embellishments are notably decorative and delicate in spite of their inherent speed and forcefulness. They necessarily bring forward a cluster of notes to form a pattern—self-sufficient to some extent in their appeal. Decidedly, they weigh in favour of craftsmanship than evocation or emotionality. They arouse admiration rather than evocation from the listener. The element of surprise which predominates also means that there is an unpredictability and some suddenness and this is what *tappa* as a genre usually offers to its listeners. This brief explanation of the nature and technique of the genre should suffice to bring out Pt. Kumar's specific way of falling back on it. Even when he was not presenting the genre he exploited some aspects of it in his *khayal*-presentation. Thus unlike in *tappa*, he was careful about adhering to the *raga*-norms or the grammatical profile but technical features associated with *tappa* were brought into play. Hence the *taans* were intricate but sharp and short, embellishments, so abundant in *tappa* were also allowed scope. On the other hand, *taan* in medium tempo, the *gamak*-mode of moving melodic lines and *bol-taans* were nearly omitted. Inclusion of specific *tappa*-aspects and keeping distance from some *khayal*-features was the dual strategy Pt. Kumar followed in effectively fusing the two genres.

In Maharashtra there is still a large class of Pt. Kumar's followers and the historical background of this situation is understandable. The Maharashtra branch of Gwalior *gharana*, led by Pt. Balkrishnabuwa Ichalkaranjikar, did not include *tappa* in its repertoire even though the parent Gwalior *gharana*-s had explored *tappa* with relish. In Maharashtra, the modified Gwalior, Agra, Jaipur and Kirana *gharana*-s drew a parallelogram of musical forces but all the four gradually became rigid in stance and structure. Under the circumstances a creative endeavour was needed to break away, both proportionately and qualitatively. Marathi stage music offered a rich alternative but that was specific to the genre. And this was the reson why the stylised twists and turns of the *tappa* proved useful to 'liberate' art music in Maharashtra and this also explains the great attraction Pt. Kumar exercised over the music-loving community in the region. The large number of younger musicians who are polarised between music of Ustad Bade Ghulam Ali and Pt. Kumar offer a corroboration of the developmetal process noted above. Pt. Kumar's music could not make a great dent in Punjab or areas in which Hindustani music was already following the *tappa*-patterning and aesthetically this was inevitable.

The Ruling Formal Principles in Pt. Kumar's Music

In sum, three basic principles in Pt. Kumar's music need to be remembered: (1) His eclecticism i.e. efforts to combine various elements from different *gharana*-s prove the flexibility of Hindustani music-making and he deserved credit for this. (2) Without going in for mystically oriented descriptions of his artistry it is possible to analyse the evocative musical power he was able to capture because identifiable formal elements in music can be identified as forces enabling emergence of a cohesive design of musical ideas. (3) His great impact on Maharashtra, a region rich in vocal art music of all sorts works as a pointer to the truth that every creative endeavour has a history. His achievement also underscores the fact that tradition always has room for change and innovation, as well as continuity or stability.

On this background it should be possible to analyse the overall effect of Pt. Kumar's music.

Musical Consequences of Pt. Kumar's Art

No music-study can ignore regional perspective and hence Pt. Kumar's music needs a close look as music that generated a large following in an area undeniably rich in Hindustani art music. However, it is not the number of followers of his music that is our concern. He requires attention and analysis because he continued to experiment as a composer as well as a performer. If an experimenter is also an effective artist he becomes more important because he not only shapes the taste but also qualitatively changes the hunger associated with it. Pt. Kumar's experiments therefore require a closer scrutiny. It would therefore be appropriate to examine Pt. Kumar's experiments in some detail.

His Experimentation

A prominent feature was that his experimentation was not confined to any one genre. It consisted of his experimentation with *tappa*, *thumri, tarana, bhajan, bhavpada, lokgeeet* and *natyapada*. All had a definite place in his interpretational experimentation. In each case he wanted to have a fresh look at the genre concerned and present it in a new light. For example, he tried to make the *tappa* evocative, attempted to establish a loose but inherent relationship between linguistic and musical profiles of *bhajan*, go back to singing *bhavgeet* as a *bhavpada* which was its early *avatar*, make efforts to extend the musical boundaries of folk songs and folk tunes, to compose new *khayal* as well as to reinterpret the traditional ones, and so on and so forth. Further, in all these he aimed at registering a new impact that can be closely and easily identified with his music. Not that all his experiments were equally successful, but what is more important is to note the wide range of his experiments. This is of some significance in itself.

The second important feature was that his urge to experiment was never based on denying the validity of the current tradition. While attempting anything 'new' or 'experimental', Pt. Kumar never suggested a complete irrelevance or obsolescence of the traditional or the older. He was intent on searching for the origins or original inspirations of the music in circulation in order to establish a positive and living relationship with it. One may say that to some extent he was thus a partial revivalist. He was certainly pro-change but not pro-revolution or even pro-evolution. He sought origins of old-new *raga*-s in folk-music. He tried locating the modern song (*geet*) in its original form i.e. *pada*. He intended to present the great Balgandharva stage-music as concert-music without the dramatic overload of the original. Reiterating the position that *khayal* was distinguished from *dhrupad* because of the liberating mode of the former, he argued that *khayal* needed to be liberated from its recently acquired rigid framework. He sensed that the major tendency of the *tarana* was to present sound-patterns in their pristine (i.e. meaningless) beauty but noted that the recent trends have nearly converted it into a speed-maniac's delight (as it sometimes happens in the '*jhala*'-phase of instrumental music). He hoped to revive the original thrust of the genre. All these features of his music did not indicate a person keen on an unquestioning following of a tradition but a person announcing an intense seeker of it.

Perhaps this search for tradition was also functioning on another level. For example, one characteristic of the romantics in literary movements is identified as their keen attraction for the past through which they want to re-view the present. Pt. Kumar provided a similar story in music. In other words, not accepting the current musical profile of Hindustani music as it was, he wanted to mount a search for its original spirit and having permeated himself with it, attempted to set up a contemporary hierarchy. In a way the adjacent past had no place in this scheme unless it too was reshaped by the earlier past that Pt. Kumar was invoking. Naturally it was inevitable that his music proved so different.

One more aspect of Pt. Kumar's experimentation needs to be noted seperately. Just as a 'new' poet (apart from writing new poetry) has also to create a new reader for it, similar is any artist's case. Pt. Kumar certainly succeeded in creating an audience for his own music. Unfortunately one suspects that it (i.e. the new audience) is expectably more rigid and stereotyped than eclectic. Pt. Kumar knew that his new music has an old traditon. His followers do not seem to appreciate this truth.

After having talked about the nature of Pt. Kumar's experimentalism it would seem logical to proceed to discuss its effects. However, this is directly related to the fact of his performing ability to present his innovations.. While his experimentalism determined his music, his effectiveness in performance made his experimentalism significant. This inter-relationship makes it necessary to devote attention to his performance.

The Reception of Pt. Kumar's Music-performance and Experiments

Those who are influenced by his performed music can be divided into two major groups—one is of singers and the other of listeners. Those musicians who can be roughly described as belonging to the earlier generation found that his singing pursued different ideals than their own in almost all aspects of music-making. In this context, the fact to be noted is that generally one tends to accept major deviation in one or at the most a few respects but it is difficult to accept minor deviations in every identifiable aspect. This is natural as minor but pervasive deviations make the process of making sense of the numerous formal or form-giving elements more difficult. Those musicians of the earlier generation who were able to undergo this process could receive Pt. Kumar's music not as an act of defiance but as a sincere attempt to re-systematise or re-map Hindustani music to a great extent and translate the intention in performing ideas. On the other hand, those many who could not undertake the process felt Pt. Kumar's music as a major example of distorting, if not demolishing the tradition, in conception and performance. This class carried a deep feeling of 'hurt'. This adverse consequence of Pt. Kumar's music should cause some worry because of the fact that many in this class have been serious musicians and music-thinkers. Of course to what extent Pt. Kumar could be held responsible for this sectional antipathy is a moot question. Pt. Kumar could have been held responsible if it could be shown that specific features of Kumar-music were directly related to some responses of the 'hurt' listeners. Admittedly it does not seem to be so. That a prominent musician's art should cause this kind of schism in taste only indicates that a deeper study of the societal taste in music is necessary.

Even among the musicians of the younger generation the responses were mixed. One very bold effect has been the tendency or even readiness to redefine the art-aspect of music-making. The performing musical philosophies in Maharashtra had become so over-defined that almost all music had become extremely predictable. The joy of surprise or sometimes even of the non-fulfillment of expectation, was almost lost. Along with the charged descriptions of the *gharana*-disciplines, methods, loyalty to *guru* etc., a process of a mechanical reproduction of the learned ideas was making its presence heavily felt in all music-making. The art of singing was overshadowed by the craft of singing. Compared to such performances Pt. Kumar's music defied pre-determination of a performing map and consequently unpredictability regained a place. This makes music-making and listening to it alert processes. It was as if Pt. Kumar was putting forward a contemporary vogue of allowing music to grow according to its own predilections. Of course this is not to suggest that a perfomring outline did not exist in Pt. Kumar's music or that it was not perceivable at all. Perhaps the better way of referring to his performing plan is to state that the plan itself had room for introducing last-minute or intuitive changes. This lessened the possibilities of sameness, mechanical approach, etc.

However, (seen in a larger perspective) for any performer reaching the limits of his innovative capacities at some point of career does not lessen the importance of his contribution. In poetry it is often seen that a new poet generates a new consciousness about vocabulary or imagery of poetry and later some other poet makes a new sense out of the same or similar resources to create a different kind of poetry. These later creations do not deny the contribution of the earlier phase. In music too a parallel phenomenon may exist. Pt. Kumar's music did not register a denial of the earlier creative efforts but added to the existing resources through new sound-imgery, and ways of making it concrete in performance. As a result the art-activity in music has been enriched. A related consequence is that the younger generation is less resistant to view art-music as having a wider spectrum than is usually accepted. Folk-music, stage songs etc. have gained a new legitimacy in their eyes as musical expressions performable on a concert stage.

Some questionable 'gains' also need to be mentioned. Musicians influenced by Pt. Kumar have unfortunately begun to put more faith in dazzling discontinuities and the attempt is to locate these as products of a fundamental principle of musical construction. As a consequence more room is given to brighter embellishing effects such as *khatka, murki*, clusters of notes posing as short *taan*. The truth that in *raga*-music these and such other effects are mere vehicles to project melodic/musical ideas, is almost ignored.

Pt. Kumar's pervasive use of the joint vowel 'ye' as the main carrier for his vocalisations cannot be considered ideal and worth-imitating. That in the totality of his music it could be ignored, cannot be interpreted as accceptance of its musical validity or legitimacy. This 'ye' sound has nothing to recommend its persistent use in place of the traditional Indian preference for the vowel 'a'. It is instructive to note that Pt. Kumar himself tried valiantly to replace his 'ye' with the conventional 'a' in his performances such as presentation of Balgandharva's flawless music. In all probability the 'ye' sound was a consequence of Pt. Kumar's health which suffered a set-back early in his career.

A trenchant observation has been made that the Kumar-followers are so intensely under his influence that they are almost intolerant vis-à-vis music made by other artists. This only means that the essence of Pt. Kumar's eclecticism is entirely lost on his followers. This certainly is deplorable though to what extent Pt. Kumar is answerable for the attitude, remains a question. It can be maintained that this is in reaction to a class of traditional musicians'views on Pt. Kumar's music. More importantly history is witness to the fact that more intense, one-sided, rigid or monochrome a view or philosophy in art happens to be, the surer is its early demise. The very nature of artistic activity denies room for closed attitudes and art successfully manages to weather the situation sooner than later.

Among his listeners there was a section of the audience for whom to attend a Kumar-music concert denoted an 'in thing' to be religiously undertaken on the lines of attending a Krishnamoorthy-discourse or a cricket match. Such sections are always interested in 'seeing and in being seen'! This kind of audience may help in giving the artist or the event some usable 'mouth-publicity' but it hardly desrves discussion in a serious consideration of artistic phenomenon as such.

But there can be a section which first turns to a particular music out of curiosity and then goes on to note its observation that the music was interesting and different but was not comprehensible. This audience may change gradually for the better in its appreciation-level but if it continues to applaud music only because of its apparent incomprehensiveness then it may prove harmful to the art-behaviour in general. The concerned artist has to be cautious about the vociferous appreciation of this non-knowing section. In the final analysis an artist has to accept a partial responsibility in cultivating the taste of an audience. Pt. Kumar's overt preference for presenting 'unknown' *raga*-s and compositions that were often composed by him perhaps needed reconsideration in this respect. Re-interpretation of more of the traditional corpus could have been more conducive in re-shaping the taste of the audience. Audience may, in general, remain more interested in re-cognition than in cognition but ultimately this needs to be discouraged.

Pt. Kumar's presentations were also characterised by a kind of dramatisation though they were not out and out theatrical. His employment and use of words was more inclined to elocution than music-making. It seemed that his attempt was to take advantage of the stereotyped or broad linguistic meaningfulness than appeal through musical suggestivity. On such occasions gradually and almost imperceptibly hand-movements and other gestures began indicating melody. The sequence of music-making and the secondary and musically optional gestural communication was nearly changed. All this lacks relevance in art music. One is reminded of the stylised theatrical-presentations that depended heavily on property, costumes etc. because nuanced acting could not be seen by the audience due to performing conditions that prevailed. As is known, this theatric tradition has its own place but in other categories of expression and not in art music.

An important artist has to be comprehensively considered with no claims to the finality of judgement. This is an attempt in that direction.

I never reviewed music concerts unless I felt that it was a part of my music-studies to do so. Pt. Kumar Gandharva's music-concerts or his thematic presentations were for my generation exciting and provoking. I found it rewarding to review them. I hold that reviewing, criticism, aesthetic appreciation and philosophical discussion are all relevant and related levels at which a work of art can be approached. This is the background on which the following discussion of Pt. Kumar's presentations is to be understood. As the period of each piece is noted it becomes an additional data for the evaluative exercise undertaken here. Most of the review articles written are of the first performances of the presentations in Mumbai.

Geetvarsha (December 1966)

In this thematic presentation Pt. Kumar Gandharva put forward 25 compositions subdivided in three parts and the total presentation time was about three hours. The three subdivisions were identified respectively as the months of *Jyeshtha-Ashadh, Ashadh-Shravan* and *Bhadrapad-Ashwin* representing the rainy phases described as '*Bauchhar*' '*Jhadi*' and '*Rimzim*' respectively consisting of seven, eight

One of the fortunate features of my work in the University Music Centre, Mumbai, was the warm feeling most of the musicians had about the place. Most of them came with an assurance that all those who love music are always welcome there. Hence artists used to come, chat, discuss music and recite/hum/sing compositons etc. Once Pt. Kumar Gandharva came and said, "Ashok, I hear that you have built up a good collection of music in your studio. Play back something good to me." Of course I readily agreed and we proceeded to the Studio. Knowing about Pt.Kumar's own collection and his careful listening to all recorded music I was wondering about what music to play back to him. I decided and played back a *khayal* in *raga Komal Rishabh Asavari* ("*Ari bir har*") sung by Ustad Vilayat Hussain Khan of the Agra *gharana*. The Ustad has rendered this composition with rare emotive power and feeling for the *raga*. Closing his eyes Pt. Kumar listened to it with rapt attention nodding with approval and appreciation now and then. When it was over he let out a sigh and exclaimed "How beautiful —the way he has maintained the emotion throughout!"

On another occasion I had gone to meet him at Mr. Wamanrao Deshpande's house at Walkeshwar. I was under Prof. B.R. Deodher's tutelage at that time and Pt. Kumar has been Prof. Deodher's most celebrarted disciple. After a while the talk turned to music and he asked me, "What is Master (this is how Prof. Deodher was known in the intimate circle of his disciples and admirers) teaching you now?" I told him that I was learning *Ramanandi Gauri* or *Shubhri Gauri*. He thought for a moment and asked, "Which composition?" In response I sang the composition "*Sughar sanehi Shyam*". He remained silent for a moment and then said, "Ashok, see how delicate this is, perhaps it is not to be sung even for a third person's ears!" The observation was accute and direct. This composition cannot be 'projected' in the usual sense of the term on account of its delicateness. This was an insight into music as a performing reality.

and ten compositions each. Of the compositions ten were classical, two semi-classical and the rest were either *bhajan* or folk songs. The advent of each new month was marked by rendering the relevant portion the *Barmasa* song from the Malwa tradition of folk music. The grouping of the songs obviously indicated a deliberate and systematic effort to structure the presentation to achieve a certain purpose. Apart from broadly similar/equal grouping of the songs into three sections the *Barmasi* song was conducive to a thematic linking of the groups. The regular *avatar* of the seasonal cycle, and its eternal, close and suggestive relationship with the human world was successfully symbolised through the *Barmasa* folk-song which entered the scene as a refrain of a song would.

A lion's share in the presentation of course belonged to Pt. Kumar Gandharva. Smt. Vasundhara Komkali, Meera Rao and occasionally Sumedha Malshe accompanied him. The first two sang the entire composition, its *mukhda* and the cyclical melodic progressions together, Pt. Kumar presented the musical elaborations and new melodic openings. This was the general plan and whenever the musical tension was likely to decrease Pt. Kumar stepped in.

Pt. Kumar's spectacular singing was the major factor in the presentation. Almost all of his vocalisation skills in his concert music were present here, except of course the elaboration of the concerned *raga* in a *mehfil*. Pt. Kumar's efforts to create a shadow, an image of *raga marwa* prior to the first song, the *malhar*-shades he rendered prior to singing compositions in *raga malhar*, or the *tappa*-style singing prior to the 17th composition almost amounted to generating a full profile of his concert-music in all its glory and richness.

However, there were some other felt deficiencies too. For example, apart from Pt. Kumar there was no other male voice.

Leaving aside the practical aspect of allowing some breather to Pt. Kumar, a balanced symbolism between rains and the earth receiving them could have given the presentation a solidity and meaningful validity as well. A significant suggestion that the spirit of being involved with the seasonal cycle consists of both male and female elements could have been better conveyed. Yet another and musically more easily perceived fault was that the accompanists moved to the desired note with more gradualness than desired. As Pt. Kumar was at the tonal centre almost as soon as he began singing the accompanists' hesitant approach appeared more disturbing. To render the compositions in the predetermined *tala* and tonal framework with precision, to begin the subsequent compositions without tentativeness, and to pick up the melodic threads left unprojected by Pt. Kumar were other matters that could be improved upon. Among all the accompanists Smt. Meera Rao appeared more confident and well set in the Pt. Kumar groove.

As far as 'singing' was concerned the programme appeared to be effective and endowed with potential. As a sample (and therefore more exciting) of Pt. Kumar's versatile vocalism the presentation was undoubtedly successful. But the presentation was based more on conceptual and philosophical sources and hence unless this aspect is examined the reviewing of the effort cannot be complete.

In Indian music, and therefore in Indian musical thinking, *raga* and time-cycles and hence *raga*-cycle and seasonal-cycle are accepted as mutually related. This musicological interrelationship has also been followed by convention. As a result, demostrating various manifestations of the seasons through the *raga*-cycle which almost moves in a parallel mode, is an idea that can easily strike roots in people's minds. This mutual relationship was stated everywhere (e.g. in the invitation itself). Consequently the audience was charged with a definite expectation. In addition, a handbook explaining the idea and difficult words in the compositions was also made available with comments in Hindi and Marathi.

In sum, *raga*-s with designated time, and textual units (i.e. words) approprite to the time/occasion are not new to Indian musical behaviour. However, the idea of striking purposeful, precise and a detailed correspondence among these components for an independent presentation was admittedly a new venture. The three constituents were designed to express one another through their own respective terms. Obviously this was the organisers' as well as the audiences' expectation. This raises two basic questions: first a musicological one, can notes and words represent each other? Another question of an aesthetic orientation is, if and when two media are involved can they really express the same experience?

To pose the questions directly in the context of *Geetvarsha* one can ask whether there is a precise, definite and unbroken relationship between physical phenomenon such as the rainy months of the seasonal cycles and *raga miya malhar.* For example in this *raga* the two varieties of the note *nishad* borrow tonal nuances from each other and thus they increase their respective intensities as well as that of the succeeding higher 'Sa' (the octave). Is all this intrinsically related to word-arrangements that intend describing the rainy season? Does our mental association of the *raga* with rainy season have any other basis than a long custom and/or convention to suppose so? If so, will it not be a distortion of music *per se* to listen to a programme based on this idea and do so with the same assumption? Are not the statements that assert this basic idea misleading listeners as far as appreciation of music is concerned? Thus to utter the word '*garajat*' (meaning 'is thundering') with perceptible vocal oscillations in order to represent the thundering clouds moves the music away from the tonal truthfulness. Do we not make music gross by seeking support from the principle of onomatopoeia in this respect? If this principle was to be invoked more meaningfully was it not more appropriate to employ the *pakhawaj* instead of *tabla* at this and similar junctures? This suggests that while conceptualising such a presentation the necessary essential basic but sophisticated thinking was not resorted to. It need not be added that convenience cannot substitute proper conceptualisation while mounting such presentations.

The second problem pertains to the inherent relationship between specific notes and emotion. This inter-relationship is too often determined by the conventional musicological relationship of time and *raga, rasa* and *raga,* etc. If an appreciative mind unconditioned by these conventions feels a relationship between specific notes and specific emotion, it does so because of the personal sensibility involved. If questioned about the general or collective perception in such contexts, the answer is likely to be quite different. It is likley to be stated that only two broad general moods are perceived in music, the mood of elation and that of dejection. In other words, listening to presentations such as *Geetvarsha* one feels that it is time to re-examine the traditional equations assumed to exist between specific emotional shades and music.

This discussion is related to *Geetvarsha* because while the compositions were being presented many listeners referred to the compositional texts and then nodded in approval. This proved the existence of the mis-conceptions about correspondence between words and music they were set to. These reader-listeners were certainly losing the joy of music. There were flowery comments intended to explain the thrust of music even though the texts and technical details have been already provided. When music began the lights in the hall were brightened. All this tended to lessen the alertness in the basic act of listening to music. That the organisers overlook this fundamental consideration evokes surprise.

In music-behaviour today, what, why and how music should be received needs to be thought about. Only that will appeal to a real appreciator and evoke a real appreciation of music from him. To some extent the music-field needs some cleaning. Due to *Geetvarsha* some serious assumptions are put forward necessitating a debate. This could be treated as an attempt in that direction.

One Kumar-Concert

If an anthology or a collection of poems can be reviewed and appreciated in detail, then why not a music concert? One Kumar-*Mehfil* (concert) proved that this can be validly and legitimately attempted.

Of course a poetry-anthology and a music-concert are different. All poems in a collection may not be related to each other at all, but this cannot be so in a *mehfil*. All compositions in a successful concert are performed as items in a link related to the previous and the succeeding compositions. For their success or otherwise the compositions are mutually dependent. Further, to concretise a *raga* or intensify the musical effect of music through evoking linguistic meaning, are the two main avenues explored by Hindustani music. Either of these two remains dominant on different occasions for realising the musical ideals set forth according to the occasion. These fundamental strategies have proved conducive to crystallisation of genres such as *dhrupad*, *khayal, thumri, bhajan,* etc. And yet in a *mehfil*-situation all that is presented influences one another. As Vishwanath had opined in literary contexts in music too each *mehfil* is a *Mahavakya*. When we say that the *mehfil* was musically successful after the interval, it can be only broadly true because what had gone before the interval and had appeared musically speaking less successful, has also contributed to the entire process of musical fulfillment. An entire *mehfil* can rightfully be treated as a larger composition.

In the *Mehfil* under discussion, Pt. Kumar presented *multani*, *marwa* and *shri* prior to the interval and *raga*-s *yaman, chaiti bhoop* and *bhimpalas* after the interval. More or less all presentations were successful and the entire *mehfil* could be counted as musically memorable.

In the *raga multani* matters were rather dull till the *drut trital* compositions began. On many occasions Pt. Kumar was off the tonal centres he was seeking and the melodic lines in the *meend* often struck as too gross /broad. But the off-colour *multani* was important in another respect. It made Pt. Kumar's technique and approach to successful music-making explicit. It was as if the method, with which he was searching for creative centres in *multani*, was in view. This kind of opportunity to perceive the nature of aesthetic music-making is rare and instructive. For example, setting aside the grammatical tenet of regarding notes *shadja* and *pancham* important in *multani*, Pt. Kumar was trying to keep notes *nishad* and with it sometimes the high *shadja* in the forefront. The *vadi-samvadi* rules or those about concentrating on the upper/lower octave-halves have also been formulated with a view to help in trying for distinctive *raga*-elaboration and ensuring appropriate emotional accent. However, very often these are taken as rigid prescriptions and other generative ideas are ignored. Pt. Kumar's above-described effort was directed at an exploration of untapped generative resources of the *raga*.

The reason why the *trital* in *multani* appealed was slightly different. In *khayal* Pt. Kumar had established the *nishad-shadja* region or the *gandhar-nishad* pair as the area of his intensified activity. The effect of intensification may be realised in Hindustani music through melodic structures or through the rhythmic patterns. In the *trital*, Pt. Kumar resorted to involved *taan* and rhythmic patterns for creating the required intensity-effect. In this manner the melodic intensities of the *khayal* provided a background for generating the rhythmic variety of intensity, indeed a case of mutual dependence.

In *marwa* Pt. Kuamr was able to locate the tonal centres in the *raga* unhesitatingly and with ease (though the *mandra dhaivat* was for a while a little suspect). The essence of the *raga marwa* lies in placing the note *shadja* appealingly in the contexts of natural achievements of notes *dhaivat* and *rishạbh*. It is customary to state that the note *rishabh* becomes *shadja* in *marwa*. But that does not deny note *shadja* its inherent sovereignty. The usually stated position only suggests that the note *shadja* functions in *raga marwa* on another level. After making a number of melodic statements with notes *rishabh* and *dhaivat* when the note *shadja* is set up it is almost as if the *Vaishnava* and the *Shaiva* fragrances are combined. In sum, *marwa* was a high point in the *mehfil*.

Raga shri which came next was however a faded effort and the reason was not far to seek. *raga shri* has notes 'Re' and 'Pa' as its creative agents and Pt. Kumar's *marwa* had already created an atmosphere with its accentuation of 'Re' and 'Dha'. As a consequence, the creative regions of both the *raga*-s became adjacent and elaborations in *shri* were experienced as repetitive. To argue that the tonal values of notes in both the *raga*-s are different and that the note-pairs involved are also not identical merely becomes an academic issue because of the broad effects concerned. Further, it must be admitted that Pt. Kumar found it difficult to consistently demonstrate the distinctive value of the note 'Re' in *raga shri*. As a cumulative effect his *raga shri* failed in its musical mission.

While presenting the post-interval *yaman,* Pt. Kumar was in full form. Two features struck home. Firstly, *raga yaman* is not just simple as it is usually described—it is also extraordinarily rich.

Secondly, like many other geniuses Pt. Kumar also denies the equation that the unknown is new, and is fortunately in favour of searching for the new in the known or the familiar. What do we mean by describing *yaman* as rich? We mean that it has immense possibilities. In many other *raga*-s one's search for creative regions is confined to certain pairs of notes or certain melodic phrases. Not so in case of *raga yaman* and similar *raga*-s. They are full of creative centres but you need somebody who can detect them.

A *tappa* followed which was not a mere series of dazzling melodic phrases. Pt. Kumar's rendereing was almost a demonstration of how attractive sound-patterns can be made alive due to their interaction with *tala*-patterns and how both result in presenting a combined dance. *Thumri* and such other genres are inclined to create intensities through byplay of meaningful words with musical units. *Tappa* emulates the strategy but with an additional dimension of intricate and decorative embellishments of musical units. The texts are in Punjabi, Pharsi etc. and hence add to the variety of sound-patterns. Pt. Kumar could decorate the *tappa* with great aesthetic abandon as even the *raga*-restrictions are relaxed in the genre. Pt. Kumar's voice was also fully cooperative and there was nothing but a liberated musical sensibility of high order in positive action.

Unfortunately the *chaiti-bhoop* that followed did not contribute much. It suggested an extension of the *raga*-frame of the usual *bhoop* but nothing else.

The last item was *bhimpalas* and what one heard was a more lyrical *bhimpalas* with its own musical authenticity. This kind of interpretation boasts of a long tradition in Marathi stage-music. Pt. Kumar gathered accolades for the lyrical quality and for the ease with which patterns in fast pace were unfolded one after the other.

After the concert I left with wonderful memories of musical delight. The vitality of the music and the musician as also his keenness to put forward his 'own' musical concepts was felt. Today musicians hardly have their own musical position on musical matters. Those few that have it often fail in presenting their position with the required courage and effectiveness. Pt. Kumar is an exception. He wants to say something different, as well as differently and he has the capacity to do so.

Triveni (Reviewed January 1968)

This is yet another programme conceived and presented by Pt. Kumar Gandharva. In it he presented altogether 16 compositions of three saints namely, Kabir, Soordas and Meerabai. Like his *Geetvarsha* this too was a choral presentation to some extent. He himself prefaced each item. The composition was first collectively presented and Pt. Kumar or one of the singers later filled in the *alap*. Apart from having one more male voice the presentation mode was similar to that of *Geetvarsha*.

In this presentation, Pt. Kumar's own voice was functioning flawlessly from the beginning. In recent times his voice appeared to be less cooperative in the lower range but not so in *Triveni*. It was a delight to witness how musical movements convince when the voice is not a barrier. Shri Achrekar on *tabla* was as reliable and solid as ever. Mrs. Komkali was sometimes tentative in intonation but on the whole all co-artists took care that the main artist's elaborations and musical designs were not punctured in any way. The audience did not have to strain itself to decide who was musical or otherwise.

All these details are mentioned to underscore the importance of even the secondary components (that are somewhat external to the main design) to ensure a musically valid presentation. All these were adequately present and functioning in *Triveni*. And still, even when the medium and the means are pulling their weight, the presentation may not attain the intended aim, which then compels one to look elsewhere to analyse the event and the attainment or otherwise.

What happened in *Triveni*? The sixteen compositions were heard as a series of *bhajan*. It was not as if one led to the other and/ or one *raga* shaded off into another, making the whole presentation a complete composition. Consequently the programme could not become a coherent whole leading to a rich artistic experience. It remained a succession of isolated musical and performing achievements in which joints or breaks were not well-concealed. Pt. Kumar put in an effort to draw attention to individual peaks but he could not depict a melody of mountain-ranges. The second failure of the presentation was that due to the total intended design even those *bhajan*-compositions which had the potential to become evocative renditions could not get the requisite space they needed for the purpose. These compositions could not be elaborated or explored in the usual manner.

Every artist is on the lookout for musical seeds with a growth-potential. Whether it is a phrase, *raga* or a composition, unless it is explored fully for its creative riches an artist cannot move on with absorption. In a presentation of serialised composition each item, unless it is explored to the required minimum height, is likely to prove an obstacle for compositions that follow, because it is only an adequately developed composition that can provide a kind of platform for the next. In the discussed programme the compositions after the first intermission were rather cursorily cast aside and this resulted in an presentational performing imbalance. In fact these were the compositions that clearly announced musical possibilities. On account of the folk idiom, the particularly attractive sound-pattterns of the folk-element and Pt. Kumar's exciting deviations from the accepted tonal values had convincing aesthetic potential—which was ignored. (As *Shayar* Jurat put it (in translation), "The anguish is more for those buds which could not bloom!")

This exposition should point to the fact that the major deficiencies of *Triveni* are not those of the musical aspect but the understanding that controlled the performance. The performance was suppressed by this understanding and its constituents. Music had to suffer because the secondary extra-musical components were in the driver's seat.

The conceptual framework underlying *Triveni* can be spelt out a little. Just as literary style changes according to the writer concerned, similarly a composer's melodic/rhythmic style also changes. Just as a writer can be identified from his literary style, a composer can also be. In the context of *Triveni* it would mean that as the inter-relationship between Kabir and Kabir's literary sensibility are determinate and comprehensible, similarly one can move to his composing style from the way he writes and explores the word-meaning relationhsip. In sum, the saint-poet's compositions lead to the meaning-aspect and the literary composition leads to their composing mode. The essence of the saint-poet's compositions become reachable when they meet their 'right' tunes.

Mr. Rahul Barpute stated this position in his own way in the anthology made avaialable at the time of the performance. Pt. Kumar's agreement was evident from the way he perfomred and presented. It was obvious that Pt. Kumar's musical assumptions and criteria for this programme differed from those he holds otherwise. It was this framework which was responsible for the blurred achievements of the programme. What was received was a series of *bhajan*-compositions and not a cohesive larger design employing the genre. In a concert one item leads to the next, which enters the scene as if by the permission of the previous item. Musical consistency is inevitable and unavoidable. In *Triveni* the individual items were judged and shaped in isolation, as if with only reference to itself. For example, questions such as the following were obviously not asked: Are varieties of *mand* presented in succession likely to be musically convincing? If *satwa* and its seven-beat rhythm are continuously employed for successive compositions, are they able to hold their attraction? Thus while during the performance musical criteria were inevitably, relevantly and automatically applied, the performance was conceptualised solely or mainly on the basis of a comparatively speaking non-universal inter-relationship between meaning and notes. In other words, musical consistency understood in a wider perspective was sacrificed.

Secondly, *Triveni* was musically speaking, uneven. *Bhajan*-compositions with musical potential were not allowed to emerge to their adequate aesthetic realisation.They could not lead to one another to suggest a complete whole. Thirdly, the assumption that each *bhajan* would have only one matching tune was a misconceived aesthetic assumption denying the essential ambiguity of music to function normally and thus open up suggestive possibilities. Kabir's *nirguna* devotion, Meera's anguished call and Soordasa's mature passion of separation can hardly be expected to come to musical fruition by composing the concerned compositions in a kind predetermined musical frame. This task was to say the least, too ambitious! To conceive a presentation with extra-musical assumptions and to expect music to fall in line could not happen and the three strands remained three separate entities in *Triveni*. It is said that the English Epic *Fairy Queen* (by Spencer) with its 12 sections, was expected to gain coherence because all the 12 had one common hero, but that could not happen and the poem became a slippery affair. So it was in *Triveni*. One common singer was the only cohering factor. Pt. Kumar could not get musically involved in the *bhajan*-compositions because of the conceptual framework which could not be firmly structured because musical criteria inevitably became functional in a performance.

With the help of folksongs Pt. Kumar tried to seek symbolic music that paralleled deep rooted psychological import in the peoples' minds in *Geetvarsha*. In *Triveni* he tried to find musical structures that paralleled deep-rooted devotional songs. He had elsewhere asserted that our art-music can find its vital juice in folkmusic and folk songs. He has taken care to put forward actual performances to 'prove' his scholastic beliefs. The processing of traditional folk and devotional corpus that he has attempted and the theoretical stance he has adopted are put forward as answers, but actually they are questions and hence very significant.

Balgandharva and Kumar Gandharva (September 1968)

Pt. Kumar Gandharva is an extremely imaginative musician and a vocalist at that. To sing thoughtfully and to think about music —he loves both the processes. Consequently he is active on both the fronts. But the story does not end there. He is not only active but tries to seek a new platform each time he is active. To present folk music after processing it, or to attempt to find the 'original' interrelationship of words and music in traditional devotional compositions are notable instances of his 'search-prone' artistry. Recently he presented a programme of Balgandharva's music aptly or suggestively entitling it "*Mala Umajlele Balgandharva*" (Balgandharva as I understood him). This too was an example of his untiring musical inquisitiveness.

In this presentation Pt. Kumar, with Smt. Vasundhara Komkali in vocal accompaniment presented compositions he selected from

Balgandharva's abundant corpus. On *tabla* was Mr. Acharekar and on the *organ* Shri Govindrao Patwardhan. In the performance in Sanghmandir which is reviewed here, Smt. Komkali's participation was much more than mere accompaniment.

Pt. Kumar had selected 16 compositions in *raga*-s generally sung in the evening and night. Pt. Kumar listened to Balgandharva's recorded music on discs, old and new, and then from different versions Pt. Kumar decided what could have been the 'original' composition Balgandharva must have crystallised and decided to present as that particular song. With him Mrs. Komkali also sang the *Natya-pada* i.e. stage-songs. After the initial and rather straight rendering of the compositions some elaboration in both Balgandharva and Kumar Gandharva styles were put forward before moving on to the next song. This was the external aspect of the presentation. I intend to put down some thoughts about the musical event, the musical questions it throws up and the importance of such undertakings.

To examine the presentation as a musical event some misconceptions must be cleared, otherwise criteria and concepts only distantly related to the effort will get tied up with the effort, and the thought-process will take wrong turns.

Firstly, the main aim of this effort was not to present singing which was *a la* Balgandharva. With his usual pithiness Shri P. L. Deshpande explained in the beginning that imitation was not the goal. Hence to compare and contrast each and every musical detail of the presentation with the Balgandharva music is totally irrelevant.

A second misunderstanding is also possible. A view can be taken that as all music in the presentation consisted of stage-songs, the presentation is to be construed and evaluated as stage-music. This approach also lacks relevance. It is to be remembered that the Balgandharva-music was performed here by one male and one female voice in a musical concert. This was a *mehfil* of Balgandharva music. (In his preface Shri P. L. Deshpande therefore rightly referred to the effort as elaboration of *pada* according to norms of vocal art-music.)

Thirdly, it should not be overlooked that as the title announced, the Balgandharva-music presented was a result of Pt. Kumar's understanding of it. In other words, one cannot reasonably assume that his interpretation of Balgandharva-music must agree with one's own. The possibility of Pt. Kumar's understanding and interpretation of Balgandharva being different from one's own cannot be ruled out. For example, an objection about exclusion of one's favourite *pada* in the presentation could hardly be accepted as a legitimate criticism of the programme.

On the whole it appeared that Pt. Kumar implied a presentation or demonstration of Balgandharva's approach or method. Even if this was not his original intention, it happened that way. Pt. Kumar reconstructed or adequately processed the available version to approximate Balgandharva's intended composition. This was first to be presented and then elaborated further as Balgandharva would have. In other words, a seed-form was performed and then followed its methodical flowering.

A nuance is to be noted. It need not be assumed that a *pada* by Balgandharva can only be elaborated according to his own method or approach. For example, his *pada* can also be elaborated and performed in the Master Krishnarao's or Heerabai's style or even in Pt. Kumar's way. In the presentation under discussion, the elaboration perceivably moved in the spheres of Balgandharva's and Pt. Kumar Gandharva's ways. Even though Pt. Kumar was not imitating Balgandharva, Pt. Kumar's pronunciation, intonation and tonal patterning often echoed Balgandharva abundantly. Hence the question is: to what extent Pt. Kumar succeeded in singing in the Balgandharva cast?

For Pt. Kumar there were some basic difficulties in registering an achievement of this kind. For example, there is a tremendous difference between Balgandharva's and Pt. Kumar's voice. The difference is so vast that Pt. Kumar cannot be expected to recreate Balgandharva's singing more than 50%! For instance, Balgandharva's '*A kar*' (i.e. the employment of the vowel 'AA' in melodic elaborations) as also the lightness of his voice are absent in Pt. Kumar's voice. Pt. Kumar's voice falters in the lower ranges and sounds rather indistinct while it cannot reach very high in the upper reaches. Further, on higher notes Pt. Kumar's voice gets thinner and pointed and sometimes fades out. In this presentation, while singing the *antara* of compositions based on the note *madhyama* as the fundamental Pt. Kumar had to leave the singing to Mrs. Komkali and the reason was obvious. The one glorious exception was Pt. Kumar's intonation of high 'Sa' (the octave note). May be due to his exposure to Balgandharva's music Pt. Kumar projected this note in an almost undistorted 'Aa'—indeed a deviation from his usual practice. As far as intonation of notes is concerned Balgandharva's principle was absolute purity of tone while Pt. Kumar's principle can aptly be described as one of dramatic contrast.

In case of *taan* too, Pt. Kumar's voice poses unavoidable obstructions. Pt. Kumar's *taan* is fast-moving and clear in its own fashion but its dynamism or the way of attaining pace is not due to the inherent vocal ease or lightness. It gets its character from the specific musical design and content of Pt. Kumar. The Balgandharva-strategy is to make a cluster of four-five notes while coming to a note, then swiftly move to the other half or part of the octave and create another cluster responding to the earlier one and thus move on. In sum, all this is achieved almost casually because the singer's voice is itself a stirring, pulsating bundle of energy.

On the other hand, Pt. Kumar's *taans* are deliberate, a product of some labour and his voice is able to weave and move only in short phrases unlike Balgandharva's seemingly unending spirals. Under the circumstances, if something is begun in the Balgandharva-way and ends up in the Pt. Kumar-way, what is likely to happen? Not only that the intended and suggested *taans* will not be realised but the performance will cause an associational friction. This is what repeatedly happened in the presentation. It may be possible to explore more possibilites in the Balgandharva-way itself without sounding imitative. But for that feat, musical consistency needs to be maintained. For example, Gandharva-*pada* and Kumar-vocalism, Gandharva-*pada* and more elaborate presentation in the Balgandharva-way were two clear possibilities. But to begin with the Balgandharva-*pada*, follow for a while in the same groove and then to switch to Pt. Kumar-mode did not click—it confused the musical content and its perception.

To add to the difficulties of keeping the content unblemished one more presentational device proved rather irritating. Mrs. Komkali, when singing independently was a musical gain but while singing with Pt. Kumar he too often made her repeat what he had sung and that was pointless. It was obvious to anybody that while following Balgandharva's mode complete synchronisation was not thinkable and so this 'public tuition' was reduced to an unmusical exercise. A Balgandharva-*pada* takes off on even a half-beat, it moves swiftly (and without a mechanical regularity) and hence it always created a kaleidoscopic musical patterning. The attempt to try to 'fix' this music in two voices was a foregone failure. The total or partial repetition by Mrs. Komkali of what Pt. Kumar had sung or attempted could have been appropriately avoided by giving more scope to Mrs. Komkali. The faulty duet-singing proved a non-starter. It failed between the two poles of

Balgandharva mode and Kumar Gandharva mode and ultimately impeded the musical flow.

These were the more fundamental of the flaws. But one smaller defect could be worked on to bring in qualitative improvement—the reference being to Pt. Kumar's pronunciation of the Marathi words. Whatever Shri P. L. Deshpande's contention might be, Balgandharva was a top-ranking actor-singer and not a classical vocalist. Hence the importance given to word-pronunciation in Balgandharva-music could not be expected in Pt. Kumar's presentation. But the Hindi-influenced '*Hriday*', or a classical musician's addition of 'H' sound to consonants (in "*Nach manasa asha*" the initial 'N' was sounding '*Nha*') or its omission (in "*Mala madan bhase*" the last word often sounded as '*base*') can surely be improved upon. As is known to students of music in, and of Maharashtra, when *Baithakichi Lavani* came to the fore the pronunciation and projection aspects in its performance underwent subtle changes as compared to the *Lavani* projection from its presentation as '*Barichi*' or '*Dholkichi Lavani*'. Similar changes take place when a stage-song is rendered from a concert stage and awareness of this aesthetic phenomenon is essential for the artistic success of the renderings.

The success of the '*Mala Umajlele*' obviously depended on how Pt. Kumar locates and presents musically creative aspects of the Balgandharva-music. Pt. Kumar achieved Balgandharva's subtle rhythmic placements and his skill in locating the tonal centres. For example, in the *pada* "*Sujan kasa man chori*" Pt. Kumar's arrival on the *sama* was as subtle as in the original Balgandharva-music. Obviously Balgandharva-influence was also apparent in making Pt. Kumar's tunefulness more transperant and pure. What he could not achieve was a synthesis of two music-s—one of the late Balgandharva and the other being his own. It is of course not impossible to bring about synthesis of two or more well-entrenched music-s (as Balgandharva himself had proved). Perhaps after some more work Pt. Kumar will succeed in doing it. What will be needed is to establish Balgandharva-music in such a manner and to such an extent that his own i.e. Pt. Kumar's music gets easily and perceptibly merged into it. At the same time enough care is to be taken to ensure that no distortion of Balgandharva-music is experienced. And this obviously is not an easy task.

The musical importance of such an effort and the questions that it rasies have already been mentioned. Balgandharva-music tended to present the most salient musical features emphatically but briefly because it was conceived as stage-music. Any attempt to elaborate what was implied but unexplored in it has to face the problem of how to maintain a positive relationship with the original mould. What changes are inevitable when stage-music becomes concert-music? If two different music-s are in their own respective ways subtle about melody, rhythm, projection etc., how to bring them together without allowing performing conflicts? These and other such questions are important.

In sum, Pt. Kumar's experiment is undoubtedly important. Balgandharva-music is facing an eclipse-situation in Maharashtra. Balgandharva was fortunate in getting loyal followers, knowledgeable appreciators but he had no disciples or performing followers meritorious enough. Nobody in Maharashtra could digest the early reformist Mr. Agarkar's writings and thoughts completely—similarly about Balgandharva! Imitators and distorters are what he has. Hence it is a musical need that a researched and reformed Balgandharva is performed authoritatively in order to draw attention to the valid musical values he had put forward so well. To put it differently, if one gets the right kind of contemporary exposure to music of the past, one gains. When an artist of Smt. Manik Verma's calibre presents Balgandharva in a different voice one takes one kind of positive step in comprehending a rich tradition. Pt. Kumar's is a different way, but equally exciting. It is one more instance of Pt. Kumar's seriousness about music and the depth of his musical vision.

Geet Hemant (March 1969)

Pt. Kumar's presentation entitled *Geet Hemant* is actually an inevitable culmination of the creative position he had assumed while presenting *Geetvarsha*. Both these performances have been motivated by an urge to musically highlight the association of ideas between a certain season and music.

Though the presentational techniques were similar if not identical in both, one sensed in *Geet Hemant* a greater coordination between Pt. Kumar's and Mrs. Komkali's singing. Mrs. Komkali rightfully exploited the greater scope available to her in this programme. Compositions in *raga*-s *deskar, bageshri* and *durga* stood out. In addition, compositions in *dhanbasanti, kaanada, shiv-bhatiyar* were applauded by the listeners (obviously because they were familiar). This distinct feature of appreciating the familiar is worth-noting. After the first intermission Pt. Kumar was in his element as by that time his voice was cooperating fully with him. The main gain from the presentation was listening to some of Pt. Kumar's impressive compositions and some delightful and processed folk songs.

Now the question to be asked is: On the background of the totality of Indian music is it possible to arrive at a coherent final effect through a presentation of a collection of compositions—either on the level of musical appeal or word-meanings? In my opinion presentations of this kind are similar to those manifestations known in Western music as program-music. Hence it is perhaps necessary to put forward some points related to it. In brief, program-music means music which seeks to establish connections between a specific musical manifestation and a particular incident, idea and/or their sequence. A cumulative effect is realised as association of ideas is established between a tangible incident on a physical plane and music. The incident may be a part of a narrative or it may even be an isolated happening.

A conventional way of relating music to an incident and make the audience feel it that way is to resort to onomatopoeia. For example, suppose that the narrative consists of incidents such as a child-birth in a house, the gradual growth of the child and finally the marriage of the grown up child, then, the music may consist of church bells to indicate the child-birth, a fast or a jumping melody (to suggest the child's growth), or music imitating its crying. Thus, even if there may not be a one-to-one correspondence between specific incidents and musical phrases it becomes possible to perceive the association between particular life-activity and definite musical phrases or aspects and this helps in moving the narrative forward. Music can therefore be construed in the light of familiar day-to-day operations. Music in between such points may however be comparatively abstract.

One more feature of the Western program-music needs to be mentioned. This musical expression is mainly realised as instrumental music. Firstly because onomatopoic use of human voice has more limitations than instruments. For example to indicate marriage the church bells or *shehnai* is sounded through human voice is likely to remind us more of the mimicry performances at the time of school-gatherings! Because of the inherent or the felt limitations of human voice, program-music exploits fuller resources of the orchestra and extra instruments if need be to weave a web of sounds that can arouse memories of definite physical events as well as the audience's associations pertaining to it. They are the clues to understand the narrative, description or story.

Perhaps there is one more subtle reason for the lesser or almost 'nil-use' of human voice in program-music. It is generally perceived that human voice reaches to deeper receptive or resisting attitudes of our minds. Not only that, these responses tend to be more rigid or near-fanatic. It is normally seen that from any unknown musical culture what is more readily accepted or received is the instrumental and not the vocal music. Human voice is more intimately connected to the concerned parent culture than instruments used in the same culture.

This discussion of program-music is put down in order to clarify why and how certain conditions need to be fulfilled if the intention is to base a musical composition on an incident, a chain of events or a narrative and yet to create a coherent ultimate musical experience. In this respect the following points can be noted:

1. A one-to-one, direct correlation of an equational nature must be established between at least some physical incidents or events and phases of musical statement.
2. Towards this end, some parts of the composition must include or directly suggest sounds of or associated with some physical events that form a part of the narration. With the help of such occurances the audience falls back on the association of ideas to consciously make sense of the music. Music can thus become less abstract.
3. The inherent limitations of human voice and its capacity to arouse pro or contra attitudes among the listeners do not prove very conducive to program-music. On the face of it language i.e. words may appear to lessen the abstractness of music but leaving aside the quotidian usage of language, in other contexts it is ambiguous. Even if the written or the spoken language can be understood it continues to

> be mainly suggestive. Hence its use is likely to raise one more barrier as different individuals are likely to interpret the used language differently. In other words, the idea of program-music seems to be shaped by deciding that there is no point in substituting the ambiguity of music with ambiguity of words.

On this background it should become clear why *Geet Hemant* does not succeed in leaving behind an ultimate cohesive musical experience.

If Pt. Kumar had selected representative physical incidents from the part of the seasonal cycle relevant to the presentation and utilised the associated sounds to choose the musical compositions it would have become easier for him to exploit some association of ideas and communicate a coherent experience. However, Pt. Kumar is a vocalist and hence all sounds must be processed in a particular manner to become acceptable to him. In addition, his technique being to present the programme with only two voices he cannot explore and exploit variety in sound. As a result, he relied on words that are descriptive. But these too had to be processed according to the genre of music to make them performable to suit his requirements. In the end, words and language proved inadequate to suggest the incidents and to make a balanced presentation of the universe of the life-sounds and that of the musical sounds. What remained was a collection of songs.

That *kaanada, dhanbasanti* were applauded and *Barmasa* song evoked whispering responses meant that the audience were listening to vocal music as usual. This is not objectionable but then this satisfaction had to be rationed out in meagre quota because of the specific conceptualisation of the venture. As this appeared inevitable the questions arise: What is the achievement of the thematic *Geet Hemant*? The main achievement is the necessity of thinking about the concept of program-music is well brought out. It is also apparent that folk music would be a useful component towards such designs. *Geet Hemant* in itself is a very hesitant step towards it, and it is a good attempt at processing folk music. With these components, classical and semi-classical genres were somehow accomodated. This was the total outcome of *Geet Hemant*.

Thumri, Tappa ani Tarana (September 1969)

Recently Pt. Kumar put forth an interesting presentation entitled *Thumri, Tappa ani Tarana*.

Majority of those who attended were delighted by the music. Mrs.Komkali's role as a musician and accompanist is now artistically more satisfying. Without breaking the link of Pt. Kumar's music she is able to make her own music with confidence and independence. Mr. Achrekar on *tabla* is always dependable and he facilitates music-making. Usually no other accompaniment has any scope in Pt. Kumar's presentations.

Pt. Kumar's voice these days is uncomplaining and his music is now full of verve. This verve proved very useful in the pesentation under discussion when *tappa* and *tarana* were rendered. These genres have an innate relationship with Gwalior-music and a passing thought was that Pt. Kumar's music these days tends to move nearer to the Gwalior *gharana*.

In the performing sequence *thumri* was first, but as far as successful music-making is concerned it certainly ranked low. There are two reasons for this. Firstly, Pt. Kumar overlooked the fact that among genres aimed at evoking specific but generalised emotions through a particular way of using words, *thumri* works its way almost like the *khayal*. Like *khayal*, there is methodical melodic elaboration involved and notes are to be 'developed' through formation and embellishment of clusters. In the absence of this strategy the experience is fragmentary and somewhat incoherent. In *thumri* the texts use conventional words to evoke conventional feelings of love, separation, etc. and this bridge allows listeners freedom to relate to the experience at deeper personal levels and make the genre appealing. But this is as far as the 'word-meaning' aspect is concerned. Here the artist has not much work to do. But the musical aspect is entirely his responsibility. As *raga*-rules are less stringent and because *tala*-s with different rhythmic designs are available, the artist has creative challenges to face. Pt. Kumar neglected the musical elaboration in *thumri*-compositions. Though not highly sophisticated the emotive character of *thumri* is constantly evoked and it is to be gradually built up by the singer. Pt. Kumar could not succeed in this task.

A corollary also followed. While singing *thumri* and *tappa* one after the other, the later *thumri*-compositions got heavily influenced by the *tappa* and in the final analysis all compositions appeared to have a *tappa* face. Originally the quiet movement of *thumri* was overlooked, later it was perceptibly replaced by the *tappa*-movements and in the process *thumri* lost its distinct character almost entirely.

The tappa-renderings were a highpoint. The dazzling *taans* were not merely exercises in speed, they were vital and imaginative components in the larger sound-patterns. The sound-patterns that Pt. Kumar wove were intricate and Pt. Kumar's skill as well as imagination were abundantly in evidence. While executing such complex designs with speed, Pt. Kumar never faltered in attaining the *sama* with admirable precision. His musical bearing was proud and confident and for right reasons. In *tappa*-singing an artist's intention is not just to fill the available places, he wants to create such places and people them with delightfully complex and crafty embellishments which compel listeners to hold their breath. To execute melodic /rhythmic designs even when apparently there is no 'duration' left for them, to move from one half of the octave to the next with agility and similar devices constitute *tappa*-artists masterstrokes giving a surprising jolt to the listener's expectations. Pt. Kumar was completely at home in creating all such moments, exciting the audience a number of times.

Second to the *tappa* was the excellence of *tarana*-renderings. On most of the occasions *tarana*-compositions consist of *raga*-music employing meaningless but exciting sound-syllables in delightful patterns. *Tarana* may in a way become a movement towards abstract music. Some major tendencies of the genre are to offer/gain freedom from the codified *raga*-frames and move away from the conventional linguistic sounds of Braj etc. to seek new pastures of sound-forms from other languages such as Farsi. So in a way it carries on the task of melodic elaboration of the *khayal* but in a different direction. Understood in this perspective to confine *tarana* to fast tempo is to encroach on its own genre-rights and artificially limit its field of operations. On this background it was highly satisfying that Pt. Kumar sang *tarana* in a medium tempo. That Pt. Kumar sensed the presently unexplored aspects of the genre once again proved his musical insight and capacity to detect performing nuances. As the medium tempo *tarana* takes up its cues from *khayal* it will be truncated if it is not provided the accomodative tempo. This of cource does not mean that Tarana should not be sung in a fast tempo. The contemporary lop-sided treatment of *tarana* needed a course-correction and Pt. Kumar's rendering exemplified it. The *tarana* in *Bhoop* was a beautiful model of a *tarana* in medium tempo and it was a pity that it was rendered when the programme was nearing its end.

As noted earlier the programme was all the time under the shadow of *tappa*. *Tarana* is intrinsically similar to *tappa* due to its reliance on non-sensical syllables or on melodic units formed from different, unfamiliar sound-patterns of unconventional linguistic sources. In a way *tarana* looks at two directions—one that of *khayal* and the other pursued usually by *tappa*. Consequently to attentively listen to the *tappa* was comparable to examine the Mogul/Persian decorative paintings etc. that sometimes go beyond being subtle! Each *tappa* was individually attractive but the *tappa*-ness was everywhere the same. In conclusion the *tappa* proved its transience. There are inherent limits to its elaborational capacities. Beyond a limit the *tappa* decidedly becomes a blurred entity. In no way can it be considered to be equal the *khayal* or *thumri* in accomodation of musical ideas. This must be remembered while placing it on the performing arc.

Now one must turn to the philosophical/theoretical or conceptual position that determined the nature of the programme. The performing aspect was first examined to avoid the contingency of being affected by the discussion of the conceptual position. Pt. Kumar had written it down and he read it out prior to launching into music-making. Did he intend that the sequence was to be the order in which receivers were to approach the venture?

In this context Pt. Kumar's position was not very enlightening. It contained the conventional statements about the usual presence of love-sentiment in *thumri* and *tappa*, and the briskness of *tappa* and *tarana*. Why these specific genres formed the content of the presentation was not well-explained. Similarities and contrasts between the selected genres was 'palpably' felt through his singing. The aesthetic hinterlands of these forms need examination and often their boundaries enjoy overlaps—these features become clear. Hence *tappa* can be broadly classified as either *khayal*-oriented

Pt. Kumar was not a bookish artist but one who can read music! This was once again proved when he presented the programme under discussion. Pt. Kumar is not known to have received *talim* in *tappa*-singing. I knew that generally the genre is not a part of his performing repertoire. So I was curious about the sources he had tapped about the *tappa*. When I met him I asked him a question about some particular composition he had sung because according to my guess he has referred to Pt. Rajabhaiyya's anthology of *tappa*. He explained to me his views on the matter and then told me, "Ashok, you know Pt. Vishnu Digambar had also brought out a book on *tappa*." Then he kept quiet for a while. His eyes became somewhat misty and he said, "Ashok , see how honest these people were. Panditji it seems knew only the *sthayi* of a compositon. You know what he did—he notated the *sthayi* and then wrote a note, 'I know only the *sthayi,* so this can be a complete composition only after learning the *Antara* from somebody who knows!' " This is how Pt. Kumar was—a sympathetic but a studious reader!

or *tarana*-oriented. This meant that the faster *tarana* could have been grouped with the *tappa*. The venture in actuality could have been a presentation of *thumri* and *tappa* to be followed by the *tarana*. This would have resulted in better experience of musical forces.

There is no evolutionism in case of musical genres. To say that one genre has originated from the other only means certain dormant or unexplored tendencies in one form get more scope in another related genre. To explore such features of the musical potential leads to enrichment of musical experience. In this manner all musical forms are complementary to one another. Viewed in this larger perspective logically it can only be said that some genres are nearer to one another than some others. Each genre has special powers and relationships to lead to experience. To perceive this fact leads to a greater understanding of music. Pt. Kumar's persistant efforts to find a new way to see the totality of music is therefore a welcome 'insistence'.

Folk Music and Pt. Kumar Gandharva (July 1970)

Like many other arts sometimes music too becomes stereo-typed. An artist endowed with independence of spirit feels the oppressive condition. For him it becomes inevitable that he seeks a way out. Depending on the industry, energy and the quality of creativity of the individual concerned, he succeeds in finding a way out and thus reaches a new height in artistic expression.

This can be achieved in various ways. For example, in Hindustani art music one may listen to music of other *gharana*-s with more alertness, or listening to musical genres other than one's own specialisation is yet another strategy. It is also possible to bring to bear on oneself altogether different influences, may be of unfamiliar origin, to make a new synthesis. His genius is lit up again and can thus become active with redoubled energy as the musical flow becomes a reality again. Pt. Kumar Gandharva sought to loosen the oppressive stronghold of somewhat mechanical thinking on music in circulation and in this effort folk music helped him in more ways than one.

What is important is that the stimuli and the influences that help in this liberating action also have after-effects that extend further and this brings in a consequence, almost through the back-door. The artist starts feeling a sense of special love for those influences, stimuli or components that have helped him in attaining new peaks of creativity. Next is a sense of gratefulness for them and a somewhat uncritical evaluation of their inherent capacity. In all this process he tends to forget that formation of new moulds or frameworks never vanish in art, rather they are reborn again and again. In other words, forces that loosen or diminish the hold of a mould or a cast are also engaged in pushing forward a new one. Under these circumstances, rather than spending more time and energy on a self-absorbed and autobiographical thinking about the process (of how one arrived at the new mould) it is advisable and meaningful to keep searching for a newer and more relevant cast or framework. Usually the inevitability and urgency of this follow-up action is forgotten because of the temptation to set up a legitimising theoretical, conceptual structure pertaining to the influences that have proved helpful at a critical moment. One develops a sense of loyalty for the framework and the attempt begins to invest it with an impersonal, theoretical and aesthetic value in art-activity in general. Consequently it becomes an additional responsibility of the interested parties to examine the theoretical, intellectual or musicological validity of the new creative model set up. The responsibility is dubbed as additional because it is also possible that the input of understanding the theoretical assumptions is not relevant to the realisation and appreciation of the specific artistic effort involved. Somewhat paradoxically the effort could be an artistic success even when the theoretical assumption is of suspicious validity. Hence the involved artist's thought-process and his theoretical position on the issues need to be further evaluated. On this background the examination attempted here, firstly of the relationship between Pt. Kumar's art and folk music is followed by the review of his presentation entitled *Malwa Ki Lokdhune*.

Pt. Kumar's approach to his own art is not merely influenced by folk music. It is also not true to say that apart from Pt. Kumar no other artist has taken inspiration from folk music. And yet the interrelationship of Pt. Kumar's art and folk music is to be examined because he has been more deliberate and musically conscious in his recourses to folk music. (Other influences on his art are discussed elsewhere.) No other artist appears to be so deliberate and consistent in relying creatively on folk music as Pt. Kumar does.

The first feature that strikes one is the 'folkish' way of presenting the material. This very general description points to those characteristics of folk music that are integral to it but occur occasionally as embellishment on other kinds of music, including art music. The use is not experienced as jarring or musically inconsistent but the inevitable feeling is that the concerned features are 'outsiders' to the music presented. For example, the words are pronounced rather 'straight' i.e. as in folk music. Not to soften or blur the sound contours of the words in the interest of musicality or easier pronouncibility is a known and pervasive feature of folk music. This is one instance of the 'folk touch' in art music. A liberal use of dialectical words is another way of bringing in the 'folk touch'. Also to be marked is the way of vocalisation that is half way between recitation and singing and one which may strike as almost monotonous (i.e. repetitious use of small and simply constructed melodic phrases etc.). Not to elaborate either the basic rhythmic or the melodic patterns is also a recognisablc folk feature. The point is that when Pt. Kumar employs such folk-features in his musical manifestations he is not making folk music but offering a whiff of it. The original folk expression is here processed by the art or classical music. Only this processed version can aspire to aesthetic stature though there are seeds of artistry present in folk music. Why these aesthetic items cannot become fully realised aesthetic entities in folk music itself has many reasons with roots in diverse disciplines. On most of the occasions when we praise some folk-feature as beautiful we are in fact taking it out of its total and original design and processing it.

This means that Pt. Kumar is taking some isolated musical features or aspects from folk music which will suit his own specific musical endeavour. Before inclusion or use in Pt. Kumar's music suitable folk musical features are selected, 'cleaned' and processed. Pt. Kumar detects musical 'means' in folk music. That he finds many *raga*-s or their origins in folk music is to be understood in this perspective. In folk music not *raga*-s but melodic structures that have a potential to become *raga*-s are found. These are taken out of their original frame for a further processing in order to develop them in the context of art music and then they may arrive at the *raga*-stage. Seeds of *raga* in folk music can become realised *raga* in art music. The qualitative distinction between a seed of a *raga* and a realised *raga* must be carefully noted before further arguments are put forward.

In addition to getting some stylistically attractive intonations and some new points of musical take-off (e.g. seeds of *raga* or rhythmic patterns) Pt. Kumar also gained in the matters of vocabulary and content of compositions. Pt. Kumar's own compositions make their distinct thrust perceivable when one notes the content of folk music which directly touches various phases and aspects of the human life-endeavour and compares them with the stereotyped content of compositions in art music. Inevitably the difference in content is also followed by a difference in vocabulary and texts. As words are simultaneously patterns of meaning as well as sound, Pt. Kumar has also gained from folk music in this additional dimension. Pt. Kumar's music is differently effective because its components also differ in some important respects. This is how the word component makes multiple contributions to Pt. Kumar's music-making.

On this background the weak links in Pt. Kumar's theoretical exposition that prefaced the presentation will become apparent. Even though rather sketchily presented, the theorisation needs to be examined because often a musically successful experimenter's theorisation is also assumed to be valid as a thought process and expected to be a sure pathway to further musical successes. This may lead many students of music and serious listeners astray in their respective pursuits. This kind of situation is fraught with aesthetic dangers. In translation some of the statements in the preface are as follows:

1. "To introduce a folktune in a art music concert as a change of taste and to present an entire concert of only folk music —are two completely different things."
2. "The aesthetic content of *raga-sangeet* in general is limited to a disciplined traditional framework. But the beauty of the folk tunes that I am going to present in the concert lies out of this framework."
3. "But the origins of the beauty of the *raga* are not permanent because these origins are also from the same framework."
4. "All the folk-songs are presented as they were found. Whatever music-making emerges from them is their self-originating music."

Now let us briefly examine the statements one by one.

1. Are the usual illustrative singing of a folk-song in a concert of art-music and a full concert of only folk music entirely different as Pt. Kumar says? Pt. Kumar does not use any other instruments than those employed as the usual musical partners of art music, namely *tanpura*, *tabla* and *harmonium* accompaniment. While singing the folk songs he continues to use the *taan*, attractive rhythmic variations and selection of some compositions for elaboration of musical ideas, i.e. he falls back on the same strategies as

are commonly employed in *raga*-music. Not only that, he is careful enough to select a folk song in *bhairavi* to end the concert! In an art music concert, the elaboration is of the *raga* whereas in folk music concert it is of melodic phrases from the folk composition. In an art music concert, the selection is of a *raga*, whereas in a folk music concert it is of a folk-song and in both presentations techniques employed are the same. This is the total situation obtained. Perhaps when presented in a classical concert the folk-song may be elaborated as a *thumri, bhajan,* etc. while in a concert of folk music it would be less so, but that is all the difference.

2. This statement is less slippery than the first. It is true that folk music has aesthetic locations that are not found in *raga*-music. But to say that this beauty which he has pointed out to us is not from *raga*-music is only technically correct. Because in folk music the framework was provided by the folktune and the elaboration was based on this and was also introduced with reference to it. In other words, the difference only consisted in having a different framework but the strategy or method of musical development remained the same in both the cases.
3. The statement of the impermanent beauty in *raga* is too gross! *Raga*-s come in vogue and go out of circulation because singing of *raga*-s and the rules or codifications that accompany them have a relationship that is characterised by forces of mutual attraction and retraction. A 'new' or an 'unfamiliar' *raga* comes into circulation because it is unlike those which are already in circulation. Thus it has deviated from a customary or conventional expression. After a while this *raga* also becomes conventional. Its grammar solidifies and its rigidity results in suffocation or suppression of new ideas and somebody has to take up

the task of ameliorating the situation by bringing in new structures relying on different rules. One may say that when a *raga* makes an exit it has presumably attained the peak of its attractiveness. A movement away from it will also reach its limits asking for an altogether new placement in the *raga*-corpus. It should be obvious that this same process will take place about a '*dhun*', i.e. folk tunes. *Raga*-s have been dynamic, changeable even though a majority of artists present them as if they are rigid and mechanically repetitive. Such general misconceptions about *raga*-s should not be taken as ground-rules to determine what the entity of *raga*-s actually means. The non-permanence of musical beauty is in reality ascribable to the '*dhun*'-s. *Raga*-s such as *bageshri, yaman, bhairavi* have limitless possibilities as is borne out by the musical behaviour of the society and cultural groups that explore them.

4. The fourth statement that Pt. Kumar has made contradicts all the earlier statements and it is also contrary to the actual performance which he planned and presented. To say that in this presentation folktunes have been presented as they are, is true in only a very limited sense. For example, the words may not have been changed but they have been pressed into service for an act of 'singing'. The tunes may be the same as they are in original but the entire focus has been on embellishing or decorating them. One may say that only a (sur)facial resemblance to the original continues to exist. In short, the selected folk tunes have been processed on various levels and in different ways. That their music is inherent is also equally deceptive because every expression used in music has seeds of growth or the potential of elaborated performance. Music is not imposed on any musical expression from outside, it is allowed to emerge

according to its inner merits.

Malwa ki Lokdhune

So this is it! As hinted earlier one needs to be cautious that objections with Pt. Kumar's theoretical exposition do not overlook the quality of his performance. It is true that the organisers' insistence of reading aloud the theoretical preface (both in Marathi and Hindi) made it a part of the programme and hence it demanded attention. But evaluation of the musical performance is a separate issue.

Pt. Kumar presented the folk-tunes methodically and seriously. The 'singing' aspect was kept vital without overlooking the pro-life stance of the content and the songs. Towards this end he sometimes employed tempo suggested by the content and sometimes also exploited the onomatopoeic capacities of pronunciation of some words. His own voice was less pointed than usual but the harm this would hace caused in presenting *raga*-music would have been more damaging. One reason is that in this kind of presentation and musical material there were more breaks and also pauses due to the number of compositions included than in a concert of *raga*-music. The second very important factor was that *raga*-music would have inevitably meant slower tempi conducive to melodic elaboration and also the dependence on the use of vowel 'a' for vocalisation. This aspect is considerably reduced in presenting folk music. And yet there was a suspicion as to the reduction of range of Pt. Kumar's voice.

To emphasise that he was presenting folk music, Pt. Kumar wisely employed certain devices and this helped preparing the audience's receptivity to a great extent. For example, he prolonged the durations of notes or locations in-between in the higher ranges and it was felt to be so. As recitation is an important aspect of folk music, this helped. The momemt one moves towards 'singing' these 'in-between' locations disappear. This became noticeable in this presentation too.

The second device was the more abundant use of a more accomodative *meend* in folk music. In *raga*-music the connecting movements between two notes never touch all the notes located in-between. This is imperative as the *raga*-restrictions about inclusion and exclusion of specific notes are in full operation. In folk music the movement becomes one that touches all notes. This feature was emphatically brought into play from the beginning.

Accompaniment of Mr. Achrekar (*tabla*) and Mrs. Komkali (vocal) added to the merits of the effort. Mrs. Komkali now discontented with merely repeating what Pt. Kumar has rendered, performance-wise makes the term '*Saath*' more meaningful. In his every presentation Pt. Kumar provides evidence of his intense efforts to look at music from a new angle. This 'hunger' is now so rare that he deserves compliments even on that account. In addition, he detects and focuses on the artistic aspects of every new presentation. And more often than not, barring the inevitable performing ups and downs, he maintains a high level of creative and capable singing. Both he and his listeners should be happy and grateful about this.

Geetbasant (July 1971)

With the presentation of *Geetbasant* Pt. Kumar has successfully concluded the revolution of the seasonal cycle of Hindustani music. When he initiated the project it had proved his inventiveness and industriousness. He would get the rare credit of having completed something begun with ambition and hope. For anybody searching into the musical universe, to stumble upon a concept with potential, shape it into effective performing material and finally put up the performance, are important achievements. But of equal importance is the maximum exploration of the original conception. Unless this is achieved it is not possible to know the scope of the concept or thought, to experience the technical problems and sense ones own adequacy to meet them. Finally the nature of the gain in the totality of musical sensibility, all remain question-marks unless the venture is brought to its logical end namely performance. After having completed the cycle of seasonal music, Pt. Kumar should certainly be eager to look back in satisfaction and examine the entire effort.

In my opinion, the re-examination should certainly include some items. Firstly, did he conceive these programmes as mainly of performed and performable music and secondarily of researching into music-based literature? For example, did he intend that the audience should listen to his music while ruminating on questions such as: is there a correspondence or otherwise between notes and words? Is the tune of a song determined by the action-ritual-descriptive content and are there extra-musical reasons for it? Pt. Kumar should first make a decision about this educational angle of the effort. One wonders whether keeping the hall lit to facilitate simultaneous reading of the texts was not a deliberate act. If one loses sight of the fact that analysis comes after experience, the entire experiment is possibly 'de-focussed'. In all programmes in the series this obstacle surfaced.

If the programmes were intended as researches into music-based literature, a very different issue arises. How and to what extent was this aim helped by the loose translation of the compositions printed below the song-text, or Mr. Barpute's reading aloud of his own (already printed) embellished preface? Would it not be more helpful to select fewer songs and explain them by giving their background? This could have made the programmes more precise. What is proved by the fact that Pt. Kumar had to drag the ends of two of the three programmes? To begin majestic processions like those in the princely states and then to scatter because of the sudden rains, this is how the last song-items suffered. This could have been avoided. In programmes where there is no musical elaboration but only neat guided tours to predestined and relevant musical locations, no waste of time and distraction of listeners' attention can be allowed.

And in case the goal was to attractively present folk music by classifying it according to a broad thematic principle, process it a little without disturbing its musical content—then different problems arise and these are mainly about the technique of such presentations. How can such programmes be presented without well-designed contribution of folk instruments? Folk music and folk musical instruments do not come together because of mere convention (they are inherently connected to one another through musico-cultural import). On the melodic dimension folk music nonchalantly explores those sounds or pitch-locations not recognised and /or accepted in art music. Similarly, it also explores the idiophonic (*ghana*) and membranophonic (*avanaddha*) instruments as well as plucked and bowed chordophones (*tata*) with their sharp and sometimes harsh sounds, thereby adding to the quality of the presentation. To include them is to change the entire spectrum of experience. To overlook this valuable aspect reduced the presentations to somewhat surfacial and an aesthecially suspicious attempt to project 'folkish' music used to present unrealised art music. Pt. Kumar certainly did not ask for this!

The programmes also lacked purposeful presence of collective singing or manifestation. When collective singing accompanies folk instruments, the variety of tonal colour increases ten-fold. This is the first advantage. Secondly the entire performance gets more body and solidity which Pt. Kumar never exploited. One may even say that folk music employs instrumental tonal colour, and solidity and emphatic quality of the collective singing as if to compensate for the lack of its musical elaboration. The entire series of the presentations showed almost no appreciation of this vital fact. The experimental spirit never touched this dimension.

In a linked context, the presentations also lacked synchronisation of Pt. Kumar's singing and the action of other components. It was almost assumed that when more than one person sings at a time, lack of synchronisation is justifiable. This resulted in blurred images of the compositions concerned. Collective renderings do not allow improvisation. Their strength lies in the precise, timely and quick entry-exits of relevant components. This is the backbone of such ventures.

On this background, inclusion of *dhamar* and forms of art-music in *Geetbasant* appears to be of questionable value. Was it designed to show how the *Basant ritu* (spring season) appeals to all sections of the society? This would be a position of a music-based sociology and it cannot be validated in this way. Even if music is placed in the context of specific event, society and period, the criteria applied to it are not of sociology of music. The criteria relevant are musical, musicological and musico-aesthetic. As a consequence, inclusion of *dhamar, khayal,* etc. can be validated only if these genres appear in their respective musical glory. If this cannot take place in a programme, to present the bare contours of compositions in the genre does not contribute.

Geetbasant was a lukewarm presentation. Pt. Kumar's voice was in full form but the amplification was faulty. Accompaniment on the whole lacked coordination. Smt. Suman Dandekar found it difficult to come out of the set Pt. Kumar-groove of singing.

In spite of having four male voices participating in the venture, their presence was not meritoriously felt. The occurance of the *Barmasa geet* in all the presentations is also questionable. In later programmes it could have been included more suggestively. The novelty was already lost and there was no possibility to musically elaborate it and hence it became just repetitious, which is harmful for all concepts sought to be transformed into performance.

SMT. MANIK VERMA
(26-5-1926 TO 10-11-1997)

19

Smt. Manik Verma

(26-5-1926 to 10-11-1997)

Brief Life Sketch

Daughter of Smt. Heerabai Dadarkar (a musician herself), Manikbai had her first song recorded in 1939 at the tender age of 13 under Datta Dawjekar, a renowned composer. The song was "*Jamalya paha vani brijbala*". Her voice was fresh and sweet though the singing struck one as of a novice. Heerabai wanted Manik to be an educated and properly trained musician. She later received guidance from Pt. Sureshbabu Mane, Ustad Inayat Khan and Pt. Bholanath, but more rigorous *talim* was from Pt. Jagannath Buwa Purohit of Agra *gharana*. Around 1945, she made her debut and won recognition for her sweet, tuneful and light voice coupled with a surprising ability to do justice to numerous musical genres with equal affection. Her audience went on increasing. She was also equally successful in all modern media such as disc-recording, broadcasting, films and the modern *mehfil*. Her music fitted them all.

A Versatile Artist

There was a time when *dhrupad*-singers looked down on *khayal* singers, who in turn tolerated *thumri*-singers, who in their turn turned their back on *ghazal-qawwali* singers and all these were at the most patient about theatre-singers or those who rejoiced in presenting modern songs! If all this distribution of petty intolerance was prompted by the desire to be real specialists, one could have interpreted the underlying motive as a drive for perfection. But soon this narrow focus born out of musical humility developed into an entirely unjustifiable caste-system among musicians. Musicians began assuming that what they sang and knew was the only music and that was the best as well as the greatest.

But fortunately there were great art-musicians such as Ustad Manji Khan who could not accept this oppressive self-centred attitude. That an artist's greatness does not depend on what he sings but more on how he does it, was their ruling idea. In Maharashtra art-musicians equally keen on *khayal*, stage-singing, *bhavgeet*, *thumri*, *bhajan* etc. made effective entry on the performing scene. In the modern period Smt. Manik Verma can be described as that rare musician who presented numerous musical forms with notable insight, skill and effect, and remained in the forefront.

An Open and 'Sound' Voice!

In the beginning Smt. Manikbai had received grounding in the Kirana *gharana*. Compared to other ruling philosophies of music, Kirana has been more open to the idea of making music in an array of varied genres. Ustad Abdul Karim Khan, the main protagonist of the *gharana* used to sing *thumri* and stage-songs to some extent. Smt. Heerabai was the next to do the same more comfortably and widely. In that case how can Smt. Manikbai's versatality be singled out for special praise? To answer the question a more detailed study of her music is necessary, *ab initio*.

In brief, it could be stated that in matters of intonation, methodical melodic elaboration (which is different from merely lingering on different notes) and clarity of *taan*, Smt. Manikbai has succfessfully moved out of the Kirana orbit.

It could he heard that in order to avoid the somewhat hollow artificiality produced by the resonance of the enveloping 'O' vowel, she had accepted and actualised the usage of an undistorted 'Aa' vowel as a dominant component of intonation. The natural openness, lightness and the easy production of voice is easily recognisable in her music irrespective of the genre presented. Virtues of her intonation were easy to recognise in the middle and high octaves. Most of the times she also succeeded in utilising a slight nasality in voice to advantage. She could have of course used it more generously to make the high notes more effective but that kind of use creates a musical inconsistency as elsewhere music sounds more different than it is desirable. Similarly, she was not inclined to use her voice 'dramatically', i.e. by contrastive use of the dimension of the volume. In sum, the effortlessness of intonation and ease of projection was a special feature of her music. It is to be remembered that many other Kirana vocalists as also musicians in other major *gharana*-s in Hindustani music have not succeeded in this respect. Thus Smt. Manikbai easily stood out among her contemporaries irrespective of *gharana* and musical idiom concerned. (In this context perhaps Pt. Basavraj Rajguru and Pt. Sangameshwar Gurav can also be remembered.)

As far as the *alap*-phase is concerned Smt. Manikbai made strides. To put it briefly, her *alap*-s were more *raga*-centred than note-centred. She certainly allowed enough time to evoke the magic of a single note but more importantly she cared to keep in view the note-fields that mattered in the *raga*-design. This made the *raga*-design more perceptible and the *raga* would then appear as easy to grasp or convoluted, as intended. It is true that in *raga*-s such as *todi* and *ramkali* she used notes that were slightly higher in pitch than usually heard. But she was consistent in her usage and hence that could be accepted as her intended projection of their respective values. You may not agree with her interpretation of their values but then artists have a right to be different if they are consistent. On the whole her *alap*-s were convincing and they certainly appear to be out of the Kirana groove.

A Slightly Loose Arrival on the *Sama*!

Somewhat surprisingly she was on a slightly slippery path when relationship of the melodic elaboration with the *tala*-circle was concerned. Her arrival on the *sama*-point was less than precise. The same happened more glaringly in her *bol-taan*. As the *sama* acts as a significant form-giving element in music this feature became a negative factor in her music. Perhaps a basic weakness in perception of the rhythmic aspect of music also makes her *tihai*-s too artificial and rather unoriginal. Compared to other Kirana musicians her repertoire was richer and that also meant that she utilised more and different *tala*-s than they usually do. But all the same, *talas* and related aspects generally appear to be 'weak' in her presentations.

Welcome Absence of Exhibitionism!

Her *taan*-process had also moved much beyond the Kirana ambit. Firstly the 'A' vowel based voice-projection continued in all segments and the experience to the listener was of a natural ease. Whether it was ascending or descending movments the story continued to be the same. The ease in *taan*-execution has always been a pleasant surprise in a majority of cases. What is more important was that in a performance this easy projection and movment was never accompanied by even a single gesture of exhibitionism. In fact even though sometimes accentuation of dividing beats in a *tala* is conducive to realise a pattern in *taan*, she did not use any accentuation, so flowing was her *taan*-action. Perhaps in this context, ease denied her a patterning device. One can be a loser due to excess of a musical virtue, it seems!

Benaras-*Thumri* with a Poise

As has been already suggested, her ability to perform forms as varied as *thumri, stage-song* and *bhavgeet* was a special feature of her accomodative musicianship. She was not among those musicians who keep and sing some *thumri*-compositions in the repertoire because 'some listeners like *thumri*'. In other words, to sing *thumri*-s is for them a marketing-strategy. This was not so in Smt. Manikbai's case. Whether *thumri*, stage-song or *bhavgeet*, all three genres were for her equally legitimate platforms for communicating musical ideas to music-loving public. It is known that in Maharashtra, in addition to a kind of native and improvised *thumri*-singing and the *khayal*-oriented Kirana-*thumri*, more traditional *gharana* in *thumri* singing such as Benaras, Patiala and Lucknow gained acceptance rather late. From these Smt. Manikbai preferred the Benaras which is full of poise. It is emotional but still full of restraint and moves through the elaborations with a dignified gait. It lacks the dazzle and overt passion of the Patiala, decorativeness of the Lucknow but chooses to touch the listeners with melodic permeation and evocative power. It seems obvious that in this case the *thumri*-type agrees with the personality profile of the artist concerned.

Singing of *Bhavgeet*—The Modern Song

As a singer of *bhavgeet* she gained tremendous popularity and that too very early in her career, when she was known as Miss Manik Dadarkar. She ruled over her audience consisting of young girls, impressionable and endowed with some aptitude for music. The singing ease, naturalness, restraint in music-projection and emotion were her discernible features. The freshness of voice that struck every listener in the early songs such as "*Savlach rang tujha*" was in later years replaced by confidence and musical sureness. Even when she was a mature musician the novelty of her musical evocation was never lost. However, what is more important is that even in *bhavgeet* which otherwise is a song composed in great details, she never lost the touch of an improvising art-musician. When her *bhavgeet*-singing is compared and contrasted with other pre-eminent singers such as Lata Mangeshkar and Asha Bhonsale it becomes clear that unlike them, Smt. Manikbai was not rendering or performing a thoroughly pre-composed song. Her singing of the *bhavgeet* included possibilities of melodic change and elaborations different from those already determined. Her predecessor Smt. Heerbai Badodekar's compositions (e.g. "*Vinvit Shabari Raghuraya*" or "*Ghanshyam nayani ala*") were conspicuous for allowing melodic elaboration. Smt. Manikbai's popular songs belonged to that category in the sense that they were not entirely pre-determined with orchestration as Lata Mangeshkar's or Asha Bhonsale's are. A detailed account of the modern song in Maharashtra should distinguish between *pada, bhavpada, geet* and *bhavgeet*. What is to be deduced is that Smt. Manikbai's *bhavgeet* were 'sung' feelingly and not merely recited effectively. Whenever she sang *alap* without *tala* or introduced them even when the *tala*-cycle was in action, or when she was rendering the embellished phrases, she achieved all that with a 'free touch' as compared with Lata and Asha. The difference almost borders on performing 'pre-learnt' or the 'free-learnt' song.

In a way, one more of Smt. Manikbai's contribution to Marathi *bhavgeet* was to add more of the northern touch to the music. In the abundant Krishna-songs she had recorded, this is very effectively brought home. She had sung tunes with the distinctive Patiala-touch but without the overt passion, or tunes with a decorative touch but still not as in the Lucknow *thumri*. Her *bhavgeet* too are identified by their Benarasi poise, evocative spirit and musical accomodation. In a typical song for example, the tune would have ascending phrase followed by a Patiala-type descent, succeeded by melodic lines and elaborations creating shadows of *raga mand, chandrakansa, madhuvanti* etc. Her composers for the *bhavgeet* have been Shri Sudhir Phadke, Shri P. L. Deshpande, Shri Madhukar Golwalkar and Shri Solunkurkar—all steeped in Hindustani art music. The emotional sepctrum covered by the songs is not very extensive and their essence has been an ambiguous sweetness. Smt. Manikbai had especially sung songs about Krishna and his flute to create an era in the development of Marathi *bhavgeet*.

Stage Songs

Smt. Manikbai turned to singing of Marathi stage music rather late in her career but she was immediately at home in singing it. It is reported that earlier she wanted to learn from Balgandharva himself but he stipulated that he would teach her only if she acted the role of Kanhopatra, a devotional drama he was acting in. As Smt. Manikbai was not keen on acting this could not happen at that time. But when Smt. Manikbai turned to Balgandharva-music she was swimming in known waters. Her first disc in Balgandharva music was the famous song "*Nath ha maza*" and then commenced a success story. Sweetness, ease of projection, emotional restraint and rather stylised but attractive elaboration were delightfully represented. As the Balgandharva-music of the yester-years was performed and presented in a contemporary voice, the appeal was widespread as befits a rich tradition.

Mild and Warm Accomodation

None of the musical effects Smt. Manikbai created with so much validity included anything dramatic. Whatever she has achieved in different kinds of music does not appear on the surface because uncomplainingly she has maintained links with the tradition while subtly moving away from it. She made it easier for female art-musicians in Maharashtra to sing in various forms and styles.In her music, values appear to be changeable without challenging them! To sing with full involvement without making a show of it was her forte. Perhpas it is better to end the evaluation of her art by a brief analysis of an example of her good *raga*-music.

Bhatiyar

The *raga*, derived from the fecund *marwa thata*, can be counted among the rare or less known *raga*-s in Hindustani art-music. The name, suggesting relationship with the legendary Bhartrihari certainly arouses curiosity. Peace, spirit of renunciation, an anguish of having lost that which is to be gained and a quiet acceptance of what comes is the spectrum of effects expressed. Allotted the morning hours, the *raga* has no special conventional relationship with any specific region or particular season. Technical demands on the performers include keeping the rendition away from *raga bhankar*, to present an interesting interplay of the two varieties of note *madhyama* and through certain linking movements (*meend* as they are called) and create evocative centres. Notes *madhyama* (ma) and *shadja* (sa) being the *vadi* and *samvadi* the *raga* makes available a balanced frame for musical elaboration. *Bhatiyar* is an expansive melody and allows exploration in all octaves and tempi. The *raga* is not easy to present and not many venture to perform it. Two main sub-types are known as *khamaji-bhatiyar* and *bhairav-bhatiyar*.

Smt. Manikbai has presented a delightful *chhota khayal* in *teentaal* in the *raga* and the performance brings out all of her musical assets. Her sweet, light and slightly nasal voice ranges over all parts of the scale and yet maintains the evocative tone. Smt. Manikbai is able to adequately accomodate all phases of elaboration such as *alap*, *bol-alap*, *bol-taan* and *taan* even though the presentation is short and brisk. She is able to convince us that inspite of adherence to the codified grammatical restrictions about the *raga* and the genre, one can produce attractive music.

I came to know Smt. Manikbai personally because we participated in a programme on her musical achievements.This was when the Bombay station of Doordarshan was launched in the 70s. Years rolled on. In her last illness she was in a critical condition—almost in a coma. I went to see her but there was no hope that she would respond to what we were saying. But suddenly some relative mentioned it and we hummed something. Her toes responded in rhythm to the music! So ingrained was music in her personality that one felt like simultaneously crying and happily exclaiming at the miracle!

Appendix

Kirana Gharana : A Wider Framework of Case-Studies

Kirana is a small village near Saharanpur in Uttar Pradesh. The Moghul Emperor Jehangir had reportedly rehabilitated many artists in this village during his times. Significantly many of the rehabilitated musicians were expert players of *sarangi* and *been*. To understand some characteristic features of the present-day Kirana *gharana* of *khayal*-music, this historical fact may prove helpful.

Today the Kirana has established itself as one of the major *gharana*-s of the Hindustani art music. On account of the pioneering work done by Ustad Abdul Karim Khan and Ustad Abdul Wahid Khan the *gharana* represents a major way to practise and interpret the intricacies of Hindustani *khayal*-music. Many other Kirana musicians have also later consolidated the work of the early protagonists. The *gharana* can truly be credited to have worked towards the spread and popularity of Hindusatni vocal art music with greater effect.

To understand the nature of the *gharana* and its contribution to Hindustani art music perhaps the best way is to assess performances of its major practitioners. The present effort is therefore limited to examination of some prominent Kirana musicians' music to get an idea of the general Kirana approach to music and know the major sub-varieties of the approach. The attempt is to provide in brief a perspective on the concerned artist with the help of some technical analysis of his music on the basis of recorded music available to all those keen on it. The efffort is to avoid a coyingly sweet comments and dry pedantry. Like the music, thinking about it should also be accessible to all.

Pt. Sawai Gandharva
(1896 to 1952)

Pt. Sawai Gandharva (1896 to 1952)

Shri Rambhau Ganesh Kundgolkar was the full name of Pt. Sawai Gandharva, which suggests the place in Karnataka namely Kundgol (dist. Dharwad) where he was born. (Some have noted that the original name of the family was in fact 'Saushi'). Rambhau's father sensed his liking for music and had some training given to him by Shri Balwantrao Kolhatkar, though it was mainly of *dhrupad*. But at the age of about 12, Rambhau heard Ustad Abdul Karim Khan's music for the first time. That decided for Rambhau his life-work in music and the *guru* who will initiate him into the musical mysteries. Whereever Ustad would perform, Rambhau would be present. However it was only in 1900 that he could begin getting Ustad's *talim* and it continued for about eight years. Apart from Ustad Abdul Karim Khan, Rambhau also received guidance from Ustad Nissar Hussain, Rahim Bux, Murad Khan, Pt. Bhaskarbuwa Bakhale and Pt. Ramkrishnabuwa Vaze. He was influenced by Ustad Rahimat Khan and Ustad Manji Khan. It is not surprising that with so many varied influences his music also displayed many colours. To enable himself to project the Kirana music and especially the soft intonation it was known for, he had to work on his voice a lot after it 'broke'. He used to present *khayal, tarana, thumri, bhajan* and stage-songs with characteristic musical quality and earned a name rightly for his versatility.

He earned fame on the music-stage after doing roles of Subhadra, Tara, and Sant Sakhu for over 14 years. His achievement was notable because at the time he stepped on stage, Balgandharva was the ruling artist and still Rambhau could impress an idiom of his own. This is the reason why Shri Dadasaheb Khaparde, a patron and a well-known leader during the Tilak-age described Rambhau as Sawai Gandharva and since then the description remained. However, with hindsight it could be said that Rambhau had to pay a heavy price for it. Because in female roles he was compelled to sing in an unusually high fundamental and this strained his voice unimaginably. After 1930 Marathi music-stage was on the decline and Rambhau had to turn completely to concert music when it became clear to him that his voice had suffered heavy damage. This meant that it required long hours and untiring efforts to 'warm' it. Yet after this arduous task was over, the music that Pt. Sawai Gandharva made was of exceptional quality.

His music could reach a high quality because he had a good musical imagination and the stage-experience had only sharpened it. He was able to generate more and varied tonal colours than his *guru*. Further, the emotional spectrum that he could weave in his music was also more extensive than his *guru* and the usual Kirana variety. Consequently his music was definitely richer. For example, his slow tempo melodic elaboration was more methodical and extensive. His *taan* carried more variety of patterning. Unlike his *guru*, Sawai Gandharva had more than one tonal colour and that allowed him to avoid an enveloping sadness in all his music (which otherwise appeared in Kirana-*thumri* too!). This also enabled him to put forth enthusiastic or ostensibly energised singing of *tarana*. Further his music could also become more 'intellectual'. In the rhythmic aspect too he could become more aggressive and this is brought out in his music. In sum, he was not averse to and perhaps liked to move away from the usual music of his *gharana*. And finally even after accepting so many influences he could maintain a music of his own. He had a different musical personality and he was aware of it. Perhaps his experience on stage had enabled him to create and play roles in music-making too!

In 1942, he suffered a severe attack of paralysis, and lost his voice completely. For about ten years he was a silent musician and then left this abode. His main disciples are Pt. Phiroze Dastoor, Smt. Gangubai Hangal and Pt. Bhimsen Joshi.

Hindol: Composition—*"Lal Jinkar Ho"*

The *raga*-name carries suggestions of a swing, spring season and the associated sentiments of joy and enthusiasm. Derived from *kalyan thata*, the *raga*-time codification allots to *Hindol* the morning hours. Early mention of the name suggests its ancientness. It is mainly elaborated in the middle and high octave-regions and the internal tempo ranges from medium to fast. Expectably it is enthusiastic in movements and ascending phrases may dominate. With only five notes included, there is abundant use of the linking moves, i.e. *meend*. It appears to be simple but it may not prove easy to keep it distinct from *raga basant, puriya* etc.

Pt. Sawai Gandhrva's *hindol* is traditional and yet it provides some characteristic features of his music. Firstly, musicians from Kirana *gharana* are not heard to favour *hindol*. It obviously goes against the introvert and slow-moving temper of the *gharana*. *Hindol* expects energetic, bright, bouncingly extrovert musicianship. Pt. Sawai Gandharva begins with quick steps. After presenting the full composition he plunges into quick-moving melodic phrases to create the image of the *raga*. Then he increases the fast tempo to make it faster. Next in line are *taans* that match this tempo. The composition describes colour festival to celebrate a joyous occasion. Pt. Sawai Gandharva ensures that the music he creates matches the import.

Puriya: Composition—*"Piya Gunwanta"*

Derived from the *marwa thata,* the majestic and grave image of this *raga* has certainly created a kind of artistic awe among performers. Rendered at late evening hours or at night, *Puriya* accomodates multiple inherent tempi and prefers exploration of the middle and lower octave. With a resonant note such as *gandhar* as its *vadi* the *raga* is full of attractions. As the grave and dignified temper is also inclusive of some sadness, the artist has the responsibility to effect a rare emotional synthesis, a challenging task indeed. There is a general agreement that Puriya invariably turns out to be a melody that touches listeners.

It has scope for abundant linking movements that include subtle touching of a number of intervening notes too. The progression is convoluted and it needs alertness to keep it separate from *marwa* and *sohoni* due to the fact that all the three have similar scalar frameworks. *Puriya* has no special regional or seasonal relationships and it offers enough scope for all phases of elaboration. *Puriya* can be leisurely rendered and presented without repetition, provided the artist's creative imagination works with full power.

While listening to Pt. Sawai Gandharva's rendering of the *khayal* "*Piya gunvanta*" one is struck by the close similarity of his tone and emotive projection of the late Ustad Abdul Karim Khan. And yet there is an unmistakable presence of some intellectual element. In some measure one is happy that the whole presentation is not awash with emotion! Pt. Sawai Gandharva catches the *raga*-image in a few phrases, sings the full compositon thus etching the listener a total melodic map of the *raga*. All aspects such as melodic contours, rhythmic patterning and the textual implications thus become known entities. Purposeful *alap*, *bol-alap* and *taan* are introduced at right moments.The *raga* is thus fully developed. Even the high octave notes are perfectly intoned and their evocative power is maintained. One is reminded of his *guru* but one is also conscious of the disciple who is in full control of himself.

Puriya Dhanashri: Composition—"*Paar Karo*"

According to many authorities this *raga* is derived from the *marwa thata*. Even though the name sounds as if it is a *raga* combining two, namely *Puriya* and *Dhanashri* it is not so and to that extent the name is a mystery. Presented in the late evening hours *Puriya Dhanashri* has no seasonal or regional associations. The main sentiment is that something has been expected for a long time but something has also been lost for a long time—but everything is accepted quietly. It is an expansive melody exploring all the octaves and allows many internal tempi. The linking movement between the notes 'Ni' and 'Pa' is its special mark. *Puriya dhanashri* is not a rare or an unfamiliar *raga*, though care needs to be taken to keep it distinct from *raga poorvi*.

Even though Pt. Sawai Gandharva presented a composition which is known almost to all, his presentation attracts and there are reasons for that. One reason is of course the characteristic tone of his voice, but more importantly, he is able to project music which is emotional but not swamped by emotionality. The *raga* is appropriate for a composition which speaks of devotee's prayer to the deity to accept his pleas. Pt. Sawai Gandharva is able to attend to both—the broad content and the musical nuances. Rendering of the composition, *alap, bol-alap,* use of high notes and *taan* come in sequence. There is imagination and variety in *taan*. They have a design and it is projected with clarity and musical efficiency. Rather unexpectedly the artist increases the tempo at a later stage but the mood remains intact.

Nata-Malhar: Composition—"*Banara Byahan Aayo*"

This *raga* is an interesting combination of two *raga*-s—*Malhar* and *Nata*—and it is derived from the *bilawal thata*. As the name suggests the *raga* has connections to the *malhar*, a *raga* with an obvious musical personality and a mood of its own. On the other hand, *nata* strikes as a somewhat dry scalar arrangement with no easily perceivable mood of its own. The combined *raga* is more brisk than both component *raga*-s but it is not very expansive and it is not easy not to allow either to overshadow the new entity emerging from the combination. *Nata-malhar* does not allow much linking of notes and the convoluted movements are an intellectual challenge. Consequently *nata malhar* is counted as one of the rare *raga*-s and not many venture to perform it. It has no regional associations. (One may say that this *raga* smiles but does not laugh with joy!)

Pt. Sawai Gandharva's presentation is symptomatic of his inclination to step out of the Kirana cast. He begins with phrases indicative of the two component *raga*-s with *malhar* looking downwards and the other looking up. The darker colours of *malhar* are judiciously mixed with the brighter melodic phrases of the *nata*. After inadequate slower *alap,* are presented *taan*, fast, full of energy and rather cerebral in appeal. Some mixed *raga*-s certainly only bring together two profiles, yet keep them separate.

Komal Rishabh Asavari: Composition—*"Preet Na Kijiye"*

Earlier there were differences of opinion about the name of the *raga*. Whatever the academic controversies may have been, today almost without exception it is stated that *raga Asavari* consists of the *Komal Rishabha* and *raga Jaunpuri*, the *shuddha* variety of the same note. In other words if you use the name *Asavari* it is tautologous to add the words *Komal Rishabh* to it.

Both *jaunpuri* and *asavari raga*-s, are derived from the *asavari thata* and performed during the morning hours. They explore all octaves and multiple tempi. The *raga* under discussion carries a constant shadow of compassion and tranquillity, and invariably affects the listener. It is full of delicately etched linking movements and to do justice to them is a challenge to the artist's creativity and powers of unerring intonation. It needs to be kept separate from *gandhari, bilaskhani todi* and *bhairavi*. *Asavari* has no special regional or seasonal associations.

From the Carnatic system of art music *raga asavari* is similar to the *raga* under discussion.

It is not surprising that the Kirana *gharana* should feel a special affinity for the *raga*. But Pt. Sawai Gandharva's presentation, though impressed by the Kirana spirit, also maintains its own touch. It is tuneful, and the pronunciation of words as also the *Sargam* is evocative, with no loss of musical quality anywhere. The time of recorded singing is obviously limited, tempo cannot be too slow and yet the composition is fully presented. Creation of the *raga* image and loyalty to the method, both are successfully accomplished—a tribute to the artistry indeed!

Tilang: Composition—"*Tab Se Sakhi*"

The name announces relationship with a region—the Telugu-speaking Andhra Pradesh. According to the ancient tradition many *raga*-names in Hindustani music are related to regions but apart from deducing the name nothing more musical can be described in many cases. It is certainly so with *Tilang* which is a region-related *raga*. In addition, it is to be remembered that Andhra Pradesh follows the Carnatic system of art music. *Raga tilang* might be a comparatively new entrant in the Hindustani *raga* corpus.

Though of limited expansive possibilities, *tilang* is a sweet *raga* and encourages a beautiful interplay of the two varieties of the note *nishad* as well as many linking movements from these notes. The internal tempo of the *raga* ranges from medium to fast and melodic exploration is encouraged in middle and high octaves. Though inclined towards sadness, hope is not excluded from the emotional spectrum expressed in the *raga*. Performed during late night hours, it is not associated with any specific season. It seems apt to have genres like *thumri,* associated with the *raga* in a major way. Even though it is expected to be kept distinct from *raga jog,* the genre in which it is mainly employed ensures freedom from *raga*-restrictions of a grammatical nature.

As presented by Pt. Sawai Gandharva, it can cause a pleasant surprise. Composition in a genre known as '*bandish ki thumri*' is presented and thus a briskness (with a letter per beat movement) is almost inevitable. The performance never drags. It almost suggests room for a kind of *abhinaya* (acting) full of decorative tenderness. In spite of being a follower of the Kirana musical ideology the artist makes no compromise with the specific gait of the genre and its propensity towards dance. In other words, the artist is aware of musical compositions that are intended to reach beyond music. He therefore employs accentuated words, devices like singing in the double tempo, repeated enunciation of certain words and distribution of delicate embellishments of a certain type in the presentation. He is also able to use the words to underline the amorous content in a dramatic fashion. Set in *drut ektala* the composition announces its special import clearly and the artist enables us to sense the slightly different composite thrust of the projected music.

Dhani: Composition—*"Kahe Raja"*

The *raga* derived from the fecund *kafi thata* is regarded as '*Kshudra*' i.e. minor if not insignificant in musicological codification. Expectably it boasts of numerous compositions in what is described as 'light music'. Compositions are attractive, fast-moving and it becomes clear that the *raga* is not expansive. There are no scalar locations where one can enjoy sustained notes and linking movements have no scope. Internal swiftness of tempi and diminished importance of major notes such as *madhyama* and *pancham* practically makes *Dhani* a 'five-notes' *raga* and it strikes as bright but quick-moving to the extent of sounding unstable. It is significant that artists often tend to import the note 'Re' in the *raga* to avoid this predicament. With no regional and seasonal associations, it is to be kept separate from *raga*-s *palasi* and *bhimpalasi*. From the Carnatic system of music *raga*-s *udayravichandrika* and *shuddha dhanyasi* appear to be similar to *dhani*.

Pt. Sawai Gandharva has sung a *bhajan*-type composition and has proved his versatility in one more way. As required by the compositon-type it was necessary for him to keep a delicate touch constantly functional in his treatment of words, tone, pronunciation etc. and he certainly does so to perfection. More importantly the musical ideas included in the presentation had to appear light in themselves. In his singing he has ensured keeping the lilt of the *tala kehrawa* in tact and immediately attracted our attention. He is able to emote with short melodic phrases that follow with speed and with a lot of ease. Pt. Sawai Gandharva thus reminds us that he also knew the stage-music idiom well and reaped advantages from his wider musical vision.

Adana: Composition—*"Jo Teri Raja"*

The *raga*-name is not suggestive of any specific region or individual. In fact the verb '*adana*' in Hindi means 'to create obstacles'. In a way the *raga* is full of difficulties. Derived from the *asavari thata* the *raga* is moderately expansive but all its elaboration is to be on high notes in high ranges and that too in a fast to faster tempi!

Notes 'Sa' and 'Pa' are respectively *vadi* and *samvadi*. It omits note 'Ga' in ascent and note 'Dha' in descent. A slower tempo immediately starts signalling presence of *raga darbari kaanada* and thus no 'warming period' is allowed to the artist. As the *raga* has almost all genres of Hindustani art music the *raga* can be assumed to have a long tradition of performance behind it. Expectably the emotional spectrum aroused is of bright aggressiveness projected forcefully.

Adana is allotted late night-hours for performance and there is no *raga* in Carnatic music that strikes as similar.

Even though the *raga* goes against the grain of Kirana *gharana*, Pt. Sawai Gandharva has presented the quick-moving composition with a practised ease. The required extrovert and aggressive music is efficiently created. He copes well with the overall fast tempo and enjoys the fast tempo of the elaborations too. Without being repetitious he has imaginatively created *taan* patterns of great variety and sparkle.

To some extent the content of the text which is prayer to the Almighty includes some humility. The overweening condition of employing fast tempo and the accompanying aggressive tone deemed to suppress it.

Bahar: Composition—*"Kaliyan Sang Karat Rangraliyan"*

The word *Bahar* in fact brings together the essence of two other words—delight or joy and flowering or blooming. The latter 'natural condition' creates the former sentiment. This is the reason why the *raga* contains numerous compositions that describe the spring season and events related to it including the life-giving exchanges between man and nature. *khayal, tarana* and *thumri* genres celebrate in this *raga* quite often. Hence the *raga* is stated to be from the post-Islamic times in Indian history.

It is instructive to note that the musical tradition did not seem to be too eager to give this melodic structure the status of an independent *raga*. Any delightful deviation from any *raga* was treated to be sufficient to earn it a name in which the word *Bahar* was included. For example, names such as '*Bhairav ki bahar*', '*Adane ki bahar*', '*Basant ki bahar*' were in circulation. Thus the effort only indicated a performer's realised desire for a musical tour of attractive deviations. It is true that even today all *raga*-s associated with the word *bahar* are less severe about sticking to the codified structures.

What is current today as *bahar* is brisk and moves in all octaves. It sounds joyful and the connection with the spring season is made obvious. On other occasions the late night hours are alotted to its performance.

Pt. Sawai Gandharva sings a composition bordering on '*Bandish ki thumri*' and the description of the spring and its natural manifestations appears recognisably. The artist pronounces the words with clarity in spite of the fast tempo. The playful rhythmic patterns are emphatically conveyed and he purposefully repeats selected words or phrases towards this end. As in *thumri* he decorates some words with perceivable embellishments and a spirit of gay abandon prevails.

Roshan Ara Begum
(1910 to 1982)

Roshan Ara Begum (1910 to 1982)

It is unfortunate that not much is known about this extraordinary Kirana musician. Born in Calcutta in 1910, her early training was from her mother Chandra Begum and then from Ustad Abdul Haq. For some time she also received some guidance from Ustad Laddan Khan from Farrukhabad. However, her true grooming was under Ustad Abdual Karim Khan. Till 1947 she was based in Bombay. Later she left for Pakistan and expired in Karachi in 1982.

Shankara: Composition—*"Mathe Tere Dhar Raho"*

Raga Shankara is mythologically related to Lord Shankara as the name suggests. Lord Shankara's name is linked with arts, creation and the final end of the world. This should explain the vigorous, manly and somewhat awe-inspiring nature of the *raga*. The *raga* is explored by all genres with grave and serious import (e.g no *thumri* is found in the *raga*). The upper half of the middle, and the high octave are its favoured fields of exploration.The internal tempo ranges from medium to fast to extra fast. Expectably *taan*, accentuated *bol-taan* etc. are employed in profusion. Due to these demands the *raga* proves difficult though it looks simple in construction. Late night hours are allotted for its performance and it has no special regional or seasonal associations. Two rarely known sub-types are *shankara karan* and *shankara aran*.

The two compositions presented by Roshan Ara are clean and bold examples of her great artistry. The *bada khayal* "*Mathe tere dhar raho*" is addressed to Lord Shankara but the composition is full of challenging nuances. The import is thought-provoking. Disguised as a wandering monk Lord Shankara has come to Parvati to beg for alms and Parvati falls in love with him. However, she knows that even if he has come to her he does not belong to her or to anybody. Thus in an apparently virile *raga* we have a composition full of emotional shades.

Roshan Ara Begum does justice to the *raga*-structure with a confident, brisk and dynamic rendering using her quick-moving, tuneful voice which has no barriers. Through a lustrous tone and rightly distributed vibrato she suggests the intense emotional content even though the composition is not sung in its entirety.

Basant: Composition—*"Ab Man Dekhe Sapne"*

Basant is a major *raga* derived from the *poorvi thata*. In the spring season it can be performed at any time and on other occasions the late night is allotted to it according to the tradition. Along with the emphasis on the upper half of the object and high notes it consists of an interplay of two varieties of *madhyama* and additionally the *pancham* note is to be placed with special effect. These features and the internal tempi ranging from medium to fast make the *raga*-movements convoluted and thus the *raga* is not easy to expand. It is also to be kept distinct from *raga paraj*. All in all the *raga* though not of the rare category is difficult to present. It is culturally significant that the ancient Hindu festival of *Madana* (Cupid) and the *Sufi* festival aptly called *Rang*, invariably employ it.

From the Carnatic system of art music a *raga* called *vasanth* is similar to it.

One does not know how to adequately praise Roshan Ara Begum's presentation. This non-traditional composition is set in *ektal* and the *tala* moves in slow tempo while the elaboration is fairly fast. Apart from her quick-moving, tuneful and obedient voice she also has in imagination, otherwise the slow *tala* and fast-elaboration technique would have easily backfired. Her lively placements of note *pancham* in varying contexts create an additional tonal region for melodic elaboration. Her evocative pronunciation adds to the enchantment. She is able to be equally bright on lower as well as higher notes with remarkable ease. To make music interesting she uses a number of devices. For example, she moves quickly from lower to higher notes and vice versa. The moment she reaches the tonal destination she also creates a tonal cluster there like a bouquet of flowers. Sometimes she creates a complicated pattern on higher level and immediately repeats the same with equal effectiveness on lower levels without making a show of it. *Taans* are fast, complex and effortless. It is indeed a music-making of rare beauty.

Pt. Phiroze Dastoor
(1919 to 2007)

Pt. Phiroze Dastoor (1919–2007)

Pt. Phiroze (Phardun) Bejanji Dastoor was born on 30th of September 1919 in Bombay in a middle class Parsi family. All these details are important because in that period Parsi society was caught in a bind, to choose between a larger Indian cultural tradition or to follow the British model. Pt. Dastoor's father was an expert-billiards player and ran a billiards parlour. All kinds of people used to visit and the collection of recorded music at home was also extensive. Dastoor was an avid listener and knew how to use his pliable voice. The times belonged to the new art of cinema. Mr. J.B.H. Wadia of the Wadia Movietone was in search of a new, hero with an ability to project Urdu dialogues and music. He focused on Fardun, and Fardun, was changed to Phiroze. *Lale Yaman* (1933) to *Gul Bakavali* (1947) are the landmarks of Pt. Dastoor's film-career. He acted in about 20 films. Later, Phiroze decided to concentrate on Hindustani art music. Pt. Javkar, Pt. Kapileshvari and Pt. Sawai Gandharva were his *guru*-s and he stabilised in the Kirana *gharana*. He made his debut in Karachi in 1939, continued to sing from the AIR from 1933 to 1955. Till the end he was engrossed in making and teaching music.

He had a sweet, thinnish voice and slightly nasal and a clear pronunciation. He favoured *raga* that encouraged *alap* and was fond of singing *thumri a la* Ustad Abdul Karim Khan. He was not intent on rhythm-work but his ability to invoke the Ustad's memory was a memorable experience.

Kalavati: Composition—*"Kahe Karat Raar"*

Even if the name of the *raga* sounds as if it is of Southern origin there is no *raga* of that name in the Carnatic system. Some hold the opinion that *Kalavati* has similarities with the Carnatic *raga malaymarutam*. It is obviously a new entrant in the Hindustani system. Expectably there are no *dhrupad*, *dhamar* compositions in the *raga*. Its internal tempo allows easy *alap*-work though the fast tempo is not prohibited. Though it is pleasant there is a sense of longing in it. Late evening hours are allotted and it has no seasonal or regional associations.

Even though the *raga* is not a part of the usual Kirana repertoire Pt. Dastoor's selecting it is not surprising. Slow-moving, step-by-step melodic elaboration coupled with a sweetness fits in the *gharana* preferences. Pt. Dastoor has elaborated it with slow emphasis on notes. The *tala jhaptal* used for the composition has a small cycle and hence the *raga* can be elaborated without undue repetition. The words are pronounced with evocation. There is no insistence on singing in "A"kar. The accent is not on rhythmic complexity, intricate *taan* and the like. These features only arrive as a clue to attainment of musical climax. In this *raga* this technique does not jar on the listener.

Gangubai Chikkurao Hangal (1913–2009)

She was born in a family of occupational musicians in Dharwad in 1913. Hence music came to her easily but also with a feeling of social embarrassment. Her mother Ambabai was an expert in singing *Javali* (a genre of semi-erotic songs) as well as Kannad *keertana* (traditional Kannada religious music). Ustad Abdul Karim Khan never hesitated in learning from Ambabai—that was her stature. Ambabai taught Gangubai Sanskrit *shloka* initially and Gangubai learnt patriotic songs in the school. She earned a name and was invited to sing from the platform of the National Congress held in the area. Additional musical guidance she received was from Krishnacharya and Dattopant Desai. On her own, Gangubai used to learn by heart recorded music of singers such as Johrabai and also try to study Pt. Bhatkhande's volumes on music. Thus, she showed rare initiative in self-learning too! But her real *talim* began when Pt. Sawai Gandharva settled in Kundgol in 1937. The *talim* continued for about four years. When she had cut some discs under the name of Gandhari Hangal her voice was sweet, thin and feminine. Through sheer practice she changed her voice to a manly, broad and heavy tone—a case of musical transformation.

She preferred to perform *khayal* and Kannad devotional music. She usually selected *raga* with an inherent mood and those which allow slow, melodic elaboration.

Bhairav: Composition—*"Balamwa More Sainyan"*

This *raga* is mythologically related to Lord Shankara. The ancient *raga* belongs to the six 'original' *raga*-s in the tradition. The *raga* is connected to *Shishir* season and on other occasions it is

Gangubai Chikkurao Hangal
(1913 to 2009)

allotted morning hours. This grave *raga* is conducive to detailed elaboration and it explores all octaves and tempi. Many musical genres explore it. It is simple in movement and thus it is often taught in the beginning to a new student. In the Carnatic system of music too the corresponding *Mayamalavgaud* is taught in the beginning. It is as hinted earlier solemn, dignified, peaceful and inclined towards compassion as well as devotion. It has many sub-types and names such as *Adi, Anand, Ahir, Odav, Bairgi, Shivmat, Shuddha Tank, Naubatkhani* etc. which are suggestive of its wide reach in the Indian musical culture.

Smt. Gangubai has presented a *khayal* in the *raga* "*Balamwa more sainya*" by the well-known and pioneering *khayal* composer Sadarang. It is a composition that can be taken as a standard. It is simple and includes all the important melodic movements of the *raga*. It gives enough scope to all the elaborational phases of the *raga*. Thirdly, it is composed in such a way that if one follows it faithfully the *raga* unfolds correctly and automatically. Smt. Gangubai presents the composition with honesty, etches the *raga* faithfully, creates the sentiment of the *raga* and appropriately conveys it to us. Her daughter Krishna has a sweet, light and rather thin voice, and both together succeed in performing all aspects of the *raga* effectively. We experience *bhairav*.

Bibliography

1. *Hindustani Sangeet Padhhati*, Pt. Vishnu Narayan Bhatkhande, Popular Prakashan, Mumbai, Part I, 1992, Ed. Prabhakar Chinchore.
2. *Hindustani Sangeet Padhhati*, Pt. Vishhnu Narayan Bhatkhande, Popular Prakashan, Mumbai, Part II, 1995, Ed. Prabhakar Chinchore.
3. *Hindustani Sangeet Padhhati*, Pt. Vishhnu Narayan Bhatkhande, Popular Prakashan, Mumbai, Part III, 2001, Ed. Prabhakar Chinchore.
4. *Hindustani Sangeet Padhhati*, Pt. Vishhnu Narayan Bhatkhande, Popular Prakashan, Mumbai, Part IV, 1998, Ed. Prabhakar Chinchore.
5. *Hindustani Sangeet Padhhati*, Pt. Vishhnu Narayan Bhatkhande, Popular Prakashan, Mumbai, Part V, 1992, Ed. Prabhakar Chinchore.
6. *Sangeetacharya Pt. Vishnu Narayan Bhatkhande*, Dr. S.N. Ratanjankar, Maharashtra Rajya Sahitya Sanskriti Mandal, Mumbai, 1973.
7. *Thor Sangeetkar,* Prof. B.R. Deodhar, Akhil Bharatiya Gandharva Mahavidyalaya Mandal, Mumbai, 1973.
8. *Sangeet Kala Prakash*, Pt. Ramkrishnabuwa Vaze, Pub. Self, Part I, 1938; Part II, 1941; Pune.

9. *Riaz*, Shivanand Swami Sangeet Pratishthan, Mumbai, 1987.
10. *Riaz, Gayanacharya Pt. Anant Manohar Joshi*, G.H. Ranade, Shivanand Swami Sangeet Pratishthan, Mumbai, 1988.
11. *Balgandharva: Vyakti ani Kala*, Vasant Shantaram Desai, Venus Prakashan, Pune, 1987.
12. *Sangeetagyonke Sansmaran*, Vilayat Hussain Khan, Sangeet Natak Akademi, New Delhi, 1959.
13. *Mallikarjun Mansoor*, Sadanand Kanvalli, Tr. Dr. Prabhakar Deshpande, Satyajit Prakashan, Mumbai, 1993.
14. *Vishrabdha Sharada*, Vol. II, H.V. Mote, H.V. Mote Prakashan, Mumbai, 1975.